THE TELEVISION BARONS

The Television Barons

Jack Tinker

Quartet Books

London Melbourne New York

First published by Quartet Books Limited 1980
A member of the Namara Group
27 Goodge Street, London W1P 1FD

Copyright © Jack Tinker 1980

ISBN 0 7043 2248 X

Printed in Great Britain by
the Anchor Press, Tiptree

For Edward Smith Tinker

Contents

Illustrations

Acknowledgements

Given the Machiavellian nature of television politics and the raw sensibilities reddening in the dawn of the new redistribution of ITV franchises, my most sincere gratitude for invaluable help in preparing this book must remain reserved for those who would not thank me for publicly thanking them. Others are omitted to avoid the identification of the former by a process of elimination. And still others are omitted, as you will see, because a curious incidence of autobiography among some leading participants in the saga prevented them from co-operating. So I will confine my recorded thanks to a few personal acknowledgements of the assistance without which I could not have sifted through the tangled history of commercial television on its Silver Jubilee. My colleague Nigel Dempster generously made available to me a fascinating archive of documents and material he had collected with a view to publishing a similar project but had abandoned because of his other multifarious commitments. Ned Sherrin, Kenneth Griffith, Michael Darlow were among those happy to go on record with their version of events. Anthony Howard provided some invaluable suggestions after a careful reading of the original text which I gratefully incorporated into the final draft. My friend Roy Moseley was a tireless source of invaluable guidance and background detail from his earliest associations with the Grade–Delfont organization and later as an agent on his own account. Mrs Toni Nelson, my secretary and assistant was, as ever, indefatigable in the long labour of assembling all the material needed, typing and re-typing but most of all supplying her own inside knowledge of the subject and her own special brand of humour.

Special thanks to Bernard Levin for allowing me to use in full his entertaining article from the *Manchester Guardian* describing the opening night of ITV.

As for the rest to whom I am indebted, may their anonymity be my best thanks for their co-operation. When future franchises are dealt out may each receive the reward he deserves.

THE TELEVISION BARONS

Mammon and the Medium

1

On the night when Independent Television launched itself into the unknown, the country at large had little thought for anything but the death of Grace Archer. Wily BBC radio chiefs had offered up the golden girl of their most popular nightly soap opera as a ritual sacrifice. Almost eight million listeners tuned in to BBC Radio that evening to await the outcome of *The Archers* cliff-hanger, left open-ended from the night before.

This carefully planned incineration of the heroine of Ambridge knocked the breath out of everyone who heard it besides a great many who did not. It also took the wind clean out of ITV's freshly unfurled sails. Those few homes who had converted their sets to receive the new channel learned of Grace's death second-hand from the shock-horror headlines across the pages of next day's newspapers, and they very likely cursed their luck roundly at having missed it. The furore caused by the brutal barbecueing of a national sweetheart certainly overshadowed most of what the new arrival had to offer that night.

'ITV opened with a yawn and then woke up,' grumbled the *Daily Mirror*, voice of the very people ITV aimed most anxiously to please. Few who saw the opening ceremony, televised with the hushed self-importance of a royal investiture from London's Guild-hall, would disagree. The accompaniment of Sir John Barbirolli and the Hallé Orchestra waxing patriotic with flights of Elgar enhanced the feeling that here was history being manufactured rather than made. It was true that they had glimpsed the début of an ebullient Hughie Green heralding Britain's first-ever cash quiz show, and if they kept their sets tuned in for an hour, they were rewarded by the sighting of Britain's first-ever commercial break. To Young & Rubicam's advertising agency's clients, Gibbs SR Toothpaste, fell the honour of leading the field. Any expectations that the shops would be inundated next day with customers high on the prospect of attaining tingling freshness for their gums were quickly dashed. The fatal, fictional carnage at the Archer stables had created a smokescreen of controversy behind which the advent of the television commercial was all but obliterated. The twenty-four-hour miracle the BBC had prayed for had worked.

Bernard Levin summed up the overwhelming mood of Independent Television's first evening in his own pithy and idiosyncratic way the next day in the *Manchester Guardian*. His article deserves to be repeated in full:

> One thing must be said immediately. In 365 days' time Independent Television – if all goes well – will have been with us for a year. So far, it has been with us for a bare hand-count of hours, and although the conclusions are crying to be jumped to the temptation to jump must be resisted. The broader judgment must wait until the end of the year – or, say, until the middle of next week.
>
> Speaking empirically, then, what wonders did we see last night? The first was a black cross on a white ground which, accompanied by a high-pitched scream, persisted for some minutes. This vanished and was followed by a card bearing the legend 'Opening Night Independent Television Service Channel 9'. Then the familiar tones of Mr Leslie Mitchell, who nineteen years ago spoke the very same words at the inauguration of the BBC Television Service, declared: 'This is London.'
>
> It was indeed. Historic scene succeeded historic scene as Mr Mitchell with scarcely a tremor in his voice, intoned a commentary which appeared at times to be in verse ('A new city would have been built, had Wren but had his way'). With a last quick word about the history so far and future of the Independent Television Service, Mr Mitchell passed us over to Guildhall, where Mr John Connell was waiting to introduce the guests at the inaugural banquet.
>
> The first guest was Pitt the Younger, looking down from his niche in unmixed astonishment. Pitt was followed by Gog and Magog, and these by the Lord Mayor and Lady Mayoress, Lord and Lady Kilmuir, Dr Charles Hill (Mr Connell's voice sank to a reverent whisper), the Bishop of London, Sir Kenneth Clark, and Mr Norman Collins, looking as if London did indeed, this night, belong to him.

4

When the guests were met it was the turn of Sir John Barbirolli and the Hallé Orchestra. Sir John, who looked so composed that he could hardly have heard of Sir Thomas Beecham's exclusive agreement with the Manchester programme contractor, led the Hallé through Elgar's 'Cockaigne' Overture.

Then came the speeches. The Lord Mayor, in admirably clear close-up, looked nervous, spoke up and sat down within four minutes. Dr Hill followed him, looking and sounding, as one would expect, pugnacious. 'An immensely powerful and ever-growing medium' was what he called television, and insisted that it was here to stay. Adding that man was many-sided, he wished the ITA well and came to an end.

Then it was the turn of Sir Kenneth Clark (his were the first eyes of the evening to look directly into the camera). For Sir Kenneth, too, the picture was wonderfully clear, as he told us that television had a terrifying power for good and evil, paid tribute to Lord De La Warr, and came to a graceful close exactly at the advertised time.

Over now to 'Channel 9' for variety opening with a huge smile from Mr Jack Jackson, who proceeded to shut Mr Hughie Green into a soundproof box. On the whole, the variety show which followed was well up (or some would say down) to BBC standards. But the producers clearly believed in stimulating appetites rather than satisfying them. 'A smile, a song, and a cigar' was about all some of the artists had time for.

At ten minutes past eight came – and it came as a surprise – the first advertisement of the new service. A charming young lady brushed her teeth, while a charming young gentleman told us of the benefits of the toothpaste with which she was doing it.

Variety came to an end, and it was drama's turn. Mr Robert Morley, his startled-goldfish expression well to the fore and his magnificent eyebrows semaphoring vigorously, told us in a few homely words how surprised he was that Independent Television had ever appeared at all. But now it was here he was clearly going to make the best of it. And the best for this evening at any rate, was to be the proposal and interrogation scenes from *The Importance of Being Earnest*. (This, of course, had already been recorded on film, and one watched with interest to see how it compared with the 'live' broadcasts we had already watched. It compared very well.)

Sir John Gielgud proposed very charmingly to his Gwendoline (Miss Margaret Leighton), but it was Dame Edith Evans as Lady Bracknell that he was clearly waiting for – and so, indeed, were we. Nor were we disappointed. It is many years since Dame Edith played Lady Bracknell (that film hardly counts), and she was clearly determined to make up for loss of time. She roared her battle-cry – 'A handbag?' – like an indignant foghorn telling its mate that it had just been insulted and the rest of her magnificent

5

performance was pitched in the same key. The film around her, in so far as one was conscious of it, was admirably, indeed beautifully composed.

It was the boxing that showed us for the first time in the evening the ITA avoiding a major BBC fault. How often we have been infuriated by a description of something we could perfectly well see for ourselves. There is no need to mention names here, except that of Mr Richard Dimbleby, but anybody who has ever watched, say, a sporting programme on BBC television will be able to add half a dozen. But Mr Len Harvey and Mr Tony Van den Bergh confined themselves almost entirely to inter-round summaries – Mr Harvey sounding infinitely wistful at finding himself outside a boxing ring and letting the cameraman tell the story for us.

With the hair-trigger timing that characterized all the pro-grammes of the evening, the boxing finished (not, alas, for those who must have drama in everything, with a knockout), and it was time after some more advertisements, for the news. I surely cannot be the first to have made a joke about Mr Christopher Chataway and a running commentary? But for Mr Chataway, it was clearly no joke. Sitting in a dark lounge suit, and obviously too worried to smile, he followed Mr Aidan Crawley's introduc-tion with four and a half minutes of news.

After the labouring in the field, came the feast. The cameras, to end the evening, looked-in at the party in the May Fair Hotel, where appropriately enough our compère was Mr Leslie Mitchell, whose voice had ushered in the new era all those hours ago. (Only three? impossible!) Everybody looked happy, calm, and carefree. And on the whole, and with reservations, and other things being equal, well they might be.

So far, then, what we have seen of Independent Television has certainly not confirmed the worst fears (or hopes?) of its enemies. Television, Sir Kenneth Clark reminded us earlier in the evening, has a terrifying power for good or evil; speaking as subjectively as possible, I feel neither uplifted nor depraved by what I have seen. But perhaps the deeper moral effects will make themselves felt only over a period of years.

Twenty-five years on, who cares a crumb about Grace Archer? Her death may safely be consigned to the department of sentimental nostalgia for a time which, like innocence, has vanished. It has no more relevance to the modern world than the recollection of what it was like to believe in Father Christmas.

Those long-ago crackling sound effects which closed that episode of the BBC's bland and banal everyday story of country folk were, in reality, the last flicker of influence which steam radio managed to exert over the collective consciousness of the British nation. A

6

quick march had been stolen, but the real race had only just begun for the men who had campaigned so long and schemed so hard to break the iron monopoly of the BBC over broadcasting in Britain. Those of them who survive have spent much of the past quarter of a century since then smiling (if propriety and good taste forbid them actually to laugh out loud) all the way to the bank. And back.

There can be no disputing the fact that Independent Television has made many men rich since its first tentative appearance on a mere 188,000 screens on the evening of 22 September 1955. To the chosen few (words carefully and aptly used), it has also brought access to the most exceptional power. Television stands out alone as a force above all known means of communication. No other medium or art form is capable of making such a dramatic impact on so many of us simultaneously. No film, no theatre, no newspaper, no book, no magazine has so swift an access to the minds and imaginations of such a vast mass audience.

Norman Collins, head of BBC TV until he resigned in 1950 – and to become one of the chief architects of Independent Television as it is today – saw only too clearly the shape of things already on his own doorstep. He had been to the United States. There he shrewdly summed up the strength of the BBC's new toy and returned home to write prophetically in the April 1949 edition of the *BBC Quarterly*:

> The television public is at the moment a small one; it has no more than a hundredth part of the radio audience. Nor can the remaining 99 per cent be recruited overnight. But once television is truly national it will become the most important medium that exists. Everything that it does or does not do will be important. The very fact that it is in the home is vital. Its only rival will be the wireless, and the rivalry will not be strong.

Visionaries like Mr Collins are rare.

By the time Roy Jenkins, the Home Secretary of the day more than two decades later, came to appoint a special committee under the chairmanship of Lord Annan to assess the future of broadcasting, among the first questions the members asked themselves was still: what makes television unique and different from all other forms of communication? And the conclusion they produced in their Report, published in 1977, was exactly the same as Norman Collins's. 'The simple answer is the mass audience – it [television] possesses the unique quality of addressing the greater part of the population in their 19 million homes.'

It is heady stuff, then. Not to be handled carelessly. Not to be handed round lightly, even if you happen to agree with the disparaging verdict of that most sharp and shrewd television communicator, Robert Kee. Mr Kee blandly informed the 43,106 readership of the *New Statesman* back in May 1976 that: 'Television does not dominate the viewer as the cinema screen does, or as a book dominates the reader or music the listener. It is at worst a triviality, at best a fascinator.'

Doubtless this dismissal of television's importance brought comfort to the few thousand worried readers it reached. But for its influence on countless millions more, one only has to look at life and death in Dallas (fact or fiction) to be convinced otherwise.

The death of John F. Kennedy was perhaps more personally felt, more profoundly and immediately shocking, than any other previous assassination of a national figure. Why? Because it virtually took place on television. It is etched forever in the mass memory of a whole generation around the globe by those hazy, hand-held camera shots of the fatal motorcade, repeated over and over on our television screens until we finally believed the man was dead. His widow's bloodstained suit became an instant visible symbol of our horror and her agony. Her grief was ours almost as it grew.

Was it merely crass triviality then, or morbid fascination which huddled everyone with access to a TV set around the last, bleak funeral rites days later? We could scarcely have shared the occasion more tangibly had we been marching alongside Prince Philip, General de Gaulle or any of the heads of state who accompanied the widow and her children behind that lonely coffin. For all their physical closeness, those present would surely not have dared to imitate the camera's frank close-up scrutiny of the chief mourner's face which we saw so vividly in our own homes.

Until those moments, Jacqueline Bouvier Kennedy had been, to most people outside her own charmed circle, little more than a pretty pin-up; an elegant adornment to an already glamorous presidency. Television instantaneously turned her into a folk heroine. No matter what she might do with the rest of her life, no matter how hard she might try to shed the burden of her fame, those vivid images of her most traumatic moments are, and always will be, a universally shared experience.

Of course, the more recent allure of *Dallas*, as imported by the BBC, does in fact owe a great deal to trivial fascination. Nevertheless, the initials J.R. have become, for a moment, practically as renowned as J.F.K.'s in his own lifetime. Lord Annan hammered home this very point in his Report. 'At a time when people worry that society is fragmenting, broadcasting welds it together,' his committee declared. 'It links people, gives the mass audience common topics of conversation, makes them realize that in experiencing similar emotions, they all belong to the same nation.' For good or bad – and very probably for neither – the Saturday-night doings of the Ewing family have more than replaced Grace Archer and the Ambridge yokels as a source of national interest, news and – were it on the opposing channel, let it be added – revenue.

Ah, revenue. There's the rub.

Profit is implicit in the very term 'commercial television', and from the outset the dangers of employing so far-reaching a medium for private gain were roundly denounced. Powerful and varied voices opposed the practice, though none rings so strangely in retrospect as that of Sidney Bernstein's southern cinema chain, called Granada so that its customers would feel they were participating in some faintly exotic experience (it was the days before the universal package tour to Spain). When, in 1949, Lord Beveridge's Broadcasting Committee sat to consider the entire future of radio and television, it was Granada who soberly testified that the right to broadcast directly into millions of homes bore 'such a great propaganda power that it could not be entrusted to any bodies other than a public corporation'.

Such high-minded reservations were obviously quickly overcome. By the time the opposition had been vanquished and the contracts to wield that 'great propaganda power' were up for auction, Granada was among the first four successful bidders. They were not alone in this irony, however; three of those fortunate four first companies had begun by opposing the introduction of commercial television.

Stringent safeguards against possible abuses of their privilege were naturally incorporated into the 1954 Act which brought the Independent Television Authority into being. Yet, by the admitted nature of the medium, never before had so much potential power been so carefully placed within the grasp of so few. Never before had the ability to influence our tastes, standards, morals or emotions been entrusted so completely to the dictates of big business.

Already I hear the counter-cry: what about the movie moguls, the press lords, the publishing magnates, the theatrical impresarios?

9

Aren't many of these as rich as Croesus, and as powerful, in their ways, as Jove?

They are – but only if they are successful in persuading the public to buy their wares. No different from the butcher, the baker or the side-street tailor. Their wealth is amassed and their influence wielded either by public consent or in default of something better being available. That, surely, is an integral part of democracy; in a pure and perfect democracy, everyone has the right to speak – which is by no means the same thing as the right to be listened to. If the public will not pay to see your film, declines to buy your book, or read your newspaper, or set foot inside your theatre, you run the risk of going quickly broke. However, nothing short of the laws of libel and obscenity stops you producing that film, writing that book, publishing that newspaper or putting on that show. It is as it should be.

Mr Kee, for instance, is perfectly free to snap at the hand that has fed him by expressing his views in that organ of independent thinking, the *New Statesman*. Had the editor of that periodical declined to print his opinions, he would have remained at liberty to offer them elsewhere. If no takers could be found, he could have printed them himself, should he have felt sufficiently strongly that free speech was being shackled. The same is as basically true of the movie industry as it is of journalism, as valid for plays as it is for pamphlets. In fact, it is true of every medium, except – by the most curious irony – the most insinuating and influential medium of all.

As has been agreed by many, whatever the restrictions imposed by its governing body, the Independent Broadcasting Authority (IBA), as the Independent Television Authority (ITA) came to be called (and who are, in turn, directly answerable to the government for their actions), commercial television has the lowest risk to highest profit ratio since the Dutch settlers bought Manhattan for baubles. Once their exclusive licences are granted, that handful of carefully selected men who manipulate the destiny of the various companies – at the moment, five major networks and nine regional satellites – suffer no unlooked-for invasion on their territory and few of the economic vagaries which beset other tycoons at the helm of other multi-million-pound concerns. Certainly newspaper pioneers like Northcliffe and Beaverbrook were secure in their empires only so long as their judgement held, their papers sold and their advertisers remained faithful.

But how could Television's Big Five ever lose their lucrative

advertising revenue? Unless they were actually to produce programmes so bad that no one watched them at all, they retain what
are virtually captive clients. The client who threatened to remove
his advertising from Independent Television would end up not
advertising on television at all. So much for the risk to the companies' revenues.

2

It was the late Lord Thomson of Fleet – himself a television baron and press lord not unfamiliar with the chancy business of buying influence through the media as owner of the *Scotsman* – who first dubbed the existing formula for commercial television as 'a licence to print money'. The charge still irks the men who run the industry. It is not fair and it is not true, they claim, every time that licence – or franchise, in ITV parlance – comes under attack. As they point out, the lease on the air waves which the IBA bestows on their companies runs only six years (although the franchises granted in 1968 were extended while the future of broadcasting was thoroughly investigated in 1974 by Lord Annan's committee, and the original franchise ran for ten years). This means that the enormous investment they must make in studios and the hardware of modern broadcasting has no long-term basis. It could be taken away from them whenever their franchise came up for renewal. Such a step at so short a notice would undoubtedly be catastrophic.

Yet, despite this oft-repeated defence, it is perhaps significant that in all the twenty-five years which bring them to their Silver Jubilee redistribution of the contracts, not one single commercial company has voluntarily relinquished its right to broadcast; moreover, during the same period only one network company, Television Wales and the West (TWW), has actually been deprived of its franchise outright.

Annan's committee members were themselves highly sceptical

of the financial tightrope which the TV barons claimed to walk in fulfilling their contracts. The risks, the committee told the contractors bluntly, were much overstated in the light of the returns. When it was announced, for instance, that TWW was losing its contract in favour of Harlech's star-studded consortium, the quoted price of shares initially fell sharply from £1.30 to 80p. But the non-voting shareholders were subsequently comforted by the offer of the equivalent of £1.05 in Slater-Walker shares by Slater-Walker Securities Ltd. There was therefore little hardship among shareholders to complain about in that particular shake-up.

The spectre of Lord Thomson's cryptic pronouncement therefore still casts its shadow over all ITV dealings. Unlike any other major industry, there is no capital investment whatsoever in the very thing that is its greatest asset: the right to use the allocated air waves.

This right is granted to the companies through the IBA, and while it is true that they pay a hefty levy out of revenue for the privilege (among the Big Five, Thames contributes £2,850,000, while ATV and Granada follow with £2,250,000, Yorkshire with £1,825,000, and London Weekend with £1,800,000), up until 1979 ITV had never shown a loss since its very earliest days. It was a real dog year in 1970 when the companies' combined pre-tax profits fell as low as 14 per cent (almost £22.1 million) of their capital outlay. By 1973, however, they were happily boasting a 78 per cent (£32 million) return on investment. The books show that, over ten years, pre-tax profit margins oscillated as high as £38.7 million and never lower than £15.3 million. Few industries in Britian could match such economic stability, come inflation, recession or a falling pound.

When the old Independent Television Authority gave way in 1972 to the present IBA, the legislation which brought it into being made it plain that commercial broadcasting was *not* to be run solely for profit. It was, in its own way, to be as much a public service as the BBC, and profits should be used to further this end. It is on this in-built understanding that franchises are distributed. Yet, for all these worthy aspirations, independent producers, writers, directors, musicians and broadcasters continue to complain that Independent Television is a misnomer; that, given the restrictions of the watchdog IBA and the idiosyncracies of the men who control the companies, the truly independent voice is seldom heard. Accusations of oligarchy have persisted throughout the history of the commercial companies. Whatever grouping of interests successfully bids for the

13

original contracts, it is always the muscle of one man which eventually makes itself felt at the top.

In a fury of justifiable frustration, the award-winning author Dennis Potter quit the British television scene altogether after a long, unequal struggle to find an independent creative voice within the creative departments of Independent Television. From his long-ago hit play *Vote, Vote, Vote for Nigel Barton* to such latterly acclaimed productions as *Blue Remembered Hills* and *Pennies from Heaven*, his pedigree has been impeccable. He provided viewers with imaginative and original drama of the highest order.

Yet still his play, *Brimstone and Treacle*, fell foul of implacable censorship, becoming an instant *cause célèbre* against arbitrary banning by the powers-that-be. And still, up to the time of writing, no station in this country has plucked up the courage to let the viewers make up their own minds.

Before he left to work abroad, Potter fired off an impassioned broadside at British television in general and London Weekend Television in particular. In a full page article in the *Daily Mail* he poured out all his scorn on the medium which attempted to mould his talents to the personal whims and tastes of its controllers.

'Through rows and disappointments and awards and bannings like that which stopped viewers seeing *Brimstone and Treacle*, I have spent the greater part of my career trying to write, and get on the screen, the kind of work which assumes that viewers are not zombies and that the television set is not simply a pap-machine,' he fumed, announcing his decision to fly off to Hollywood.

To this end, with producer Ken Trodd, he, like many more, had formed a small independent company – PFH Ltd – designed to give them greater control over their own work. So when Michael Grade (nephew of Lew, son of Leslie and young scion of the House of Winogradsky from which, as we shall see, so much of Independent Television's taste has sprung) announced a joint deal between Potter's PFH Ltd and the mighty London Weekend Television, it seemed like the ultimate breakthrough of all their ambitions. Grade was the powerful programme controller at LWT, being groomed, it has been confidently predicted, to take over when his Uncles Grade and Delfont abdicate their empires.

'Creative people of this order have earned themselves the right to a bigger say in how they work,' Grade asserted at the convivial press conference called to launch the new partnership. Potter professed himself delighted at this stroke of good fortune. But his satisfaction was to be short-lived. The following Monday, Grade issued another press statement – with none of the bonhomie which had accompanied the former. It tersely broke the news that the contract had been dropped.

'You may *earn* the right to a bigger say in how you work,' reflected Potter bitterly, 'but you are damned to the eyeballs as soon as you seek to exercise it.'

His sentiments were, and have long been, echoed by all those independent artists who have clamoured to make the new Fourth Channel a showcase for an alternative choice to the run-of-the-mill fodder which presently provides British television with its staple diet. Towards this hope, Lord Annan's Committee on the Future of Broadcasting had leant their weight; but alas for men like Dennis Potter, the newly-returned Thatcher government threw the Annan recommendations overboard.

'The Fourth Channel, so long our hope and now due in 1982, has been virtually handed over to the existing ITV companies,' lamented Dennis Potter.

And the Independent Broadcasting Authority's forecast that £29,000 per hour as the price it is prepared to pay for the privilege of controlling the new channel has caused even deeper gloom among the band of freedom fighters who wanted to break the BBC–ITV duploy.

'That will buy you a two minute commercial at today's rates,' says Potter contemptuously. 'A genuine film drama cannot be made at such a price.'

The article he penned as a farewell raspberry in the face of British television probably summed up as eloquently as anything the indignation and frustration men like Potter have come to feel about the way television is administered at present. 'Take a look at LWT and other ITV profits,' he urged his readers. 'Examine the waste. Run your finger down the TV programme pages – and then ask yourself whether you get the kind of TV you really want.

'I'm afraid I cannot wait around for the answer. I have to go to Hollywood next week to work on a big MGM movie that everyone over here turned down flat. It won't be lonely – the place is stuffed full of British writers who have sore knuckles from hammering on too many closed doors in their own country.

'I may even bump into Michael Grade in Hollywood. If his face is red, it won't be from the Californian sunshine.'

Dennis Potter's weariness with the workings of the system comes despite years of desultory effort to distribute the power of television moguls more fairly and sheaves of well-intentioned reports aimed at giving viewers a better deal.

The first chill blast around the walls of the newly carved out empires came from the now largely forgotten Pilkington Report in 1962. Pilkington's committee looked into the workings of the infant industry, which was then, after only five years' existence, leaving the BBC with barely 25 per cent of the viewing audience. They loathed what they saw. The venom of Pilkington's condemnation of ITV's standards and populist policies surprised even the hard-core anti-ITV faction which had held out so volubly in Parliament and elsewhere against the introduction of commercial television into this country in the years before poor Grace Archer was burned at the ratings stake.

With the pronouncements of Sir Harry Pilkington and his committee (the report was, in fact, drafted by Dr Richard Hoggart), the puritan brigade rallied the opposition forces once again. They set off to charge at full tilt in the hope of scattering what was deemed to be the wages of sinful Mammon and a rapid descent into mindless mediocrity. In his admirably comprehensive book, *The Mirror in the Corner*, Peter Black, the former television critic of the *Daily Mail*, has likened this running combat to a power-struggle between Roundheads and Cavaliers. Sir Harry Pilkington's report certainly sharpened the Roundheads' pikes. The Cavaliers were at first in outraged disarray, resorting to all manner of curious revenges in their own defence. Peter Cadbury, whose holdings in the regional Westward TV had momentarily eclipsed his family interest in chocolates, organized a spectacular garden party at which a giant effigy of Sir Harry's report was burnt together with six actual copies for good measure.

To begin with, the Cavaliers' commander-in-chief, in the shape of the Independent Television Authority – the body originally responsible for keeping good order and discipline among the troops in the field – decided only to apply a little cosmetic surgery to the unacceptable face of capitalism as this was being revealed in the cathode ray tubes. But, by 1966, they were ready to make strategic withdrawals and to effect some sweeping redistributions of vital territories.

3

In granting the 1968 contracts, the ITA effected their first serious shake-up within the industry since Independent Television's own national network had finally been completed some seven years previously. From 1961 it had been able to compete home for home with the BBC. And, from its earliest days, there was no doubt at all in which way the viewing masses were moving.

At the portentous Guildhall opening celebration of 22 September 1955, the Postmaster-General of the day, Dr (later Lord) Hill, had assured the assembled founding fathers of the new channel: 'Television is here and an immensely powerful, ever-growing medium it is.' Only a year later they were able to rub their hands with glee at seeing exactly how ever-growing their stake in that medium had been. The 188,000 Channel 9 sets which received Dr Hill's tub-thumping address had grown to 1,550,000. The number of viewers who watched them had swollen, according to official estimates, from 658,000 to over 5 million; and all within a year.

The trend continued, unstoppable as the incoming tide or the waxing moon. Soon independent television was claiming to have captured all but 25 per cent of the viewing public. But, by 1968, the Pilkington ethic of no profit without quality, no privilege without responsibility, was coming home to roost.

The first Big Four network companies (ABC, Associated Rediffusion, ATV and Granada) became the Big Five (ATV, Granada, London Weekend Television, Thames and Yorkshire); of the two original contract companies to survive intact, ATV and Granada suffered drastically altered boundaries and/or viewing space. Moreover, reform from within was hastened by additional pressure from without. After a select parliamentary committee had delivered a post-Pilkington dig in the ribs, the output of 'serious' programmes transmitted by the independent companies perked up from 25 per cent to 34 per cent. Home-grown documentaries crept up from a meagre 4 per cent to 7 per cent of output. And the ratio of peak drama originating from ITV companies (as opposed to the old films or comedy series complained of so bitterly by Sir Harry and his stalwarts) grew from 23 per cent to 28 per cent in the programme planning. News and current events programmes were all but doubled.

To allay further criticism of enormous gains being made from shoddy goods, the independent companies would be able to point to undeniable artistic achievements over the years. By the time Lord Annan and his committee came to look into the merits or otherwise of the country's broadcasting system, they could boast some outstanding successes. The non-profit-making Independent Television News Service had, time and again, overwhelmed its rivals with its smooth professionalism, speed and incisiveness. London Weekend Television's *Upstairs Downstairs* became an international earner without ever lowering its sights; it proved as valid a commentary on the social mores of class evolution as an engrossing entertainment. Granada, though it had forfeited its early claims to be a foremost showcase for new drama, could still hold its head high with such products as *Sam* and *The Disappearing World*. Associated Television weighed in with the studiously re-searched *Edward VII*.

Thames's record for putting out adventurous television had become a most impressive roll-call: *World at War, Jennie, Rock Follies* and *The Naked Civil Servant* all provided admirable antidotes to ITV's persistent stereotype of endless give-away quiz shows, tired variety formats, old movies and silly domestic comedy series. Meanwhile, as their sharp sports team might say, up at Yorkshire rests the crown Granada once wore as king of the drama and controversial documentary departments. Yorkshire TV's harrowing *Johnny Go Home* case-history into the plight of vagrant teenage boys in London was investigative journalism of the highest order. The resulting official clean-up and public outcry once again proved, if proof were still needed, how immediate is the effect of such

18

exposures of social evil on television when compared, say, with the equally thorough and exposing researches of Henry Mayhew into the lives of London's poor over a century before.

Emboldened by their success with *Johnny Go Home*, the same production team at Yorkshire created an even greater sensation, resulting in a parliamentary hue and cry, into the treatment of mental patients at the government's criminal mental hospital, Rampton.

With something much akin to relief, the Independent Broadcasting Authority was moved collectively to reflect: 'That there is some dross in this output is not surprising; it is gratifying that in recent years viewers and critics have recognized such gold.'

It is certainly no intention of the present author to sit like a Pilkington committee member in judgement on the artistic virtues or otherwise of commercial television. Lord Hill himself – having been elevated not only to the peerage but also to the post of chairman of the Independent Television Authority, after presiding over its creation as a former Postmaster-General – declared it was not difficult to assess the financial strength of the various companies which bid for the authority's contracts; the greatest difficulty was rather to judge between promise and performance. Yet, even to assess performance, is to impose one's personal taste. So, although Lord Annan's Report opined that, 'severe as our criticisms of the BBC have been, they still, in our judgement, give a better all-round service to the public than does ITV', the statement remains the subjective verdict of that particular committee.

Slightly mystifying, however, is the somewhat airy way the Annan committee members dismissed one of the most prickly questions in the whole thorny issue of protected profits. There is something which smacks of Pontius Pilate in the way they shrug their shoulders and say: 'Whether or not the ITV companies give the country the service it deserves *in view of the profits which they make* [my italics] is a debate to which there is no end.' As most of us understood Lord Annan's original brief in 1974, it was this very debate which his committee was appointed to bring to an end.

Quality, however, is not here a prime concern; but fair dealing is. If we are to argue the case for democracy in terms of television, then it must follow that, if everyone has the right to speak but not the right to be listened to, those who listen must also be free to hear what they wish to hear. Like the idealist who will disagree with what you say but defend to the death your right to say it, the present author must meekly stifle his own innate distaste for such hapless entertainment as *Crossroads* so long as there is sufficient viewing public demanding to see it. What seems of greater concern is Lord Annan's finding that the advent of a rival channel to the BBC's monopoly, has not, in practice, created a wider spectrum or broader vision for the viewer to enjoy, but has achieved exactly the opposite.

> At present [runs Annan's summary of things as they stood before the 1980 battle for a Fourth Channel was resolved] the BBC and IBA pursue similar objectives. For that they are not to blame. Parliament set them similar objectives...but the effect has been to narrow the range of choice for the public.

Was it for this that, as will be seen, a handful of businessmen catapulted themselves into a rarefied class of protected international tycoonery and acquired the means to a life-style to rival any potentate's? And always with wealth comes access to power. No one could or ever has claimed that any one of these men has behaved like a latter-day Goebbels and abused the undeniable influence from which their wealth is accumulated, except perhaps by default in the standards attained by their programmes. And, against this subjective charge, there is in the end a double safeguard. Given the nature of their operations, the first and regrettably the most persuasive defence is plummeting viewing figures. In the absence of any other competitor for television advertising's multi-million pound revenue, the only way the companies can render their lucrative monopoly worthless is by demonstrating that their clients are whistling in the wind. That is exactly what they would be doing if they were to pay vast fees to promote their products on a medium which most customers ignored. Money may talk, but public indifference is also capable of answering back.

This is, of course, not an argument which the businessmen who masterminded the contract companies like to pursue too prominently. It smacks of control by the sponsors, and in the United Kingdom, at any rate, as Lord Annan discovered to everyone's relief, there is hardly any evidence for individual advertisers attempting to influence the content of programmes on ITV. Why should they? They simply keep a close eye on the ratings and adjust their purchase of prime advertising time accordingly. Certainly nothing causes so much consternation along the corridors of independent television's scattered empire as proof of having lost favour with the viewers.

Nothing shocked the bosses of Independent Television more fundamentally than the notable failure to woo back a mass audience from the BBC at the end of the long and costly dispute with their engineering unions at the end of 1979. Populist as their policies have invariably been, the inevitable conclusion to be drawn was that absence had not made the public's heart grow fonder. They had hardly been missed. Their humiliation in the eyes of their advertisers was complete when Thames TV televised the British Academy of Film and Television Arts Awards for 1979-80. Out of the ten top awards for individual excellence, the combined might of the five principal networks and the nine regional satellites could snatch only one from the parade of BBC personnel who filed back and forth in front of Princess Anne and the cameras. More shaming still were the expressions of scorn from the television critics next morning for the dreary way Thames had stage-managed the actual presentation. These were some of the disparaging remarks made by Herbert Kretzmer of the *Daily Mail*.

> It is ironic that a programme honouring superior achievement in the screen arts should itself prove barely watchable. Award ceremonies, if we must have them, are themselves media events and should aim at least to be as credibly professional as the shows which get the prizes...Princess Anne had concluded her strained opening remarks with a breezy assurance that 'things can only get better'. But they got immediately worse. By the end the Wembley audience appeared to be stunned by the tedium of it all like bored schoolchildren in a vast classroom waiting for the sound of the bell.

Only Melvyn Bragg's *South Bank Show* saved the ITV companies from complete annihilation by winning an award for its producer-presenter, Mr Bragg himself.

Such cynical considerations aside, there is the second fail-safe against the worst abuses or misuses of the power and wealth which an ITV franchise brings. This is the Independent Broadcasting Authority, and it is to them that the TV bosses themselves prefer to point when the taint of owning a licence to print money is raised against them.

21

4

The Independent Broadcasting Authority acts rather like a Star Chamber over the feudal commercial rights of its TV barons, though you will find no one openly to admit it. 'The Authority has one moment of supreme and lasting influence over programmes: when it decides who will produce them and who will not,' maintained Sir Robert Fraser, the flamboyantly expressive original director-general of the ITA. 'The Authority sees them as partners to be trusted not agents to be instructed.' Sir Robert was quite innocent of the way the winds were to blow. The IBA gradually evolved into one of the most curious of institutions imaginable: part publisher, part censor, part impresario, part arbiter, part Santa Claus, part Wicked Uncle. It is the giver of contracts and the receiver of levies. By some painful contortion it must put itself in the position of official benefactor to the barons and impartial watchdog for the public. In gambling terms, its roles cover shuffling and dealing the cards as well as holding the bank and interpreting the rules.

Against these charges of conflicting interests on the part of the IBA, it should be pointed out that they are the only publishers in any media to be answerable directly to Parliament. Even the British Broadcasting Corporation is free of this formidable onus.

Exactly how such a confusion of responsibility came about is as difficult to pin down as a canary in a cornfield. But the effort is intriguing and ultimately rewarding.

*

It all began long before the Television Bill that was introduced into the House of Commons on 4 March 1954, finally to break the BBC's monopoly on broadcasting. To bring that complex Bill into being there had been the strangest coupling of bedfellows. On each side of the fence, lions lay down, albeit awkwardly, with lambs. Lord Hailsham, the clamorous champion of High Toryism, found himself, for example, penned in with practically the entire Labour Party, an experience which may have accounted for his subsequent outburst on the subject; in the House of Lords, deputizing for Lord Halifax, he worked himself into enraged Reithian rhetoric, denouncing the advent of sponsored television as being as lethally contagious as 'smallpox, bubonic plague and the Black Death'. Even his most ardent admirers thought he had gone a bit far.

The Parliamentary Labour Party remained resolute in its distaste for what their leader Clement Attlee denounced as allowing television 'to pass into the hands of private profiteers'. Even here there was one solitary dissenting voice to the general stand: that of Anthony Wedgwood Benn. Whereas Christopher Mayhew proved to be the party's most vociferous voice of conscience from first to last, it was Mr Wedgwood Benn, the implacable thorn in the side of any who were later to stray from the narrow stony path to true socialist doctrine, who advocated compromise. He sought to reconcile those who were most deeply troubled by the BBC's monopoly of this most potent means of communication and those who shied away from the market-place of commercial television. His proposed solution was that the BBC 'be reorganized in such a way as to avoid many of the monopoly dangers'.

The Conservatives, the party of free enterprise, were much more deeply divided. Crucial, perhaps, in their state of flux for or against taking away the BBC's monopoly was the ambivalence of Sir Winston Churchill himself. The old warrior, so quick in the recently won global hostilities to exploit every trick in the trade of mass communications in the interests of national morale, was inclined to regard television as nothing more than a 'peep show'. He was neither atheist nor agnostic on the matter, but adopted an élitist's pose, as if shying away from the tiresome attentions of an unseemly rabble. It was left to others within the Conservative ranks to pioneer the cause of commercial television.

Lord Woolton, the party's chairman from 1946, was its most persuasive advocate. He it was who welded the forces of change together. From his influential post in the party, he represented a

23

new breed of Tory sitting on the backbenches; the first post-war election had set no fewer than a hundred fresh faces among the Conservative ranks in the Commons. Under Woolton's subtle leadership, there was born what might be called a practical Conservatism as opposed to the old Establishment brand. If Churchill was to dismiss television as little better than an intrusive toy, as Professor Hugh H. Wilson strongly suggests in his exhaustive survey on the foundation of ITV, *Pressure Group: the Campaign for Commercial Television*, Woolton did not. He marshalled his troops and bided his time.

That time came about almost by accident and default. The Beveridge Committee set up by the Attlee government had rejected the case for breaking the monopoly, not because it challenged those who, like Anthony Wedgwood Benn, wanted to end the monopoly, but because, with the means available, there would appear to be no prospect of improvement if they did. (Thirty years on, Lord Annan's findings both roundly support that contention, even now when the means are at hand, and put the blame on Parliament for setting the BBC and IBA such similar tasks.)

Beveridge made a hundred recommendations that would tame 'the brute force' of the BBC's monopoly without causing it any harm, but his findings were rendered redundant practically before they were published.

The year after the Beveridge Committee came into being, the Labour government's overwhelming majority in the Commons was slashed to six by the General Election of 1950. As the socialists limped on through a bleak winter of strikes and cabinet revolts, ill-health joined hands with bad luck to thwart them further. A series of physical afflictions within the cabinet had as far-reaching an effect on the future of commercial television as it did on the short-term life of the Attlee administration.

Herbert Morrison, who had been placed in charge of broadcasting affairs after the war, would later declare himself to be, on balance, in favour of the BBC's monopoly. But, in the meantime, he was hastily switched to the Foreign Office as a result of the illness of the then Foreign Secretary, Ernest Bevin. Bevin nominally took over Morrison's brief on broadcasting, but was far too much of a sick man to make his presence felt. On 10 April 1951 he had one significant meeting with Lord Simon, chairman of the Board of Governors at the BBC, and Sir William Haley, the director-general, to discuss broadcasting's future. He died four days later.

24

Responsibility passed into the hands of Patrick Gordon Walker, not nearly such a heavyweight in cabinet as Morrison or even an ailing Bevin. With the Korean conflict abroad and a growing economic crisis at home, he found it impossible to settle the future of the increasingly worried British Broadcasting Corporation.

By the time Attlee again went to the country, in October 1951, death and sickness had sapped the strength of the real muscle within the Labour Party. Sir Stafford Cripps had had to resign from the Exchequer in the first October of that brief Parliament, Bevin had died in the following spring, and Attlee himself was referred to hospital with a duodenal ulcer, the classic symptom of a man under pressure. Between the presentation of the Beveridge Report, with its overwhelming support for continuing the BBC's monopoly with modification, and the advent of the new Conservative government, the outgoing Labour government had not found time to review the BBC's Charter, due to run out at the end of the year. The new men renewed it for six months while considering what to do.

While the whole issue was thrown back into the melting-pot, Lord Woolton by no means managed to stir things all in his own direction. When he had stood up in the House of Lords the previous July to speak in favour of ending the monopoly of the BBC and had asked his colleagues to consider, 'within a reasonable distance of time from now', creating or leasing some station 'that would permit sponsored programmes', he was a lone voice. Not a single member of the Lords who spoke in the debate supported his views.

He was scarcely better served on the cabinet committee set up to work out a policy to fill the hiatus left by the previous government. The four-man committee immediately went into deadlock. Woolton, as Lord President of the Council, and James (later Lord) Stuart, Secretary of State for Scotland, were known to back commercial broadcasting. Sir David Maxwell-Fyfe (Home Secretary and Welsh affairs) and the Marquess of Salisbury (Lord Privy Seal) needed convincing. In the actual cabinet, support for the views of Woolton and Stuart was even more sparse. Only Lord Simonds, then Lord Chancellor, added his open advocacy to their arguments. However, in March Woolton replaced Lord Salisbury as the man master-minding the government's attitudes on broadcasting. By the time the committee's White Paper was published in May, the radical wing among the new 'practical' Conservatives, ably assisted by Lord Woolton, had caused to be placed in it a small paragraph which was, in effect, a ticking time-bomb under the BBC's entrenched rights. It read meekly enough, however, to cause little consternation among the enemies of commercialism. Indeed, it asked no more than that 'in the expanding field of television, provision should be made to permit some element of competition when the calls on capital resources at present needed for purposes of greater national importance make this feasible'.

Elsewhere in the White Paper there was plenty to soothe the fears of the BBC lobby, not least the assurance that the corporation must have first claim 'when labour and materials become available'. Moreover, the document was adamant in its view that any new station should be subject to the supervision of some controlling body, and that political or religious broadcasting were definitely not to be allowed. So the worries of those who feared the prospect of the puissant new medium of television falling into the hands of propagandists were also banished.

But, with the phrase 'some element of competition', the bomb was in position and primed.

Norman Collins, the man who had in the earliest post-war days of the BBC served on his colleagues notice of his belief in the Titan strength of the medium, was first to light the fuse. Having resigned from the BBC, he set about showing his erstwhile colleagues that he intended business. With Sir Robert Renwick, C. O. Stanley and the backing of Lord Bessborough's merchant bank, Benson, Lonsdale & Co., Collins formed the first commercial television consortium. It was an impressive union of interests, even by the standards with which we are familiar today. Stanley was the chairman and managing director of the vast Pye conglomerate, whose interest lay mainly in the hardware of communications, being manufacturers of radio, television and electronic equipment. Renwick brought with him an equally wide range of interests in the electrical industry, as well as his invaluable experience as controller of communications at the Air Ministry and controller of communications equipment at the Ministry of Aircraft Production. Allied to Lord Bessborough's banking interests, the group, calling itself the Associated Broadcasting Development Company, was the earliest object-lesson in how to assemble a television consortium. It has been the prototype for all those that have followed.

If one combines the financial assets of a respectable merchant bank with the proven administrative ability of a public figure, then

26

adds a vested interest in the responsible expansion of the medium to an undeniable and recognized artistic flair, there is on the face of it an instant recipe for a fair bid for any commercial television franchise when it comes up for the taking. As it transpired, Mr Collins could have been luckier in choosing his backing bank. Their caution was to cost him his slice of the cake when the time came for it to be cut.

Collins himself always claimed that he was forced into the direction he took by the BBC itself. Certainly his views on the future of broadcasting diametrically conflicted with those of Sir William Haley, and could not possibly have co-existed within the same organization. Furthermore, the reasons for his resignation as head of BBC TV only served to convince many fair-minded people, both inside and outside the cradle of democracy, that the corporation's control of our broadcasting system had become a most dangerous threat to the fundamental rights of free expression.

What started it all was a mildly satirical trifle of a play – how trifling may be judged from the title – called *Party Manners* and written by Val Gielgud. It poked fun at politicians and implied that socialists also had itchy palms willing to be scratched. For this heresy, Lord Simon, the Chairman of the BBC, decided to scrap the transmission of the live repeat of the play (there were as yet no tele-recordings of the traditional Sunday play). He could not have demonstrated more clearly the iniquities of the monopoly had he crossed the floor and joined Lord Woolton in his solitary campaign. The largely Tory press roared disapproval at the ban, and the *Sunday Express* – part of the Beaverbrook stable which remained super-sensitively opposed to independent television long after it became a reality – gave Collins an entire page on which to argue his case when he walked out of the corporation a week later.

Cannily, and not without just cause, Collins assumed the mantle of the martyr who has voluntarily put his head on the block. 'The man who resigns from the BBC knows perfectly well that in the present circumstances he can never again engage in the control or direction of any broadcasting service within these shores,' he told readers of the *Sunday Express*. He went on eloquently to encapsulate the plight of the artist, writer or communicator who finds himself without a platform on which to take a stance or a means to make his voice heard. On the subject of the BBC's monopoly, he wrote:

It is unhealthy for the corporation because it means that some members of the staff remain there, patiently and miserably working out their time, for the simple reason that they know only too well that their single, specialized talent is totally valueless and unsaleable outside. It is equally unhealthy for the person who resigns. He is apt to fall into the dangerous mental state of believing that he is the only one in step. He may have been. Or he may not. The one thing that is certain is that he will never know, because there is no wholesome corrective alternative employment that might disabuse him.

It was Collins who thought up the very name 'Independent Television' once his 'wholesome corrective alternative' became a definite gleam at the end of the 1954 Television Bill. The term was a master-stroke of propaganda in its own way, coined during informal chit-chat at the Reform Club. At a stroke it sweetened the image of the enterprise by removing from it the taint of blatant commercialism.

Blessing the rose with another name, however, was not enough to convince its die-hard opponents that sponsored television would be all that Collins so earnestly and honestly desired. It is instructive to find so many of his arguments for free expression being fulminated over again when Lord Annan was set the task of deciding what form a wholesome alternative to the duopoly of the BBC and ITV should take.

'If I am free to say anything I want to say except the one thing I want to say, then I am not free,' Anthony Smith, that persuasive historian and broadcaster, informed the Annan Committee. 'If the medium is to be managed how can there be any democracy? A single prohibition on a national broadcasting authority or within it tends to corrode the whole output.'

The sentiments could just as easily and aptly have been penned by Mr Collins in the *Sunday Express* the week after he quit the BBC thirty years earlier.

5

'If we hadn't fired Collins there would be no commercial television now,' grumbled Lord Simon. He was wrong on three counts. First, Collins was not fired; he resigned. Secondly, Collins never really believed Parliament would swallow sponsorship whole, which was why, out of all the founder fathers, he was the most interesting and least lucky. And thirdly, with Lord Simon himself adding the most inflammable kind of fuel to the fires of the Conservatives' over-heated notions about left-wing bias within the BBC, something had to give when Labour lost the election. Censorship can be a two-edged weapon.

In the event, when it made its appearance, the Bill seemed to please nobody. It was condemned by those who most fervently sought to end the BBC's monopoly as 'a sorry compromise'. The Roundhead faction, who continued to see the dawn of commercial television as the opening of perdition's gates, naturally regarded it as anathema. Patrick Gordon Walker pledged that the Labour Party – whose election defeat and failure to ratify the BBC's Charter had paved the very path they were now being dragged along – would abolish Independent Television immediately on being returned to office.

Interestingly enough, as the clever Mr Collins had anticipated back at the Reform Club, the name of the new animal excited tremendous interest. What it should be called fermented as much keen debate in both houses as how it should be constituted. Behind the debate, camouflaged but ever-present in the undergrowth, was one very British sentiment: 'Gentlemen don't earn money, especially money from advertising.' So far as I can discover, the name of Christopher Tietjens was never mentioned in the debates, but his memorable old Tory sentiment from the novels of Ford Madox Ford underlay the entire proceedings.

Those who took Mr Collins's advice and fought for the title 'Independent Television Authority' found themselves opposed because it carried the implication that the BBC was not independent. Those who wished to dub it the 'Commercial Television Authority' were accused of wishing to load it with a term already pejorative to the general public. None of its parliamentary sponsors wanted the new channel to be linked in the minds of potential viewers with the sleazier aspects of commercial hotels or commercial travelling. 'Independent' might not be an entirely accurate description of the newcomer, and by the time the powers of the authority were defined it most certainly was not, but it had a wholesome ring to it.

'Alternative' television was, of course, the word Norman Collins had first used in his *Sunday Express* article, and the one he wanted us to have. (What we got eventually, as Lord Annan was to admit twenty-five years later, was largely more of the same disguised with advertising breaks. By that time, however, Lord Annan's most far-reaching recommendations towards Utopia were ready to be swept aside as Beveridge's had been in their own day.) To our ears today even the term 'Alternative' as applied to the media has become tinged with an odour of impossible dreams from damp cellars and lunatic fringe publications. No doubt if anyone attempted to dub the embryo Fourth Channel with such a title, they would also be accused of trying to discredit it, despite the fact that so many independently minded broadcasters, writers and communicators have looked for so long towards that innovation with much the same aspirations which Collins hoped to achieve with the coming of the Second.

The Bill grumbled its way on to the statute books with nobody quite clear over exactly what mandate had been given to the emergent ITA, apart from the gift of the contracts and the promise of £750,000 a year to put on any programmes which it felt might, in exceptional circumstances, not be fitting subjects to be surrounded with advertisements.

'The ITA is not intended to be a broadcasting organization at all,' the noble Lords were told by the Earl of Selkirk on behalf of the Paymaster General when the Bill and its myriad of amendments landed in their laps. 'It is a regulating organization set up to handle the programme contractors.' And despite all the Lords' cogitations over the desirability of removing coverage for royal, religious and educational events from the maw of commerce and placing these safely in the lily-white hands of the new authority, that was what the ITA eventually came to be. The Act which received the Royal Assent on 30 July 1954, however, was exactly what Dennis Lloyd, Quain Professor of Jurisprudence at London University, dubbed it: 'A collection of vague and ill-defined duties' – duties which were made no clearer by the dust-dry wording of the crucial clauses in Section Three, Sub-section One:

It shall be the duty of the Authority to satisfy themselves that, so far as possible, the programmes broadcast by the Authority comply with the following requirements, that is to say –

(a) that nothing is included in the programmes which offends against good taste or decency or is likely to encourage or incite to crime or to lead to disorder or to be offensive to public feeling or which contains any offensive representation of or reference to a living person;

(b) that the programmes maintain a proper balance in their subject-matter and a high general standard of quality;

(c) that any news given in the programmes (in whatever form) is presented with due accuracy and impartiality;

(d) that proper proportions of the recorded and other matter included in the programmes are of British origin and of British performance;

(e) that the programmes broadcast from any station or stations contain a suitable proportion of matter calculated to appeal specially to the tastes and outlook of persons served by the station or stations;

(f) that due impartiality is preserved on the part of the persons providing the programmes as respects matters of political or industrial controversy or relating to current public policy; and

(g) subject as hereinafter provided in this subsection, that no matter designed to serve the interests of any political party is included in the programmes:

Provided that nothing in paragraph (g) of this sub-section should prevent –

(i) the inclusion in the programmes of relays of the whole (but not some only) of a series of the British Broadcasting

Corporation's party political broadcasts.

(ii) the inclusion in the programmes of properly balanced discussions or debates where the persons taking part express opinions and put forward arguments of a political character.

What offends good taste or decency is as imponderable a conundrum as what constitutes good taste and decency. What is a 'proper' balance of subject matter? Whose standards of quality will be used to measure the ambiguous term 'high general'? What proportion of British-produced programmes is considered 'proper' and by whom?

The Act posed as many questions as it answered. Even the manner of allocating the contracts – which were being openly predicted by the advertising industry to yield a revenue of between £5 and £10 million a year – was little better than open-ended. So much so that Lord Hailsham, never far from the thick of the fray, was moved to expostulate:

> When I see the Government proposing a system of television the effect of which may be, as far as one can tell, to erect a series of local monopolies over the country for the purpose of television, I am bound to enquire of the Government how that squares with the principles of competition as against monopoly? Because these three broadcasting stations [London, Birmingham and the North of England were the first bases planned for the new service] will not, in effect be competing against one another or against the BBC.

His point was as sharp as his language was blunt. It stung a more satisfactory definition of the new service from the Paymaster General who assured Parliament that the best system – 'and I mean the best system from the point of view of introducing genuine commercial competition and also for the commercial success of the scheme' – was a time-sharing arrangement under which the whole network would be divided between several main contractors, each of whom would have sole use of it for a set number of days a week. These would then be supplemented by smaller local companies for the individual regions.

In other words, give or take a few shifts in the boundaries and the time schedules, this is what we have today. It only remained for the Independent Television Authority to be constituted (under director-general Sir Robert Fraser), to agree on the powers they had been given and how to administer them, and the following advertisement could be placed in the newspapers of 25 August that year:

THE INDEPENDENT TELEVISION AUTHORITY INVITES APPLICATIONS FROM THOSE INTERESTED IN BECOMING PROGRAMME CONTRACTORS IN ACCORDANCE WITH THE PROVISIONS OF THE TELEVISION ACT. APPLICANTS SHOULD GIVE A BROAD PICTURE OF THE TYPE OF PROGRAMME THEY WOULD PROVIDE, THEIR PROPOSALS FOR NETWORK OR LOCAL BROADCASTING OF THEIR PROGRAMMES, SOME INDICATION OF THEIR FINANCIAL RESOURCES AND THE LENGTH OF CONTRACT THEY WOULD DESIRE.

There was, oddly enough, no mad rush to reply. A mere twenty-five companies availed themselves of the ITA's invitation. Of course, there remained enough uncertainties to scare away the timid. The contracts on offer were for ten years, but no one could yet make a guess on how long it would take to earn back the £3 million or so calculated to be needed to launch a new station. If the contracts were a licence to print money, few were eager to risk the money it took to acquire one. There were, it seemed, few enough people to share Dolly Levi's optimistic view that money is like manure: the more you spread it around the more it makes things grow. But to the bold goes the victory. Soon the original twenty-five contenders had shrunk to five: Associated-Rediffusion, Prince Littler's Incorporated Television Programme Company, Sidney Bernstein's Granada cinema chain, an alliance made up of the Kemsley Press and Maurice Winnick and, of course, Norman Collins's Asociated Broadcasting Development Company. Of the five principals, perhaps only Collins believed one hundred per cent in the garrulous Sir Robert Fraser's sweeping assertion: 'This is free television in a free country and the people will get the television they want, as they get the press and government they want.'

The fact, of course, is that no one can possibly ever know what the public wants with any degree of certainty. As Lord Annan was to point out, if they did, there would be no marketing disasters, no unsaleable goods, no failures in the cinema, no remainders in the hands of publishers. The impenetrable conundrum, 'How do I know what I think until I hear what I say?' is just as valid when it reads: 'How do I know what I want to see until I see what I have?'

It was to explore this fundamental freedom that Norman Collins walked out of the BBC and pioneered his vision of a wholesome alternative. How depressing it is, then, to read what Lord Annan's committee thought of the staple diet which had been fed to the public in twenty-five years of giving them what they want. 'Much of

ITV's output seems settled in well-worn grooves, safe, stereotyped and routine in its production,' the Annan Report dismally recorded.

They could just as easily have been speaking about the progress *The Archers* had made by the silver jubilee of Grace's death as the bold new experiment which Collins had virtually launched on his own. The competition between the chief operators themselves hardened into business rather than artistic rivalry; the battle with the BBC degenerated into a ratings race. As events fell out, as events will where men and money mix for private gain, Collins's hand was not to be the one that took the tiller to steer the craft he helped to design. Ultimately it was an ex-booking agent and former Charleston champion, the boss of a northern cinema chain, an ex-airline pilot, a former British Ambassador and a media whizz-kid who steered the fortunes of independent television into the harbour where Lord Annan found it.

The booking agent was Lew Grade.

PART TWO

Up Graded

6

There are few people inside the entertainment industry who do not hold Lew Grade in high professional regard, and there are many who view him with real and warm affection. They may not like everything he does, but the manner in which he accomplishes it leaves even his most partisan critics in a certain state of awe. His simple aim in all his dealings is to offend nobody and to sell to everyone. This is nothing sinister to be found in that, unless you take elitism to its most repugnant extreme and totally oppose the ethics of trade. 'I have hundreds of rivals but no real enemies,' he is often pleased to say, and he probably tells no more than the truth.

It was, however, Hugh Jenkins, MP, when he was Labour's Minister for the Arts, who gave the most succinct expression to misgivings about the system which enables men like Lew Grade to consolidate such an empire.

'I agree Lew Grade is a nice man,' said Jenkins without much fear of contradiction, 'but what is dangerous is that such a concentration of power should rest even in the most moral hands. It is a dangerous situation in which a man has such power that the question of whether he's a nice man or not is not important. Even Lew Grade is not immortal.'

When a government minister expresses his alarm in such strong, unequivocal terms, it is worth while to examine more closely the causes for his concern. Niceness and straight-dealing are not the issue; nor is plutocracy. Something far more difficult to define, yet all the more insidious for that, is at stake. 'The greater the power, the more dangerous the abuse,' said the eighteenth-century philosopher Edmund Burke two centuries before such a force as television was ever imaginable. Even the high priest of free enterprise, Benjamin Disraeli, qualified the Victorians' unswerving belief in personal empire-building by writing: 'I repeat that all power is a trust – that we are accountable for its exercise – that from the people, and for the people, all springs and all must exist.'

To justify his own position, Lew Grade can point to his ratings. If that is not power from the people and for the people, what is it? He is genuinely perplexed by the sophistication of Mr Jenkins's arguments, and will maintain with sincerely wounded feelings that the accumulation of money is the last thing he thinks about. 'Multimillionaire? Baloney!' he protests, a small, finely boned hand raised in horror so that the gold jewellery winks away up to his cuffs. 'I have no money. I spend my money. I have perhaps been very generous with my money, but let's not go into details about that. Making money, having power, that's just an incidental part. If people let it change their lives, they don't love their work.'

All this, as we shall see, is the case. He *does* love his work. He *is* nice. He *does* produce popular programmes. He *does* give the public what they seem to want. He is *not* interested in amassing wealth for wealth's sake. He *is* the benefactor of countless untold good causes. The epitaph he once asked for was: 'I always kept my word' (subsequently altered to: 'I didn't want to go'!) But go, one way or another, he must. He himself has fixed his retirement at the year 2000. Be that as it may, as Hugh Jenkins points out, even the most moral men are mortal.

However or whenever he goes, he will leave behind that 'dangerous concentration of power', and given the vagaries which put it into those sensitive, delicate hands in the first place, who can tell what manner of man will succeed him?

When Lew Grade finally emerged from the fascinating early musical chairs at Association TeleVision, his company's assets stood at £9,400,000. Within the first ten years of his single-minded stewardship, this tiny, rotund and genial man had husbanded his empire so shrewdly, and with such canny flair, that its assets topped the £35 million mark and its interests spread around the globe. By the time the centre of his all-consuming interest had shifted from television

to the making of movie spectaculars and he took the title of presi-
dent, it is fair to say that he had stamped his personal mark on all
branches of the entertainment industry from his vast office in ATV
House, Great Cumberland Place, adjacent to London's Marble
Arch; he had become a showman mogul cast in a heroic mould, as
Lord Annan was to agree.

By then the chances were that when you turned on your radio,
went to the cinema, bought a record or a theatre ticket, relaxed at
home in front of the box or merely whistled a tune, this amazing
man would own a slice of your consumption. For his £210,000 a
year president's salary, he brought a Sam Goldwyn touch to the
television industry. No other man has been so successful in selling
what the public wants to buy. There are few who would deny Lew
(later Sir Lew and latterly Lord) Grade the status of the real
founding genius at ATV. The one man who might have put in a
counter-claim was Val Parnell, and Val Parnell is dead.

Grade himself enjoys telling how he first came to be in television.
Like most stories concerning him it has a nub of truth and is
packaged with a showman's relish for the quotable anecdote. It
started, he says, with the advertisement placed by the ITA inviting
interested parties to tender for the original contracts. His version of
what followed has all the hallmarks of his own bravura simplicity:

'Now it was bandied about at the time that you needed £3 million.
I said how was I going to get that kind of money? Well, my friend
said he had someone who could find £2 million if I could find the
rest and a board consisting of people well known enough in entertainment. I said "Okay" and I told my brother Leslie he was in the
entertainment industry.

'At that time we hadn't got much money. We put in all we had –
about £15,000 each. Then I rang Val Parnell and told him: "You're
in the television business" and he put in £10,000 to £15,000. Then I
called other friends and we virtually formed the group.'

Among the most influential of those other friends was Prince
Littler, chief of the Moss Empires variety chain. It was an impressive showbusiness consortium by any standards. There are people
who remember hearing Val Parnell tell a similar story with the calls
reversed. Exactly who picked up the phone and called whom is not,
however, the real point. It is a good story and it is a revealing story,
for it demonstrates lucidly what a modest outlay was needed for
these leading showmen to buy their way into the ground floor of a
multi-million pound venture. It is also some indication of how

much (or little) they judged that new industry to be worth.

For what Grade's throw-away anecdote disguises is in fact how *slow* any of them was to pick up the phone. It was certainly not a case of sizing up the potential of the new service, as both Norman Collins and Lord Woolton had done five years before, and rushing in to bag a claim. The bandwagon had been rolling, albeit bumpily, for a long time before Lew Grade jumped aboard. He actually missed the ITA's advertisement in the newspapers. And even after it had been brought to his attention and the cavalier phone calls had been made, there was no direct route to the handsome blue-carpeted office with its table-tennis sized desk which was to become the seat of all power within ATV. It was a circuitous and quite improbable series of events which finally brought him there.

When the ITA advertisement appeared, Lew Grade (as he then still was) was totally immersed in the business affairs of his vast theatrical agency. It is both his strength and his weakness to be almost obsessively absorbed in his own current project. Part of the project he was then concerned with was a tour of the American singer Jo Stafford, and it was two of Miss Stafford's entourage who played the most prominent roles in launching him into television. Her manager, Mike Nidorf, over in London from the United States to iron out various details of her contract and her performance schedules, spotted the advertisement and enthusiastically outlined its possibilities into Grade's receptive ear, one of his most abiding qualities being his willingness to listen to new ideas. It is, indeed, among his proudest boasts that his office door in Great Cumberland Place has always remained open to anyone from tea lady or office boy to top executive if they have an idea which they think might be useful to him.

Lew listened carefully as Nidorf argued how, once it got under way, commercial television would have about as much chance of losing money as a fruit machine in Las Vegas. He was backed in his assessment by a most persuasive lady, Suzanne Warner, who was also prominent in the Jo Stafford ménage. Added to her obvious Californian glamour was a spirit of daring enterprise. It was, in fact, Suzanne Warner who 'had someone who could find £2 million' to put alongside Lew, Leslie and Val's £45,000. By one of those happy chances, the stuff that television's dreams are made of, she was being treated by one of London's most fashionable medical practitioners, who also happened to number among his patients one Mr H. Grunfield. Mr Grunfield was a senior partner in the merchant banking firm of Warburg & Company; what is more, he had already formed his own shrewd conclusions as a banker that commercial television in Britain could be as big and bountiful as it had been in the United States, if used effectively.

It took only an introduction from their mutual doctor to fuse the ambitions of Suzanne Warner to the resources of Mr Grunfield and to deliver them both at the doors of Lew, Val and Prince. Thus was the Incorporated Television Programme Company born, and no one who had any part in it – except, as it proved later, Dr Nathaniel Mayer Green, the accommodating practitioner – had any cause to rue their participation. Their company was to become the most profitable of all the commercial empires, and when it did so, Dr Mayer Green sued both his former patients for a portion of the fortunes they had amassed from their founder shares; shares which he had at the time declined. The cases were settled out of court.

Compared to the slippery, rock-strewn trek they had to make to reach the top of the mountain, the doctor's litigation was merely a pebble to be cast lightly aside. By then they had survived far worse vicissitudes. When the ITA came to award contracts, the Incorporated Television Programme Company was the only one of the five competing contenders whose bid was rejected. The first three, announced on 27 October 1954, went to Lord Kemsley's alliance with the television producer Maurice Winnick; to Associated-Rediffusion; and to Sidney Bernstein's Granada chain, those former pious opponents of allowing anything but a public corporation to invade the sanctity of the home via the cathode ray tube.

Before going in with Lew Grade, however, Prince Littler himself had begun by vehemently mistrusting the advent of commercial television. He saw it as a real threat to his theatre empire, and in this proved quite correct. But he rationalized his fears with a businessman's innate instinct for survival. He realized in time that, if television was going finally to complete the erosion of popular variety which the cinema had begun, he would guard his interests better by exerting his influence from within the enemy camp. He quickly became chairman of the board of the Incorporated Television Programme Company. A similar logic must also have had as much to do with Sidney Bernstein's *volte-face* as his undeniable socialist desire to make his mark on the progress of the new mass culture. And though Associated-Rediffusion were the only experienced operators in the broadcasting field, they too had gone on record as believing that commercial television would not be in their best interests before waking up to the inevitable and putting in their bid.

Norman Collins, perhaps the only one among the contenders who was not counting the possibilities of the new service in terms of business expansion, was offered the franchise to broadcast London's weekend programmes and weekday to the Midlands. That he should have been awarded such a rich base for his Associated Broadcasting Development Company was only to be expected, and was only fair. His role had been crucial in bringing the ITA into being.

Had he been more of a businessman and less of an idealist, had he seen his new brainchild in the same light as his competitors, he might well have hung on to that franchise. It was, however, significant that he took a week longer than the rest to accept the offer. Benson, Lonsdale & Co., the bankers Lord Bessborough had brought into his deal, were already dragging their feet. Their over-hesitant caution caused them to under-invest and ultimately cost Collins his contract. Winnick's group was also in dire financial need. His Kemsley backers developed cold feet at the last minute and withdrew. The financial hiatus took Winnick, the clever operator who had introduced the popular panel game *What's My Line?* to the BBC, out of the running before the starting-pistol was even fired.

The collapse of the Collins enterprise – on the face of it, the safest and most public-minded of all the companies – gave Prince Littler's conglomerate the breathing space it needed to regroup for a fresh attack. Lew Grade's explanation of their failure to capture one of the four contracts was probably the correct one. 'It was the result,' he said, 'of too great a publicity campaign in which we made it look as if we owned the world.'

The ITA members were deeply reluctant to hand over one of their precious contracts to such a daunting array of vested interests: the complex web of the Grade Agency (of which more later) allied to the might of the Moss Empires variety chain along with the commercial radio interests represented by Harry Alan Towers and the powerful spending potential of Warburg's merchant bank.

It is still a part of Lord Grade's charm that the best stories against him are invariably the ones he tells himself. 'As far as I was concerned, Warburg's might have been a chocolate company when their name was first mentioned to me,' he confesses. 'So I called up a friend of mine, Sid Hyams, and asked him if he's ever heard of them. He said: "Yes, they're merchant bankers."' Which was also how Warburg's became part of the act.

The ITA held out for many months against the Littler-Grade-Warburg conglomerate. But a neat side-step, as neat as anything Lew Grade ever accomplished in his early days as a novelty dancer on the variety stage, shook the authority's determination. Littler, having started as a reluctant recruit to the joys of commercial television, had grown incensed by the ITA's refusal to recognize his group's claims. He began to fight an ever more determined campaign, and when Norman Collins finally had to capitulate to the parsimony of his bankers and bow out, Littler was ready to advance his forces. The remnants of Collins's Associated Broadcasting Development Company merged with Littler's light entertainment giant, and the weight of Collins's reputation clinched the matter. In the spring of 1955, ITA announced that the newly formed Associated Broadcasting Company – almost immediately the title was changed to Associated TeleVision (ATV) – would fill the breach by taking over the contract to broadcast London's weekend programmes and the weekday schedules in the Midlands. Littler, Parnell, Grade and their holdings were in the race after all, and again it was Collins more than anyone who had made the success possible, though he could hardly be expected to feel altogether happy at this outcome to events. In such company he had effectively lost control of his own brainchild.

7

For a man of such remorseless energy, Lew Grade maintained a surprisingly low profile in the early days at ATV. The centre of his focus remained the theatrical agency he had built up with his brothers Leslie Grade and Bernard Delfont. By his own admission, he was at the outset nothing more than a part-time partner in the new television enterprise. All that was to change when the company's first balance sheets landed on his desk. In the first seven months of transmission, ATV had lost something in the region of £600,000. These enormous initial losses challenged his showman's pride and unleashed a huge reservoir of resourcefulness.

'By January, I had moved in full time,' he recalls tersely. He moved at the crucial moment. The money had almost run out. By April it *had* run out, at least so far as their initial capital went, though to pretend, as the companies did later to Pilkington, that the summer of 1956 saw them all on the verge of collapse is to over-state the dangers. Too many people had too strong an interest in keeping the network afloat until they could move into the black to contemplate a total shut-down so early. Moreover, almost £4 million-worth of advertising time had been sold by the three existing contract holders (Granada, being late on the scene, escaped the worst anxieties of commercial television's first summer). Of the pioneer clients, eight of the most important commercial giants were sufficiently aware of the importance of television advertising to invest over £100,000 apiece in it.

For the television hardware manufacturers, too, the new channel meant a rapidly expanding market. The number of receiving sets was increasing enormously. In the first three months of transmission, the sales of ITV sets had more than doubled to reach 500,000. But here, also, there were set-backs when the government's clamp-down on rental agreements some months later put an unexpected damper on the industry's natural growth. (As part of his stern fiscal measures, the Chancellor of the Exchequer demanded nine months' rental be paid in advance on any new sets for hire.)

At the outset, in any case, the ITA had calculated that their contract-holders should expect to show heavy losses in their first year, lose a little less in their second year, begin to break even in the third, and only then move into the promised land of profitability. It meant that six years of plenty were left for rich harvesting within their ten-year franchises. During the initial crises, though, as may be imagined, there were frenzied attempts to bail out bathwater in order to hold back the flood of disaster. There were also many willing hands ready to stop any of the babies being thrown out at the same time. Cecil King, chairman of the Mirror Group of newspapers, was only too anxious to offer his support when ATV's hour of crisis came.

Floating out with the displaced bathwater at ATV went Harry Alan Towers, their original controller of programmes. He had come from commercial radio and went having made no great splash, leaving behind him scarcely a ripple. His going, however, paved the way for the serious entry of Parnell and Grade into the day-to-day planning of the station's schedules. It also marked the start of a curious allegiance between three light entertainment magnates and an austere Wykehamist captain of industry, Cecil King. King had been awaiting the call to serve the cause of commercial television rather as De Gaulle waited at Colombey-les-deux-Eglises for the call to serve the state. He had let it be known that he would 'await the first two bankruptcies' among the ITV franchise-holders, and then move in the financial might of the Mirror Group to clean up the mess. In the earliest stages, he set about trying to encourage the bankruptcies he had rashly predicted by mounting a scornful campaign against alleged right-wing political bias among the four original contractors. Certain memorable *Daily Mirror* leaders denounced the franchise allotment and indignantly demanded that the ITA should call in all the contracts and start from scratch. But soon he saw that time was running short. He stepped smartly in with over £400,000-worth of investment from the Mirror Group, the last outsider to be admitted into the charmed circle of the new Big Four.

It was a lucky break for King; the capital investment was never called on and the Mirror Group picked up a healthy 36 per cent of the shares, which brought them within one per cent of Chairman Littler's holding. The story still persists among the apocryphal legends at ATV House of how Littler stage-set a vast empty office with prop chandeliers, carpets and dining suite for his lunch-time meeting with King and his men, and then returned all the parapher-nalia to the property department after business was concluded. It demonstrates how desperately the ATV board hoped to impress this prospective partner, even though everyone concerned swears it is simply another television fable.

These events, however, were to draw Lew Grade even further into the hurly-burly of the business he had been instrumental in founding. But he remained the junior partner in the trio when it came to administrative weight. Littler and Collins had announced on the departure of Towers that Parnell would take sole control of programme planning. In practice, it was to be Lew's brand of showmanship which showed through more and more. The combin-ation of himself with Parnell ensured that showbusiness was ATV business. Val Parnell's *Star-time* was leaving any competition the BBC put up against it with something between two and four per cent of the viewing figures. By the time Parnell relinquished his grasp on the controls of the company – in circumstances which are still mystifying – Lew Grade's judgement was holy writ. He had proved, whatever the promises made in his company's original agreement with the ITA, that he above all others knew how to make television box-office. Whatever the ITA may have envisaged the contractors' programming should be, it was Lew Grade's show-man's instinct which directed what it in fact became.

'I seemed to have the knack of knowing which acts would suc-ceed,' he once disarmingly told the late Nicolas Tomalin. He was speaking of his previous success as a booking agent, but he might equally have been explaining his dictates for the early days of commercial television. He, more than any other individual, tipped our culture into the lap of 'Americanization'. He it was who resolved the dilemma of the Sunday-night top spot, dominated for so long by the ritual of the BBC's weekend play, by introducing the spec-tacular *Sunday Night at the London Palladium*. By doing so, he not

46

only boosted their ratings but capitalized on their assets. The London Palladium, through ATV's holdings in the Stoll–Moss Empire chain, belongs to his company, and inevitably many of the top acts televised from there came from brother Leslie Grade's agency – the most powerful in Britain at the time – of which Lew himself remained the largest single shareholder. It was a pattern of business dealing guaranteed to set his adrenalin flowing.

But the interlocking of the Grades' entertainment business enterprises was already causing grave concern in many quarters. 'He says he keeps his interests segregated,' as a fellow impresario complained, 'and certainly the industry hasn't felt any real harm from it. But it's a public company and when he dies someone else takes over. *That* could be very bad for the industry.'

It is true to say that, with the disappearance of Val Parnell and the subsidence of Norman Collins's platform of influence within the company, Lew's word came to be law. Lord Willis, who worked with him closely on many projects at that time, is in no doubt as to the reason. 'He's been right so often that even the accountants respect him, though they may groan. His tastes are not mine and you can say that all the series are the same with a different title, but he's never wanted intellectual acclaim, never wanted to play Hamlet. He just wants to be Lew.'

Being Lew meant that he managed to run everything himself, and he achieved this super-human feat because he worked harder than anyone else, because he was the first person properly to grasp the tangled finances of the network system, and, as Tomalin was to observe at the height of Grade's power at ATV, because he would always win in a competitive deal. He has always loved to sell; he can market anything from an idea to a multi-million pound series. In the eight years up to 1977, he had sold television programmes to the United States which had earned the company $238,887,000. Yet he always maintains that it is the sale motive not the profit motive which fuels his energies.

'I've never been in the entertainment business to make money,' he will tell you severely, not a little hurt at the suggestion. 'It so happens, what I have done has made money. Listen! If I was after the money for myself I could do two pictures a year as an outside producer and make two million dollars a year. As easy as that. I could live in a country where I paid only 50 per cent income tax. But that doesn't mean anything to me. I live off the excitement of doing things the best way possible. I was determined to prove that British

47

programmes were the best in the world – and I did it. Look at the sales figures!'

In reaction to Lord Thomson's accusation that he holds a licence to print money he is highly indignant, and has been known to thump the table when the quotation is brought up. 'It is a disgraceful thing to say!' he protests. Those close to him agree that he means every word. But it does not disguise the fact that, doing things the best way possible, means doing them his way, and that being the best in the world is measured in terms of selling the most.

The persuasive power of Lew Grade's brand of sales drive is eloquently told by Shirley MacLaine in the second volume of her autobiography, *You Can Get There From Here*. She confesses that it was Grade, by then Sir Lew, knighted in recognition of his services to the industry, who sold television to her. Until then her experience and artistic expression had been confined mainly to the stage, and, of course, to Hollywood, with which she had grown increasingly disenchanted. But who could resist someone who (in her estimation) is worth $400 million and begins a business meeting by saying: 'What would you like, Shirl, dear? Anything your little heart desires is yours.' Not even the level-headed Miss MacLaine.

> He paced the spacious, stark office, relighting the cigar, gesturing with a sort of ceremonial mischievousness, knowing, like any good performer, just how charming and neatly effective he was with his repertoire of old country humour. I can't remember everything he said. His words were a blizzard, a storm, a Hurricane Zelda of his promises, dreams, visions. His head turned on his egg-shaped body as he giggled and danced on the thick blue carpets of that office over Marble Arch.

Miss MacLaine's recollections, written down much later, may well be tinged with the chagrin she felt about the way those promises and dreams and visions materialized. *Shirley's World* – the programme series which was the outcome of their first affable meeting – was an artistic and financial fiasco; one of Lord Grade's major errors of instinct. Nevertheless, she accurately reflects the way he works. Her nose, she maintains, 'twitched' even then at some of the sentiments he expressed, not least the assurance that her talent was super, but, 'What interests me about you, Shirl, is your fame.' Yet she went ahead and bought what he was offering. Why not? Before she left the plush executive suite of ATV House, she was assured that she would be paid 'more than any American network can afford'. According to Miss MacLaine's account, she was also told how she would be stimulating employment in Britain', that a movie deal would be worked out, that he would finance two pictures a year for her on any subject she chose, and that she need only shoot four months a year for television. It left the sort of glow any girl might be expected to enjoy, even a Hollywood movie star.

There was never any suggestion in all the bitter catalogue of disappointments which she published subsequently about her association with *Shirley's World* that these promises were anything but genuine, or that they were not kept. Grade's proudest boast throughout his entire career has been that his verbal agreement is as binding as a contract; wouldn't his chosen epitaph read: 'He always kept his word'? Yet, as she was to discover, a handshake from Lew Grade might be as firm a guarantee on matters of money as could be wished, but it was no safeguard of artistic merit. At the end of the series, she declared her experiences at ATV to be 'akin to what Vietnam must have been for Kennedy, Johnson and Nixon'. By the time it had dawned on her that her scripts were not as inspiring as the advertisements which interrupted them, and not nearly so pithy, it was too late. She called her agent early on to instruct him to get her out of her agreement, only to discover that the ebullient Sir Lew had been even better than his word. 'There's more involved with this series than you think,' her agent told her soberly. 'Riding on your face right now, I would say conservatively is – oh, $20 million with advertising and air time combined.'

Spending on this scale overwhelmed any artistic consideration. 'Cesspool wise, I was up to my knees,' lamented Sir Lew's international star, and protestingly dragged herself from location to location, battle to battle. When the sorry tale came to be told, Grade had his answer ready; on the very day Miss MacLaine's book was published, detailing all the horrors of the series as she had experienced them, Grade countered its damaging effects with the bold announcement of his £50 million investment in movie making.

Lord Grade was again moving upwards and outwards. His basic values, however, remained the same.

8

'Images! Images! I'm not worried about images. Whatever I do, I do well,' Lord Grade retorted somewhat testily when someone sought to query his judgement. Nevertheless, he does have a very clear image of himself, and he projects an even more distinct one.

In the 1950s the *Daily Express*, following Lord Beaverbrook's sour-grape editorial policy, printed a picture of Lew Grade which *Private Eye*, the satirical magazine, continues to give currency to with its constant references to 'Low Greed'. The *Daily Express* caption read: 'Is this the Man you want to choose the programmes for your children?' It showed the inevitable 7⅞-inch cigar, protruding from generous sensuous lips, drooping jowls, fleshy nose and bald head; not the prettiest portrait of a mogul. Yet, in all probability, Lew Grade had sanctioned its distribution for publication; certainly he had allowed it to be taken. He is, as everyone will tell you, the very first person to enjoy the countless tales which depict him as a tough-dealing tycoon and repeats them willingly against himself. There is the favourite old chestnut in which he's asked: 'What's two and two, Lew?' 'Are you buying or selling?' he is supposed to have replied. He also encourages the Goldwynisms which add a touch of the frontiersman to his brand of showmanship. Accused of not doing enough to promote religious programmes on television, he is reputed to have retorted: 'We put out the Saint. What more do they want?'

When he's through laughing at them, he shrugs them aside,

50

protesting innocently that he could never think up clever answers spontaneously enough to live up to his legend. 'I only wish I was as sharp as the Lew Grade they tell stories about,' he beams.

Another favourite self-projected portrait is of the benevolent paterfamilias running a family business. He likes his employees to call him Lew and he maintains that he knows them all by their Christian names, which in fact he does not. How could he? His employees run into thousands. Even so, he does conduct his affairs with jealous paternalism. 'At ATV we have 1,000 managing directors,' he is fond of repeating, and even the disenchanted Shirley MacLaine could not help noticing that the staff there do in fact treat him rather like a rich, benevolent, awesome uncle.

'I don't give ulcers,' he has assured many of the journalists he puts at ease with those pale blue eyes which never leave the face of his listener. 'My staff can tell me to go to hell any time they like if they have a grievance.' He does, if challenged, modify this to: 'Well, not exactly tell me to go to hell. But they'll say I'm talking a load of nonsense and that we shouldn't do this or that.'

Certainly he earns their respect by his staggering example of industry and energy. From the beginning of his omnipotence at ATV House, he established the habit of arriving for work before 6.30 each morning, his wife, Kathy, having risen with him at 5 a.m. to make him a cup of tea before he left. He is chauffeur-driven through the empty streets and the grey dawns between his Knightsbridge penthouse and Great Cumberland Place in a Rolls-Royce which, as befits his status, is complete with personalized number plate (LG 10) and radio telephone. Around that phone is another of the myths which cling to his image. He had it installed, his more mischievous detractors allege, the moment he heard that Lord Bernstein of Granada had acquired one for his limousine. As soon as it was fitted into his Rolls, the story goes, Grade lost not a second in calling his rival on his newest toy – only to be told by Bernstein's chauffeur: 'I'm sorry, you'll have to ring back. He's on the other line.'

The truth is that he lives by the phone, no matter where he is. There are three installed in every room of his penthouse (including his sauna). One of each trio has a blank dial, the number of which is known only to Grade himself. Not even his wife is aware of its secret dialling code; nor, she says, does she want to know, in case she incurs his wrath by accidentally giving it away to friends. Lew's explanation for his mystery hot line has, like so much of his dealing, the bravura innocence of a tycoon mind. 'I might be on two phones,' he explains, 'and want to phone out.' Even the patient, adoring Kathy has qualified her assertion that she sees more of her husband than many wives by adding, 'Usually he's got a telephone glued to his face, but I see him.'

If he has phoned no one on his way to work, the chances are that his telephone will never be far from his grasp once he is at his desk, the night porter still his sole companion in the building until the secretaries and executives begin to arrive after eight o'clock. Business problems must be settled the minute they present themselves. Calls are fired off around the world irrespective of time-differences or the importance of the person on the receiving end. Business is more vital than somebody's beauty-sleep or private moments. Lew's public face is his private face; there is no guile about it. His affairs are so international that he calculates everything in dollars ('It saves time that way'), and work is his stuff of life. Seldom will he stray further than the South of France for the twelve days' holiday he allows himself each year, and this he always breaks up into six-day stints.

The desk, that massive focal point of his empire, is invariably immaculately clear; a sign not of how little industry is generated from behind it, but exactly the reverse. It is the mark of a meticulously ordered mind, an outward symbol of its occupant's dislike of cluttered thinking.

Even when he leaves the office that is dominated by a portrait of his son Paul and lined with trophies won by his various productions (mostly his films, for his television series win audiences rather than prizes) he has not finished. In the comfort of his penthouse (said to have cost around £300,000 in 1972) with its strong wall colourings and its profusion of large, silky, chintzy sofas and armchairs, his mind is seldom away from the running of the multifarious business interests he holds – which range over two television studios, cinema film-making, video production, a world-wide distribution network, Pye Records, piped music, bowling, Bermans & Nathans, theatrical costumiers, and the chain of variety theatres. Over the weekend he thinks nothing of sitting down to watch six to eight video tapes of films and programmes in which he has some concern. At night he reads a pile of scripts and synopses before retiring to bed at around 10.30.

The Grades also have a large rambling house not far away in Wimbledon, but he rarely visits it. Kathy's mother lives there, and his wife pops over most days to see to its gardens, which are her hobby. Around the penthouse, too, there is evidence of her green fingers in the collection of hand-made chimney-pots which she uses as flower containers out on the terrace. She likes them because they *are* hand-made; the thought of some obscure artisan having cared enough to embellish them with his designs appeals to her. For the same reason, she collects cast-iron fireplaces and decorated manhole covers and dots them about her garden at Wimbledon.

She met Lew when she was a seventeen-year-old singer, and her belief in him has never wavered. The gold bracelet that dangles from his wrist is a present from her. It is inscribed with the insignia of his war-service, '1123014 Lance Bombardier Grade L. With All My Love, Darling, Kathy 1941', and commemorates his cunning in having contrived to have his discharge papers left undated, thus giving him the opportunity of bowing out any time he chose. In his office is another engraved gold token of her abiding belief that this man can achieve anything to which he sets his mind, 'except win an Olympic Gold Medal'. It is a replica of that Olympic Gold Medal which even she concedes is beyond his prowess. On it she has inscribed the words, 'Yes, My Lord', to celebrate his elevation to the peerage when he took the title Baron Grade of Elstree.

It is not therefore surprising that, with so much activity to cram into his day, he drinks very little, and that if he has to entertain at business lunches, they are taken in the dining room alongside his own office. The sixteen huge cigars he lights each day are his only creature indulgence.

It all helps to perpetuate the image of the father-figure, watching over his favourite 'sons' among the top executives in his industry, setting his minions the supreme example of hard work and application. And he, himself, of course sees his employees as belonging to one big family.

'The secret of our success,' he told Tomalin, as his powers at ATV became absolute, 'is team work, hard work and mutual trust. I know the names of everyone here and they know me. They can always come and tell me their troubles.' Those on whom such an overwhelming brand of paternalism is practised, however, have always found it to be double-edged.

'There are two Lew Grades,' one of his executives complained. 'One is the father of the family who'll do anything for you if you're in trouble or appeal to his sense of loyalty. The other is the business-man who'll cut your throat to keep down expenses or make a neat deal. He'd rather *give* money than spend it. Ask for £500 because of some personal crisis and it's yours. Ask for £500 extra on the budget for some vital programme – not a chance.'

There are, too, those who suspect it was the second Lew Grade who was responsible for the resignation of Val Parnell in 1962, leaving the way clear for himself to take over completely. Parnell resigned quietly and with little fuss. But, a week before Parnell relinquished his post, one of his employees, Roy Moseley, was dining at his house to discuss some business. During the main course – roast lamb – at about 8.30, the telephone rang. It was Lew.

'Val Parnell left the room and took the call. When he came back after a very short while he was – well, I can only describe it as ashen. He sat down and just said to Aileen Cochrane: "Lew's fired me." Fired or sacked, I forget which, but I know neither I nor Aileen, who he later married, were under any misimpression. We simply didn't know what to say. All he added was: "I'm not going to go without a fight." But it wasn't until I got home that I realized that Parnell was Lew's boss on the board at ATV. From his expression at dinner I was certain that he had made his mind up not to go, and couldn't at that time see any possibility that he would be unseated by a junior partner. But a week or so later he did go. I never found out what they talked about on the phone that night. It hardly took more than a few minutes, whatever it was.'

9

Though Val C. Parnell's entry into showbusiness lacked the smell of the greasepaint and roar of the crowd that accompanied Lew Grade's, it was nevertheless in the time-honoured tradition of the self-made tycoon. He began as office boy at Moss Empires in 1907, five years before the Winogradskys set off on the trek which brought them to Stepney. Though his career there ended in furious public acrimony with his partner Prince Littler, his reign as managing director and controller of the Palladium made him one of the single most influential showmen in the country for more than two decades.

His philosophy coincided exactly with that of the up-and-coming Grade Agency. Popular entertainment for the masses was what Parnell dealt in. And the Grades were ready and able to supply it. Though his office was besieged by agents most of the day, trying to sell him their acts, it was with Lew that he struck up a long-term business relationship after he took over sole command of the Palladium on the retirement of George Black at the end of the war.

This was the time when he was approaching the peak of his power in the entertainment industry, and he was taking the Grades ever-upward with him. The son of a ventriloquist act, ten years older than Lew, and in the business since he was a lad, he was in every way the senior of the two at the outset. His life-style could not have differed more markedly from that of the workaholic Grades. His custom-built silk suits, his taste in expensive wines and women to match, his liking for leisure weekends on prime golf courses or in luxury love-nests, were not in Lew's line at all. Moreover, unlike Lew, who in his day could boast that though he had countless rivals he had no enemies, Parnell's power and *modus vivendi* made him not only feared but heartily disliked in certain quarters.

He was eventually to settle down with the strikingly beautiful singer, Aileen Cochrane, and eventually married her after he had resigned from both Moss Empires and ATV. He left the latter only months before his second wife, the former adagio dancer, Helen Howell, sued him for restitution of her conjugal rights in a flurry of unwelcome publicity. There was, of course, no secrecy about his genuinely loving liaison with Miss Cochrane in the circles in which they moved. But the permissive society had not then reached semi-detached suburbia or the family audiences Parnell liked to cater for in his theatres and at ATV. In those more prim days, as managing director and virtual programme controller of such an influence on public morality as Associated TeleVision, he was almost as vulnerable to any irregularities in his matrimonial arrangements as the Archbishop of Canterbury. Not many years later, one of the BBC's director-generals, finding himself about to make an appearance in the divorce courts, was discreetly to resign his post.

Lew Grade, with his exemplary home life and his adoring wife Kathy, never voiced his views abroad about having his senior partner living a domestic life so precariously close to public comment. He was, indeed, most vocally loyal when the storm-clouds began to gather around both Parnell's business dealings and his home life.

As his deputy managing director, it was Lew who gave Parnell all credit when ATV entered the lists for the joustings over the Third Channel that became BBC2. He himself, he avowed, never took any decision without consulting Parnell. 'Some guy gets a great idea and comes in here with it. I say to Val, "What do you think Val?... It's going to be expensive." And Val says, "Yes, but wouldn't it be great at 7.30 on Sunday? Let's do it." And we do it. Mind you, Val is a genius.'

To Parnell he attributed the introduction of the mobile 625-line camera at Elstree to tie in with the American system; the cost of a single camera unit being around £100,000 at the time, but the profits over the years immeasurable. All this was when ATV's total advertising revenue was topping £9.7 million a year, and when their profit returns were £5.3 million. For Parnell as managing director in that summer of 1960, things could not have looked more secure to any casual observer.

But, as Guy Fawkes' night approached, the fireworks that exploded around Moss Empires's executive offices out-did anything the bonfires could offer. Prince Littler, Parnell's partner at Moss Empires and chairman at ATV, was aghast to discover how Parnell was backing a £5.7 million takeover bid for the theatre chain. Concerned with the magnates Charles Clore and Jack Cotton in the boardroom bid was Bernard Delfont. Not for the first or last time was internecine strife to cloud relationships between either the three musketeers at ATV, Prince, Val and Lew, or between the brothers Grade and Delfont themselves. (The ramifications of that remarkable family are gone into in more detail in the following chapter.) Lew and Bernard have always maintained that they kept their business interests strictly separate and secret; after both moved on into film-making, they were locked in a cut-throat race to the box-office with two multi-million pound versions of the self-same subject: the *Titanic*. (When Grade heard that his brother was floating the same notion and planning an earlier launch, he barked down the phone: 'What are you trying to do to me? *We* had the idea first!')

It is, however, improbable that he was unaware of his brother and managing director being hand in glove over the proposed Moss Empires takeover, even though Prince Littler himself was caught totally unawares. Littler's reaction to the bid was swift and quixotic. He marshalled all his financial resources and bought up enough preference shares to ensure control of the company. While Parnell was out of the country in Geneva, Littler effectively quashed the deal behind his back. City experts estimated it had cost him between £500,000 and £800,000, and he used his own Stoll Company as the base to swallow up Moss Empires. 'It is clear you wish to wrest control of Moss Empires from me and my associates,' Littler wrote cryptically to Clore by special messenger. 'I regard it as my duty to shareholders to take such steps as are within my power to defeat your object.' Unknown to Parnell, his own 1,300 preference shares were voted over to Stoll by his fellow directors.

By the time Parnell returned to hold a hurried press conference on the steps outside his Hyde Park apartment, it was clear he had been outflanked. The friendship and business association between the two men, which had lasted a quarter of a century, was effectively finished.

Parnell threatened to sue. He claimed that he had telephoned Littler personally before he flew out of the country to ask specifically if there was 'anything of importance' to be discussed at the Moss Empires's board meeting, and was told there wasn't. As a director he had every right to know, of course. Littler countered coolly that he had not noticed Mr Parnell's absence from the crucial directors' meeting that blocked the Clore–Delfont bid. Asked, incredulously, how the absence of such an imposing figure as Parnell could be overlooked, Littler replied tersely: 'He was often absent.' The implication was unmistakable.

Bravely Parnell assured the waiting reporters: 'It is impossible for Littler to force me out of my job as managing director at ATV. I'm fireproof.'

But the crack in the fabric of his power-base was all too visible, despite the bravado, and he was deeply hurt by Littler's manoeuvre. 'To me,' he said, 'it is an astonishing thing to have happened. I was instrumental in getting Littler on to the board of Moss Empires and getting him into television in the first place. Prince Littler has a lot to thank me for.' Littler thought otherwise.

Two days before 1960 drew to a close, Parnell was out of Moss Empires completely, and out of his precious London Palladium, too. He sold his shares and resigned from the board. It could not have been the best of Christmases for the showman who had once been king of Britain's seasonal cheer in the theatre.

Time was clearly running out for Parnell. Alienated from Littler at ATV, he was to continue there as managing director, with Lew as his deputy, for under two years. He may well have considered himself to be fireproof, as he told the reporters when he returned to vent his wrath on Littler over the Moss–Stoll share dealings. But he was sixty-eight. His private life was about to erupt in public statements and lawsuits by his estranged wife; it cannot have been pleasing for a man of his flamboyant image to find himself being sued for the restitution of conjugal rights long after having left to live with somebody else.

It is possible that he was temporarily reassured by Lew's public and sincere praise of his abilities. Even considering Lew's gift for hyperbole, it is extremely gratifying to be dubbed 'a genius' by one's peer. Whatever he assessed his strength to be within ATV, however, the phone call he took from his deputy managing director as he sat down to dinner with Aileen Cochrane and Roy Moseley in the comfort of his Hyde Park home, shook him. Once again he was to repeat his intentions of hanging on to his post, come hell or high water. But he was obviously a spent force in the boardroom. He resigned on 26 September 1962, with twenty-one months of his contract still to run.

'I thought it about time I should be relieved of some of the arduous tasks that go with the managing directorship and give the younger ones a chance in this very modern field,' he said in a press statement. To draw attention to the toughness of the job, to the modernity of the medium and the need for younger blood at the helm, indicated something of his own state of mind. The fifty-eight-year-old Lew Grade stepped into his shoes on 1 November. Both men were earning identical salaries (£8,000 a year), plus a share in the profits when Parnell retired. Parnell retained a seat on the board and the right to present *Sunday Night at the London Palladium*.

The following April his wife's embarrassing petition for the restitution of her conjugal rights was heard and granted. Two years later he was divorced on an uncontested charge of adultery with Miss Cochrane, who soon became the third Mrs Val Parnell.

Lew remained steadfastly loyal to the Parnell legacy at ATV, even in the most curious ways. For example, he has always been quick to defend the merits of the artistically and technically inept soap opera, *Crossroads* – and which stars Noele Gordon, a former rising West End star in some of Parnell's musical shows – against all criticism. He can, in fact, be quite terse on the subject. But not even his spirited repudiation of adverse critical opinions nor his good relationship with the IBA could save it from one most embarrassing censure from the authority. Standards had sunk so low, in their opinion, that, in 1979, they demanded ATV should cut down the number of transmissions so as to invest more time in raising their quality. This was a dreadful slap in the face for all concerned; but ATV, with Lew as its spokesman, staunchly repeated their faith in their own product.

It would have been even more awkward if he had not done so. For, among the many agreements arranged by Val Parnell in his early halcyon days in television, was the transfer of a block of ATV shares to Miss Gordon. Not for nothing is she a voice to be listened to at the ATV studios in Birmingham.

10

With Val Parnell's abrupt retirement, there was never again any confusion at ATV House as to where the ultimate authority lay. No longer merely the power behind the throne, Lew Grade was by 1962 firmly in occupation. Before examining more closely the effects of his unchallenged rule, it may, perhaps, be timely to break off and trace the development of the remarkable spirit of quest and con-quest which brought him – with his two younger brothers, Bernard and Leslie – to such a peak of eminence.

The original family name of the Grade–Delfont clan was Winogradsky, and neither of the two surviving brothers (Leslie died on 15 October 1979) has anything but a just and robust pride in the humble origins from which he grew. None of them ever pretended more grandiose beginnings for himself. Why should they? The script which fate handed the family has enough rags-to-riches romance, stoic endurance and single-minded perseverance to satisfy even Lew's insatiable taste for high-minded, all-star adventure epics. Their early, often desperate struggles could out-gross *Fiddler on the Roof* if music were added. Like so many of their faith, their instinct for survival, tenacity and family bonds were forged by persecution and poverty. The cruelties and hardships which they endured ensured that only the strong, the lucky or the clever survived: and the brothers have shown, each in his individual way, that the Winogradsky boys were blessed by possessing all three qualities of fortune.

Their father Izaak's character may also have contained the same combination of sterling qualities, but there they were mixed in a different blend. When he fled with his wife Olga and their brood from their home-town near Odessa in 1912 to escape the anti-Jewish pogroms being waged ruthlessly throughout Tsarist Russia, tailoring was his main trade. Like so many others, he finally settled in the back streets of Bethnal Green to earn a subsistence income of 8s. (40p) a week as a tailor's presser and Singer sewing-machine mechanic. Both parents loved music and sang in amateur opera, giving their children an early if shaky appreciation of the performing arts. Izaak was not, by all accounts, blessed with Lew's conservation-ist attitude to money, even such little as he earned. The traditional working man's escape from the defeating grind of a dispiriting existence, a flutter on the horses, was Izaak's great weakness. But even his raw gambling instinct was channelled more often than not into entrepreneurial ventures aimed at lifting himself and his family out of the gutter by the bootstraps. As the metaphor implies, if followed through literally, father Winogradsky's efforts invariably landed him on his rear. He did, however, bring the family into contact with the lower rungs of the showbusiness ladder by buying himself an interest in a shabby, minute, flea-pit cinema in the Mile End Road. It was a financial failure, but at least it demonstrated that their father was the first in the family to appreciate the possibilities of bettering oneself through the entertainment industry.

Of his eldest son's shining intelligence there was never any doubt. Lord Grade often boasts that the seat of his education was 'Rochelle University', his whimsical name for Rochelle Street Elementary School off Brick Street, Stepney. His surviving contemporaries from there can still remember the half-day they were given in celebration of the scholarship he won. Scholarships were rare enough to merit such bonuses, and highly prized in those early days of perfunctory elementary education. They were rarer still and even more highly prized among immigrant families like the Winogradskys who had arrived in an alien land so few years before, scarcely speaking a word of the language. What Lew remembers, however, is the fact that he was not allowed to take up the scholarship because his family were still registered as aliens and wartime restrictions were still in operation. By the time he graduated from the back-street university of Rochelle Street and the Stepney Jewish School, he had won first-class honours in resilience and the work ethic.

His younger brother, Bernard, who left school at the age of twelve with slightly less distinction – he was caught running a football pool at a halfpenny stake – describes with something akin to nostalgia the privations which built the brothers' characters: one decent suit which had to last and be passed on; cardboard in the soles of their shoes if the cobbler couldn't be cajoled to mend them with a promise to pay later.

Yet both will swear that their childhood was as happy as the best. Their father, though strict, was colourful and imaginative enough to show them the glimpses of horizons beyond the grim back streets of Stepney. And not one of the boys had any fear of, or lack of faith in, the value of hard work.

'If you didn't want to starve, you earned money,' the disgraced sweepstake holder of Stepney Jewish School was to testify after being elevated to the peerage of his adoptive land and taking the title of Lord Delfont of Stepney. 'It all bred a desire to achieve something better. That feeling came as naturally as breathing.'

From the same roots as the Grades sprang such notabilities as Sir Jack Cohen, who founded Tesco Stores, Jack Solomons, who dominated British boxing for decades, and Joe Loss, whose big band became big business. Brotherhood and the spirit of competition were inextricably bonded by their background and their upbringing. Lew had already proved he possessed a well-above average brain. Robbed of his opportunity to develop his agile intellect along any academic channels by being deprived of his hard-won scholarship, he was out in the world at the age of fourteen. He took his chances where he found them. For a boy born on Christmas Day, 1906, in Tokmah, near Odessa, in the Southern Crimea at the height of Jewish persecution, he had come a long way and was not afraid to travel a lot further still.

From East End backgrounds like the Winogradskys' there were probably only three avenues for a boy to travel in search of something better, and each one has had its famous followers; it is much the same in any deprived, immigrant-dominated community anywhere in the Western World. There is crime, there is boxing and there is showbusiness. Stepney has produced its share of celebrities in all three fields. Crime was abhorrent to the sort of family who found their pride in being poor but honest. Boxing was out by virtue of Lew's build (though he never shirked a fight),

Bernard's affability and Leslie's reticence. So, logically, only show-business was left. Oddly enough, for a boy as bright as Lew, it was not his first choice of career. He had always seen himself working with figures, and had even managed to have himself hired as a 12s. (60p) a week costing clerk with a clothing manufacturer. This was, after all, what he knew about from his father, and costing was where he felt his instincts lay. The strange whims of fortune that had brought the Winogradskys to Stepney were already pulling him in other directions, however.

He had learned to Charleston. Everyone did in those dance-crazy, jazz-baby days. But it was an ingrained part of his nature, even by then, to capitalize on any asset to hand. Self-taught, he could out-Charleston anyone on the dance floor by seventeen. Trophies he won were sold to eke out the family funds. But when he won a Charleston championship (the competitive spirit never far from the surface), a four-week engagement at the Piccadilly Hotel was the prize and he did not sell that. He was in showbiz.

Lack of self-assertion can never be said to have held Lew back. He was soon billing himself immodestly and not entirely truthfully as the 'World Champion Charleston Dancer'. As such he never wanted for engagements or partners. When the Charleston lost its currency, he was on the bills around the touring circuits of Britain, first as 'Grade and Gold, Eccentric Dancers', Winogradsky having no doubt become Grade for easier billing, as a concession to the old music-hall tradition that short names looked bigger on the bills, better in lights and saved on electricity. Brother Bernie, also never slow to seize an opportunity, soon followed him on to the boards, though the shyer, more retiring Leslie never saw the lure in the footlights. To avoid confusion with his brother's double act, Bernie and his partner (Albert Sutan) called themselves 'The Delfont Boys', which is why, eventually, there were never two Lord Wino-gradskys, or even Grades, in the Upper House together. Grade and Delfont they remained, even after Lew, with his uncanny instinct, assessed his own talents as shrewdly as he was soon to assess those of others and bowed out while the going was good.

'I'm still the finest Charleston dancer you'll see,' Lord Grade of Elstree is not slow to boast. Seldom has he ever passed up a chance to prove it. At a conference of advertisers called to hear about the new schedules for ATV's programmes, Lew knew only too well that the details had been circulated beforehand to the representatives present. So, when he arrived to address them, he brushed aside the formalities, told them it was absolutely ridiculous his coming to tell them what they already knew, and volunteered to repay them for wasting their time. 'The only way I can compensate you for coming here,' he told them, 'is to show you that I can still do the Charleston.' And he did.

'They went mad,' he recollects, and it is hardly surprising, given such a spectacle, that they should do so.

A fellow dancer and friend of all three brothers in the early days implies that, whereas Bernard had a so-so act and knew it, Lew had a so-so act which he believed to be the greatest in the world. Lew's faith in almost everything he tackles is naively all-embracing. Even so, his decision to hang up his dancing shoes seems to have caused him little or no visible heartache, despite his continued pride in his prowess as a hoofer. 'Top hat, silver cane, I did it all. But I came to realize that as a dancing star I had limitations and that the profession had limitations. So I became a theatrical agent,' is his version of how that part of the story ended.

He makes becoming an agent sound as easy as this whenever he tells the tale. To him it probably was. He always operates best where he sees fewest problems. It was the same Lew, blithely talking about dropping dancing to open an agency, as the Lew who discussed the casting of the £18 million TV epic *Jesus of Nazareth* with Franco Zeffirelli long after ATV had become a world-wide production company. Zeffirelli was wistfully musing on how Laurence Olivier would be ideal for the role of Nicodemus. 'Well, why don't we *get* Olivier to play Nicodemus?' he reasoned. '*You're* a friend of Olivier; *I'm* a friend of Olivier. *Get* Olivier to play Nicodemus…' To Lew it was all so simple. Friendship, the personal approach; these have been his constant talismans for success.

The agency he formed became his all-consuming interest after 1931. At the outset he went into partnership with Joe Collins, father of the sultry film star Joan and the passion-writer Jackie. With Collins, an easy-going man who had a well-established background in music-hall management, he built up a comfortably successful partnership. Collins described him as 'a seven-and-a-half-day a week man'. They prospered steadily in an unspectacular way.

However, when Lew was finally discharged from the army in 1943 (he had never been eligible for active service), it was with brother Leslie that he teamed. Here, indeed, was a formidable partnership: Lew, with his 'knack of knowing which acts would succeed', and Leslie, with his zest for meticulous hard work and long hours (an

64

eighteen-hour day would still leave him short of time to gobble up his meals). They set up business with a not insubstantial loan from the brothers Phil and Sid Hyams (the same Sid Hyams who was to put Lew on the right track with the Warburg banking firm when he was being persuaded to diversify into commercial television). Between them they built the biggest agency in Britain. Few agents have been so trusted, or so feared.

Wartime conditions in the entertainment industry favoured the newcomers. Theatre managements, cautious of an uncertain future, were only too willing to let agents take responsibility for producing and packaging their shows. Men like Lew and Leslie were thus, as producers, able to negotiate their own deals with, as agents, their own artists. Whatever conflict of interest this may have involved them in, it most definitely improved the firm's finances. As agents, they were entitled only to their percentage of their artists' earnings; as producers, they could not only regulate what those earnings were, but were entitled to any profits which the show made after everyone had been paid off.

It was good grounding for the delicate balancing acts Lew Grade was later to perform as controller of so many contrasting financial interests: television chief, agent, impresario, theatre owner and so forth. And it also brought him into close partnership with Val Parnell. After the war, Parnell had taken over sole control of the London Palladium. It was Lew, with his personal approach, his tenacity and his knack of knowing what was needed where and when, who provided him with the string of top-line American entertainers which restored the prestige of the establishment as Britain's number one variety theatre. Bob Hope was his first *coup*. In signing up Hope for the Palladium, Grade not only broke the monopoly of the huge American agencies but turned the Grades' agency into the biggest in Britain and gave it an international importance.

Lord Grade's arch rival as founding father of ITV, Lord Bernstein, recalls the brothers' agency from its earliest days. His family, like Joe Collins's, had roots deep in theatre management. 'Lew and his brother started producing for us thirty years ago. They honoured every contract and people trusted them completely,' Bernstein has testified. Few are accorded such tributes from former associates who have grown into competitors.

But if the Grades attracted the best stars into their stables, it was because they supplied the cleanest hay and treated top clients like thoroughbreds. Lew would be up at four or five any morning so as to be at the airport and ensure his visiting acts would find a welcome. He would personally supervise their baggage on to the train, take them to their hotel and attend to any creature comforts.

'My whole basis of life is to have a good relationship with people,' he says simply.

Thus was the pattern of his *modus operandi* established. But, by the time his business tentacles were embracing every aspect of showbusiness in Britain, an active disquiet had grown within the industry concerning the all-enveloping 'good relationships' of the brothers Grade and Delfont. Equity, the actors' union, petitioned Parliament to introduce legislation against the virtual monopoly which the three Winogradsky siblings were exerting over entertainment. More damaging still was a detailed investigation of their business affairs by the *Sunday Times*'s investigative 'Insight' team which was published in May 1966.

As we have seen, the brothers have always denied operating their businesses in one another's favour and are deeply resentful of any such suggestion. Fierce rivalry was, in fact, always a hall-mark of their relationships, especially between Lew and Bernard. Lord Delfont, the most public and accessible of them, has often pointed out that he has withdrawn artists from ATV shows because of the hard time Lew gave him during negotiations. 'He was bending so far backwards not to show any favours it amounted to victimization,' says Delfont ruefully. Certainly this was only one of the many squabbles which the brothers have had during their long business associations. In this case it took the intervention of Lord Renwick, the chairman at ATV, to smooth Bernard's ruffled feathers over an expensive conciliatory luncheon.

There probably were times when Delfont artists did not have things all their own way at his brother's television company. Yet, against this, there is Delfont's own discernible long-standing tactic of allowing the BBC to break in his up-and-coming acts for television stardom (Morecambe and Wise among them). Only after the BBC had taken the risks and turned them into household names would Delfont guide them towards an ITV showcase and the big-money salaries which their popularity could command. Such a strategy could not have endeared him to the BBC nor, at times, to his brother. Lew also enjoyed the game of buying cheap and selling dear, but was hardly likely to take it kindly when the trick was perpetrated on himself.

Yet, when Delfont came to part with the agency side of his business, he did not look outside the family circle. He sold his interest in his artists to brother Leslie for £250,000. The *Sunday Times* investigations had shown only too graphically the cross-fertilization of the three brothers' separate showbusiness empires. It availed Delfont little to defend himself against the accusations of nepotism by complaining: 'I can divorce my wife, but I can't divorce my brothers.' The evidence was there. As deputy chairman of Leslie's agency company (which owned outright the Harold Davison Group of Agencies and Impresarios, and London Management) as well as his own Bernard Delfont Managements and Enterprises Ltd and the Bernard Delfont (Agency) Ltd, he had access to talents ranging from Laurence Olivier, Edith Evans, John Gielgud, Noël Coward, Joan Plowright, Dorothy Tutin, Ralph Richardson, John Mills, Albert Finney, Judy Garland, Dirk Bogarde, Frank Sinatra, Ella Fitzgerald and Louis Armstrong to such pop phenomena as Cliff Richard and Frank Ifield. With Bernard also owning the Prince of Wales Theatre outright, together with major shares in two other West End theatres and two leading night spots, besides being the producer of six West End shows, four summer seasons *and* having responsibility for the Morecambe and Wise television series, this amalgamation alone was enough to cause serious disquiet in and out of showbusiness.

Allied to Lew's connections as managing director of ATV, it provoked a major storm. For Lew, as we have seen, was also the largest single shareholder in Leslie's agency interests. His company also wholly owned the Stoll–Moss Empires Theatre Group, which in turn controlled not only the London Palladium, where such as Garland and Sinatra could be expected to perform, but also Drury Lane, Her Majesty's, the Globe, the Queen's, the Apollo, the Lyric, the Victoria Palace and fifteen leading provincial theatres.

The most damning example used to pinpoint the brothers' stranglehold on the richest pickings in light entertainment that year was the Palladium pantomime set-up. Leslie Grade and Bernard Delfont promoted it with Leslie Macdonnell, who happened to be managing director of Moss Empires, which, being owned by ATV, brought the circle back to big brother Lew. The stars for the panto that year numbered Arthur Askey, the late Sid James, Kenneth Connor, and the pop singer Frank Ifield, all indisputable box-office draws to one section of the public or another. And all of them were clients of the Grade Agency or one of its satellites. To make the balancing of the books even more interesting, the entire spectacular was kitted out by Monty Berman, the theatrical costumiers who, I may remind you, were three-quarters owned by ATV. Once again the circle swung back to brother Lew.

Nor was Lew ever slow to reciprocate in the undeniable act of family coffer-swapping. Associated TeleVision's big audience attraction that season was Kathleen Harrison's folksy *Mrs Thursday* series. Miss Harrison herself paid her fees to her managers, London Artists – a subsidiary of Leslie's Grade Organization agency. The author of this highly popular series was Lord Willis. Lord Willis has pointed out that his tastes did not always coincide with Lew's; but here they did to the tune of a £10,000 flat fee for scripts and the original suggestion. The agent's percentage of that not inconsiderable remuneration then went to Robin Fox – director not only of London Authors (which was 99 per cent owned by Leslie's umbrella company) but also of the Grade Organization itself.

Fox himself did not deny the power brought about by such transactions. As Leslie's right-hand man in the organization, however, he was quick to defend it. 'The power itself is not important,' he protested. 'The question is, how we use it.'

According to Hugh Jenkins, who found himself, as Minister for the Arts, not unwillingly embroiled in the ensuing protests from Equity, the question was exactly the reverse. The important thing was that the power had come into existence, *not* how it was used. He was already deep in negotiations to strengthen the controls governing the fees an agent could charge a client for putting him or her to work in any enterprise in which he, the agent, also had a controlling interest.

Meanwhile, the Agents' Association's Articles of Agreement were being closely scrutinized in the interests of artists who felt themselves threatened by this incestuous agency-management mingling. Doubts were spread elsewhere. The Independent Television Authority's original misgivings for holding out against Lew's initial bid for a franchise were seen to have materialized only too visibly in every aspect of ATV's dealings. The publication of the *Sunday Times*'s 'Insight' investigations fired public debate against the cosy rut and easy options into which ITV's main programmers had settled.

Yet, for all these efforts back in 1966, the accusations of monopoly abuses have not subsided in the years which followed. When Lord Annan came to publish his report, it was on to ATV that his committee directed their sharpest attack. For example, Annan had listened carefully to the fears and complaints of composers, lyricists, musicians and the like who were *not* signed up with a music publisher associated with a main ITV programme contractor. These alleged to Annan that they had scarcely any chance of having their work used on the commercial network. Rival music publishers also aired their grievances that they, too, suffered because of ITV franchise holders like ATV diversifying into music publishing on their own account with such companies as ATV Music Publishing Co. Ltd, Northern Songs and many others, as well as owning Pye.

The Independent Broadcasting Authority (IBA), which had replaced the old ITA, had, in all honesty, to report to the committee that, of the proportion of music used on ITV and published by one or other of its own companies' subsidiaries, 'by far the highest was on ATV'. According to the IBA's figures, as much as 70 per cent of the music Lord Grade's ATV company used for his programmes came from firms associated with ITV companies. Associated Tele-Vision defended themselves against this charge by claiming that the figure of 70 per cent was inflated by the fact that it included the music regularly used with the ATV symbol itself: their daily 'sign-in' music as well as the signature tunes and end-title melodies for their *Today* section and their *General Hospital* series, not forgetting, of course, the inevitable *Crossroads*.

This plainly partisan face-saver hardly exonerates ATV from the taint of exercising an effective closed shop against outsiders. No other network company came within half of ATV's predominant use of their own or subsidiary companies' artists or their music, although Thames was accused of insisting that its musicians publish their compositions with its own EMI-controlled companies.

These admissions by the Independent Broadcasting Authority to Lord Annan were made all the more astonishing in view of the 1973 IBA Act, which, in paragraph (6) of Section 12, specifically prevents any company holding a contract if it carries on business, 'either alone or in partnership', consisting of 'manufacturing records or publishing musical works, promoting broadcasts of sound record-ings or the broadcasting of performances of musical works or of obtaining employment for theatrical performers or for people to take part in broadcasts'.

On the face of it, one would have thought that this catalogue of restrictions would have precluded Lord Grade and the directors of ATV from 99 per cent of their extra-mural activities.

For a time, however, as the storm-clouds of criticism gathered round ATV House during 1966, it seemed likely that the entire empire might be toppled.

11

The Independent Television Authority had already indicated by June 1967 which way their wind of change would be blowing when Lord Hill, now chairman of the television authority he had helped to launch as Postmaster-General in 1955, announced a drastic reshuffle. Invitations were to go out for applications for fourteen (fifteen with the Channel Islands) claims to the stations now proposed. A new networking station would be allotted to Yorkshire, its territory to be carved out of the area east of the Pennines which Lord Bernstein's Manchester-based Granada company had left fallow for fresh harvesting.

For the fifteen contract invitations extended by Lord Hill and the ITA, there were thirty-six serious bidders, including the original fourteen franchise holders, as compared to the five who had competed for the four original areas back in 1954. It was surely some indication of how lucrative the industry was now seen to be. The early pioneers' could, with a great deal of justification, claim that their profits had been born of risk, for they had risked the unknown. In their earliest days, they had seen a capital investment of £11 million swallowed up before a penny showed black in their account books. Lew Grade claimed that, by 1960, ATV had spent £2.5 million on their Elstree Studios alone before converting to the 625-line system. This setback, though it had been predicted well in advance by the ITA, was now largely forgotten and all manner of interests clamoured for a franchise. It was generally thought that

71

Lord Thomson of Scottish TV would be the one to regret his ill-received boast that a franchise was the same thing as a licence to print money by having his taken away from him; everyone in the industry realized that a sacrifice had to be made to stem the mounting tide of hostile criticism. As it turned out, Lord Thomson hung on and Rediffusion was thrown out of its envied London weekday slot (though, as we saw earlier, it was speedily to buy its way back into a 49 per cent holding in the new consortium).

Despite being a public body appointed by and answerable to Parliament, the IBA's decisions are all made in the utmost secrecy. No one ever knows quite how they arrive at their conclusions. This is one of the main complaints against the authority, particularly in the area of allotting franchises. Such far-reaching decisions to the public at large should, it is argued, be made accessible to the public. And a Select Parliamentary Committee has already urged the holding of public hearings when inviting applications or renewing contracts, as certainly happens in other countries which set high television standards, such as Canada.

What most concerned Lew Grade in his spacious office suite high over Marble Arch was the imminent carve-up of London's lucrative broadcasting stations. Lord Hill's authority had determined to split up London into a four-and-a-half day week with a two-and-a-half day weekend, which meant that ATV had to assess where best their chance of a successful bid lay: in London's weekend broadcasting or the Midland's weekday. In the end, Grade opted for the Midland franchise (where ATV was the lone bidder). His empire retrenched and focused its sights on Birmingham while he licked his wounds. He must by now have realized that the recipe with which he had wooed and won the mass weekend audiences away from the BBC in the early stages of his operation was in bad odour, both with the ITA and even among the fickle public. The loss of his weekend network outlet shook him momentously. For some time it looked as if Sir Harry Pilkington had come to sit like Banquo's ghost at Lew's feast. The spectre of the Pilkington Report's strictures once again hung heavy over ATV House.

It was an unusually subdued Sir Lew who spoke to the *Financial Times* after the inevitable reshuffle had been effected but had still produced no visible sign of improvement in quality of output: 'If you care about independent television you don't have to worry where the programmes come from as long as they come from independent television,' he opined philosophically. 'We all hoped that somehow or other the new companies would produce a miracle … and miracles are not easily produced. Everyone thinks there is some secret drawer we have filled with brilliant remarkable programmes which we store for emergencies. That's not true. Sometimes a brilliant idea can look brilliant on paper – you have to proceed with it but it does not always work out.'

Those new ideas which had looked so brilliant on paper were the ones for which Lord Hill and the ITA had awarded brand-new contracts – London Weekend Television, Yorkshire Television, Thames Television and Harlech Television. And they were already under heavy critical fire as the veteran showman spoke. Worse still was the fact that ITV's audience ratings following the radical shake-up had dropped sharply. There was a head-on, back-stage clash of opinion between the David Frost—Michael Peacock consortium – the new-broom whizz-kids at London Weekend Television – and Lew's old-brigade vision of what the public wanted over the weekend.

Lew was the man who had once caused ITV's prime drama showcase, *Armchair Theatre*, to be moved from its prestige Sunday-night spot because he considered the viewers were not in the mood to concentrate just before going back to work on Monday. 'And if they missed one important line of a play they wouldn't have a clue what was going on!' Peacock and his consortium at LWT, the new guardians of Britain's weekend ITV, had more confident notions about the public's tolerance level of concentration.

The viewing figures, however, began to argue heavily in favour of Lew and the old brigade, even before the new broom had a real chance to sweep anything but the cobwebs from the corners. A massive loss of nerve was perceptible throughout the industry, from the ITA through the advertisers to the network planning committee. 'You cannot feed people a continual diet of cultural or informational programmes,' Lew complained of the network's fresh face. 'You've got to give them some, of course, and it is our responsibility to give them some. But if you give them too much, they begin to switch off.'

To encourage the defectors to switch on again, ATV held fast to its tried and trusted formulas, and Lew simply doubled the numbers he had first thought of. He even managed to resurrect *Sunday Night at the London Palladium* for a brief spell. Exactly how

73

London Weekend and Yorkshire survived their separate baptisms of fire we will see in more detail later. The salvation of London Weekend is a sorry saga which reflects credit on few who were involved, and certainly demonstrates the television authority's singular lack of resolve when its franchise agreements come to be openly flouted. Yorkshire, which may, by contrast, have begun with rather a whimper, has gone on to give every indication of making some of the biggest bangs on the small screen.

These examples are given here only to illustrate how the collapse of the fresh policies, hopes and ambitions that followed upon the new 1968 contracts only served to consolidate Lew Grade's position as ultimate arbiter of the ITV audience's popular taste. While the new boys were busy trying to show that you *could* get revenue from the big advertisers and *still* produce programmes for more discerning tastes, Lew was scheduling fifteen Tom Jones spectaculars costing around £100,000 apiece. And once again, in Lord Willis's words, he was being proved right by the accountants. Even before the show's options were taken up, they were chalking up a profit of £1.5 million with Lew himself predicting a $50 million gross (he, as always, dealing in dollars) when the series was complete. Housewives and teenagers alike returned to ITV to watch Jones the Voice gyrate and tease with his star guests. The advertisers could hardly have been happier to welcome them back. It was exactly the audience spectrum which they were seeking.

Lew Grade could therefore afford to take a charitable view of the failure of ITV to revolutionize itself overnight. 'We all make mistakes,' he told the *Financial Times* sympathetically. 'I think the new companies are doing remarkably well considering the short time they have been in existence. I am talking about the major companies, Yorkshire and London Weekend. When independent television started, there were a lot of mistakes and people did not take too much notice because it was all beginning.

'You have to remember that for these companies the past few months were also the beginning. They had to find their feet. They will continue to be encouraged.'

There was about that carefully conciliatory speech, however, more than a touch of the elder statesman's condescension; more than a hint of 'I told you so' in arguments he was to use so much more forcibly in the back-stage network struggles to come.

From the outset Lew Grade had shown himself to be a master at steering the vital Network Programme Committee that decides on which programmes shall be carried by each of the stations. After the reshuffle he battled on successfully to maintain that valuable supremacy. Allied to his indisputable record of knowing what the public will buy in bulk went his canny assessment of human individuals. He has claimed to be able to sum up any man's character in the first five minutes of meeting him, and claimed he has only been wrong in his judgement on three or four occasions.

The committee, at all events, meets six times a year to draft its policy.On the committee sit the Big Five's programme controllers as well as the IBA's deputy director-general, who is responsible for the authority's programme services. It is their task to sift the wares on offer from the regional and network stations and to bring forth an agreed variety of programmes which will satisfy the demands of their viewers, of their regional companies, of their advertisers and not least of the IBA. The ITV companies themselves pay all the costs of their own regional productions. The budget of those networked is shared on an extremely complex scale based on so much per hour of their share in the 'net advertising revenue after levy' (commonly known by its initials, NARAL). The costs of *Independent Television News* and the films bought for networking are also shared by all fifteen companies on their NARAL formula.

But, for all this apparently fail-safe system of fair vetting and cost sharing, as so often happens in human affairs, the real decisions rest on the strength of the personalities involved. Those like Lew Grade possess the gift for getting their own way, for besting an opponent while still winning friends and influencing people and so invariably tipping the balance in their own favour. In the hey-day of his influence over British television, Grade made a point of being personally present at all planning committee meetings. This effectively cut out any middle-man programme controller from 'interpreting' the boss's wishes or trying to impose his own schemes. What ATV wanted was therefore synonymous with what its chief executive wanted. And that same chief executive was there in the thick of the fray to ensure that it came about.

One of the few battles Lew Grade ever lost completely in the Network Programme Committee was his struggle to chop ten minutes from ITN's top-rated *News at Ten*. He resolutely maintained that twenty minutes was all the public could stand of current affairs at that time of night. For once, viewing figures and critical opinion were united in proving him wrong. Elsewhere, however, he was on stronger ground. And though he publicly expressed his heartfelt sympathy with the struggles of the newcomers to the network committee after the 1968 reshuffle, they proved to be crocodile tears in practice. He gave little quarter when it came to making *his* vision of television entertainment the one that reached the screen.

It was extremely difficult for the new boys, such as Yorkshire and London Weekend, to shout him down; they lacked both the practical experience and, as the ratings were showing only too embarrassingly, the viewers. Even such a dynamo of energy and oblique thrust as David Frost (in whom Lew might so easily have seen a mirror image of his younger self given the advantage of that lost Rochelle Street scholarship) found his resolution faltering under Lew's direct attack. In committees, Grade was never afraid to strike where it might hurt most if he believed his instincts for popular appeal were being betrayed. And he it was who slammed into London Weekend's precariously balanced fortunes by kicking one of their main supports out of its crucial slot: the *Frost Show* itself. It had been one of London Weekend's whitest hopes when Frost and his consortium made their successful bid for the IBA contract. Though they maintained their faith in it by allowing it to dominate the weekend's peak viewing hours, audience figures fell away in their millions. With Frost himself sitting with them on the Network Programme Committee, not a single member had had the temerity to raise the embarrassing subject – except Lew.

I've succeeded in business by knowing exactly what I hate,' he told them without preamble, fixing Frost with his sky-blue eyes, 'and I know I hate David Frost.' *(S. Times* profile by N. Tomalin, 23 Dec 1968).

No one produced a knife to cut the silence, but the silence was there to be cut and the knife was in Frost's front. Lew had once again judged the mettle of his man with complete accuracy. There was no bluster. No heated exchange. No counter-attack. And, more importantly, no defence. The arch-exponent of cut-and-thrust, on-camera television debate, the man that critics accused of waging trials by TV, sat there meekly and took it. Eventually he broke the awkward silence which clogged the room by saying quietly: 'All right, Let's talk this subject through.' They did. When they were done Lew had won his reshuffle and the *Frost Show* was demoted in the schedules. Such opposition in the committee did not, of course, help the new companies to 'find their feet', as Lew himself had piously hoped in his interview with the *Financial Times*. Nor did it exactly match up to his pledge: 'They will continue to be encouraged.'

It did, however, help to re-establish his dominance over the mass culture of the country, and lead to his preferences in the Network Programme Committee carrying on unabated. London Weekend Television's *Weekend World*, despite its stimulating and highly praised in-depth approach to topical events, continues to be grudgingly allotted the Sunday lunch-time limbo hour. While the affairs of the nation are being openly debated, it is presumed that the majority of the nation has better things to do. When the social history of Britain from the 1950s onward comes to be written, then Lord Grade must inevitably take his place among the main interpreters and arbiters if not actual innovators of contemporary taste. While he has staunchly and strongly held out against such transatlantic habits as breakfast-time television, his over-all Americanization of ITV did as much as anything else to feed transatlantic rather than European values to a country hungry for something new and thirsting for material prosperity. The Hurricane Zelda of promises, dreams and visions with which he spun Shirley MacLaine into her nightmare adventures in *Shirley's World* reflected values in which he sincerely believed, and which on most other occasions he has been able to make come only too true. The trophies lining his office testify to his success as a spinner of popular dreams and visions.

One of the genuine Goldwynisms to come from the Grade lips sprang from his amazement when the movie, *Voyage of the Damned*, lost money at the box office: 'I had thirty stars in that one!'

If he does respect anything, it is star status and establishment opinion. When he told Miss MacLaine that what interested him most was not her talent but her fame, he told her no more than the truth. The more stars, the bigger the budget, the more spectacular the theme, the greater the faith which Lew has in his product.

When he made the six-hour television epic *Jesus of Nazareth* in 1977, he was as proud of its £18 million budget as he was of its cast. Besides signing up Lord Olivier, as well as Robert Powell for the title role, he enticed, among others, Anne Bancroft, Sir Ralph Richardson, James Mason and Olivia Hussey to lend their fame (and in some cases their talent). 'I told the Pope about it,' he would say, not unmindful of the theatrical effect thus created. 'He thought it sounded marvellous. And it is. This is a film which will last for centuries. And I do mean centuries.' He might almost have been founding a faith rather than filming the birth of one. 'I've seen it forty times and I keep on weeping during the Crucifixion.'

According to Lew, when he went to Rome to receive the honour of the Order of St Sylvester (with star), the Pope said to him of his film: 'What a wonderful thing for Christianity.' Lew, mindful of his own faith, and perhaps not wanting to restrict its box-office appeal, replied: 'No, sir. For all the world.' Then, says Lew, 'He patted me and said, "You're quite right."'

That Lew Grade came to be at the top of the pile can reflect nothing but credit on him. He saw the system as it had been created, and he used it in the best way he knew. His tastes are not inflammatory; he stands with Mrs Whitehouse in her vigilante swoops on smut and violence. The programmes he most enjoys producing are the programmes he most likes to watch.

By selling what most people want to buy, he has earned his company fortunes, but still it is the selling which enthralls him more than the money it brings. Moreover, his generosity with what he earns is universally acknowledged. Such a man is hardly likely to abuse the fruits of his herculean labours, however rich the harvest. But the system which put the ladder against the tree leaves it there for other, more cynically calculating mortals to climb.

PART THREE
They Also Serve…

12

One other founding father of independent television has also managed to stamp the indelible imprint of his own individual personality, dreams and visions on the station he created. This is Sidney Bernstein. Like his rival, Lord Grade, at ATV, he has also been elevated to the House of Lords for his services to the country through television. But, unlike Lew, his consuming interests in life are both cultural and political. He is, in practically every fibre, a direct contrast to the King of Showbiz who rules at Associated TeleVision. He came to view the dawn of commercial television with something of the same crusading spirit possessed by Norman Collins. Once he had overcome his socialist repugnance at seeing such a mighty medium pass out of public control, he was quick to grasp the undreamed-of opportunity to serve the area he knew best in the best way he knew.

Although he was born in Ilford and still spends most weekends in his Kentish retreat, he is as fiercely chauvinistic of the northerner's heritage as the most aggressive native Mancunian. He held an abiding belief that the cultural roots of northerners were stronger and their education better than any in the soft south. London, he once wrote, with the contempt of a proud provincial, was just a town for 'displaced people'.

Bernstein's conviction that Manchester could be turned into the cultural capital of England was considered by many to be the romantic fantasy of a southerner gone native, in the way that people, when they move to Ireland, become passionate Gaelic revivalists. Certainly there has always been something of the reforming evangelist in Bernstein's canny business dealings. He is given to lofty ambitions for the city's spiritual heritage. 'If Essen, Duisburg and Krefeld can house their arts decently, so can Manchester, which is bigger than any of them,' he once wrote in a rallying call to the city fathers. 'Let us have done with makeshift second best and see that the North gets the arts centre it deserves.'

A man on familiar terms with such places of artistic pilgrimage as Essen, Duisburg and Krefeld would be the obvious choice to give the North the television it deserved, too. One of the twenty-five initial bids for a contract from the ITA was Granada's. Unlike Grade's consortium, they did not frighten off the infant authority with ballyhoo. Nor, interestingly enough, did they overload their application with Bernsteinian schemes for an artistic Utopia.

'We have wide entertainment experience,' they stated baldly, 'and we can find £3 million. Just write to Barclays Bank.'

Sidney Bernstein had not picked up the telephone and talked half a dozen cronies into a deal, as Grade had done. There was no need. He had his own company and they had their own financial resources.

The Bernstein family interests in the entertainment industry were firmly established as far back as 1908 with a variety theatre at Edmonton in North London. Like the Winogradskys, the family had emerged from the oppressions and pogroms of Tsarist Russia. Alexander Bernstein, virtual founder of the British Bernstein dynasty, had escaped through Sweden and then, as a very young man, settled in Ilford on the outskirts of Sidney's despised London. In 1891 he married a local girl, Jane Lazarus. Not unusually for the times, the family multiplied prolifically; eight children were born, five boys and three girls.

They did not, however, have to share the privations that the Winogradskys were to endure in their father's adopted land. A quick-tempered individual with something of the social reformer about him, Alexander was no struggling Izaak.

Whatever he touched prospered. Although his training was in the leather trade, his business interests were wide and diverse. Among his holdings he owned a slate quarry in Wales. He also developed a habit of acquiring property at auctions, not least of

1

2

1. The helicopter has become the trademark of the television tycoon. Even the least flamboyant of them, Sidney Bernstein, uses one to ferry him between meetings.

2. Bernstein's headquarters in the heart of his self-styled 'Granadaland'.

3

4a   4b

3. Lew Grade in typical working pose – telephone, cigar and contract as ever-present accessories. 'Usually he's got a telephone glued to his face – but I see him,' says his devoted wife Kathy.

4. Val Parnell (a) after the fateful telephone call from Lew Grade had heralded his departure from ATV. His resignation as managing director was followed by a suit for restitution of conjugal rights by his previous wife, divorce and marriage to Miss Aileen Cochrane (b).

5. Parnell's protégée, Noele Gordon, as she appeared after taking over from Julie Wilson in the London production of *Bet Your Life* at the London Hippodrome. When her association with Parnell ended, Miss Gordon received a block of shares in the newly-formed ATV and now reigns at their Birmingham studios as the queen of *Crossroads*.

6. London Weekend Television pinned its faith on David Frost's ability to attract viewers each Friday, Saturday, and Sunday evenings. When the viewing public turned over to BBC in droves, LWT's ambitious plans crumbled away to nothing.

7

8

9

7. John Freeman *(left),* freed from ambassadorial duties in Washington, came in as a Mr Clean chairman at London Weekend after the IBA had objected to Rupert Murdoch's back-door attempt to take over the station. In an earlier career he had interviewed Lord Thomson *(right),* chairman of Scottish TV and the man who coined the phrase 'a licence to print money' for ITV. The programme was *Face to Face,* still the standard model for television inquisition.

8. and 9. It was on his famous *Face to Face* confrontations that John Freeman reduced BBC television's irascible star personality, Gilbert Harding, to tears. The date: 18 Sept 1960. It made television history.

10

11

12

10. The self-effacing Leslie Grade *(left),* third of the Winogradsky brothers, with co-director Robin Fox *(middle),* (father of actors Edward and James) clinching a deal with Kenneth Rive *(right),* to break the distribution duopoly on films of the giant Odeon and ABC chains. Leslie's son, Michael, went on to become programme controller at LWT and is widely tipped to take over his uncles' empires.

11. Kenneth Griffith, actor and documentary producer, found himself victim of the ITV system when his film *Hang Out Your Brightest Colours* was banned by Grade's ATV organization. Its director, Antony Thomas, went on to create *Death of a Princess* which ATV screened amid an international furore.

12. The subject of *Hang Out Your Brightest Colours* was the Irish patriot Michael Collins. Griffith intended to give British viewers an insight into the background to the Irish troubles. But with the redistribution of the franchise looming, ATV deemed it altogether too explosive an issue to show. Having commissioned the film, they locked it away.

13

14

15

13. If the late Lord Beveridge's report had been adopted by the post-war Labour government, commercial television might not have broken the monopoly of the BBC when and how it did. However, Attlee's administration was rendered impotent and voted out of office before the Beveridge recommendations on the future of broadcasting could be implemented.

14. The Pilkington Report, from the committee chaired by Sir Harry Pilkington, roundly condemned the standards of the infant independent television stations. They complained of excessive profits and lamentable standards and recommended that the whole system be dismantled, taking the programme planning out of the hands of the Big Four companies.

15. Peter Cadbury *(right)*, chairman of Westward Television, threw a garden party at his mansion to burn a giant effigy of the Pilkington Report, so furious were the bosses of ITV at its recommendations. Later on, the flamboyant Westward chief was to meet opposition from within his own boardroom. But here, in a happier mood, he shows Lord Hill *(left)* around his headquarters.

16. Noël Annan, created Lord Annan (life peerage) in 1965. He has been the chairman of the Committee of Enquiry into Broadcasting since 1974.

17. Prince Littler in the heyday of his theatre empire. His opposition to commercial television – on the grounds that it would be the death of live entertainment – quickly evaporated once ITV became a reality. He became the first chairman of ATV.

which was a run-down estate in Manor Park close by their home in Ilford. For this he paid a paltry £270 site-unseen, which, since it consisted of something like 600 houses, was nothing short of a *coup*. Whatever the dilapidation of the little terraces, or the ludicrously depressed price of Victorian property, he had bought himself a bargain.

Something of Alexander's character, and that of his eldest surviving son, Sidney, can be gleaned from the way he capitalized on these grim, dreary, dismal streets. Not for this landlord a quick return on his slum properties. The buildings were renovated, being sturdily built. Gas was installed. The district was brightened by offering the encouragement of annual prizes for the best-kept gardens. Good housekeeping was rewarded by the gift of a sack of coal each Christmas to all who had kept up to date with their rent (a popular Victorian form of paternalism at work). To give the area an air of uniform respectability, he put venetian blinds at every window. And he reinforced the image of solid security for his tenants by providing a number of free houses for policemen and their families, so that each street was adequately patrolled by its own local bobby. These streets still stand today with the names that Alexander Bernstein gave them – Selborne and Alvestone after leading judges of the day, and, more prosaically, Parkhurst and Walton.

It was his flair for social planning which, ironically, brought Alexander into touch with the entertainment industry. He had wanted to develop a plot snapped up at Edmonton into a parade of shops. It was more to create a lure for potential shopkeepers to his speculative development than it was out of any overwhelming desire to break into showbusiness that he decided to establish a theatre there. Certainly the site needed something to attract traders and customers alike. It was a refuse dump when Bernstein bought it.

Bernstein himself knew nothing about running theatres. The impresario whom he approached to take the responsibility off his shoulders, however, soon ignited his short-fused temper and sent him storming out of a meeting vowing to go it alone. In the event, and with his ire suitably cooled, he avenged himself by engaging the showman's own personal assistant in typically impulsive fashion. 'Do you want a music hall, young man?' was how he broached the deal to the astonished young Harry Bawn one day during a chance encounter in the Charing Cross Road. And the theatre which he built, strategically sited opposite the Great

Eastern Railway's Lower Edmonton station, was Bawn's, for a rent of £900 a year.

It was typical of Bernstein's style to open it on Boxing Day after a suitably philanthropic gesture to the neighbourhood. Every child in the district was invited to the Edmonton Empire for a special preview treat that Christmas of 1908. And the nine-year-old Sidney Bernstein, dressed in a smart new sailor suit along with the rest of the young Bernsteins, was driven over from their Ilford home to stand on the steps of their father's splendid new theatre to hand out packets of sweets to the audience as they came in. The excitement of the event was doubly enhanced for them by the appearance of a troupe of performing elephants and the rumour rife in the district that the weight of this novelty would cause the building to collapse into the rubbish tip on which it had been built.

The Edmonton Empire survived the elephants' act, and Alexander Bernstein found himself more and more embroiled in the day-to-day finances of the theatre. As with all things, he was not a man who practised half-measures. By the time the First World War broke out, he had built or bought up five more provincial music halls and expanded them into pleasure palaces specially designed for the new cinematic shows. While Izaak Winogradsky was speculating unsuccessfully in his flea-pit venture in the Mile End Road, Alexander Bernstein was involved in heavy and lucrative early investment in all branches of the new, burgeoning film industry. The war brought its share of tragedy to the Bernstein family. Their eldest son, Selim Alexander, was killed on active service in Gallipoli in 1915. He died something of a hero, twice mentioned in dispatches before the war was a year old.

But the war period also saw the rapid spread of the cinema, bringing instant cheer and escape to a war-weary public. When he died in 1922, Alexander left behind eight Bernstein theatres – his original Edmonton Empire; the Electrodome, Bow; the Lyric Cinema, Guernsey; and his other Empire 'Kinemas' in Ilford, Plumstead, East Ham, West Ham and Willesden. It was hardly Hollywood, but, for his twenty-three-year-old heir, Sidney, it was an auspicious enough entry into the world of mass entertainment.

13

The embryo young magnate had never been allowed to feel that he had been born with a silver – or even a nickel-plated – spoon in his mouth. If his father had brought him along to his theatre in a neat sailor suit to distribute sweets to the neighbourhood children, it had not been to fill his head with any notion of his own social supremacy. It was to remind him of his duties and obligations. Alexander Bernstein had been a severe task-master to all his children, not least to Sidney, who was, after the death of his elder brother Selim, the natural successor to his father's business interests. Alexander might have been a model landlord – even if giving bags of coal only to those tenants who could afford to keep up with his rents and withholding them from those needy enough to fall behind in their payments does suggest a lack of charity's real spirit – but he expected nothing short of perfection from his offspring.

Sidney was quickly tutored in his father's demanding standards. He had left Highlands School, Ilford, at sixteen, and, before joining Alexander's Empire Works as secretary, was cannily sent out to learn his business elsewhere. Bernstein Senior was not going to have his son making his apprentice mistakes in *his* time. Between the ages of eighteen, when he joined the family business, and twenty-three, when he took control of it, Sidney had learned his trade in the frugal fashion of the true Victorian régime: plenty of brickbats when things went wrong, and few bouquets when they went right (because that was how they were supposed to go anyway).

Even so, he had received the most thorough grounding in all aspects of the business by the time he became boss at the companies' offices in Cecil Court, just off the Charing Cross Road. And he soon began to assert himself as an independent operator in his own right.

By one of those neatly drawn full-circles which can bring such a satisfying sense of form and order to the haphazard accidents of life, Sidney's personal interest in the entertainment business began exactly in the same spot his father's had: at the old Edmonton Empire.

He was going about his late father's business, travelling to a working dinner in the country with a leading film distributor of such box office draws as Charlie Chaplin, when he happened to pass by the building that had begun its life with the trumpeting of elephants and the shrieks of over 1,000 children.

What he found inside was almost as dispiriting as the refuse tip it had been built on. Harry Bawn, to whom his father had so impulsively handed the theatre almost two decades before, was also dead by now. His widow, who had in her day been a music-hall favourite, was running it with her son, but without much future. Light bulbs had been removed from the sockets to save electricity, though this was not the only kind of gloom enveloping the premises. Young Mr Bernstein became so depressed that, first thing in the morning, he instructed his accountants to negotiate with Mrs Bawn to buy back the lease. Then he contacted Maurice King, the son of one of his father's closest business associates, and proposed carrying on the two families' connections into the second generation by asking him to help to run it.

Together they went to look the place over again, and it seemed even more dispiriting. But, being positive thinkers, they agreed that at least together they could do no worse, and therefore might even do better. With Sidney running the theatre, and Maurice overseeing the three big bars, they calculated that, with the profit from the liquor, the entire box-office takings could be ploughed back into raising the standards of the acts on stage. And this they did with some success from 1922 to 1927. It was Sidney's first independent venture. The Edmonton Empire was indeed the corner-stone of all the Bernstein family's showbusiness fortunes. In 1933, Sidney was to use it yet again, this time to expand his influence on the cinema world, but not before the theatre had carved out for itself some memorable slices of history. Not only did almost every leading

86

music-hall star of the era tread its boards – Florrie Forde, Ella Shields, Albert Chevalier, the up-and-coming Gracie Fields, Will Hay, Harry Champion, Nellie Wallace, Little Tich and G. H. Elliott, 'The Chocolate Coloured Coon' – but it was where the greatest of them all, Marie Lloyd, made her last stage appearance.

It is an interesting side-light on the sensitivity of the new young boss's nature that the star-painted door of Marie's dressing room was kept locked from the day she died in 1922 (the year he took over) to the eve of its transformation into a cinema ten years later. Mementos and embroidered keepsakes she had left there after she was taken ill were discovered when the door of her enshrined dressing room was finally opened for the theatre's face-lift.

By the time it was gutted and totally remodelled, Sidney Bernstein was important enough as a leading theatre and cinema impresario to have Jessie Matthews and Sonnie Hale, the two greatest West End and British movie box-office stars of the day, on hand to perform the ceremonial laying of the new Edmonton Empire foundation stone.

By now all the brothers had entered the business in one capacity or another, and their mother also remained an imposing presence on many of their company boards. But it was Sidney's creative energies which were directing the Bernstein's ever-expanding fortunes in the industry. He had been quick to grasp the importance of creating an atmosphere of luxurious fantasy for the customers who flocked in search of escapism and dream fulfilment. He travelled regularly to the United States to keep in touch with the latest developments in the industry, and it was New York's famous Roxy, with its choirs, its music, its pampering to the customers' creature comforts, which fired his imagination most. 'Never', declared the young showman realistically on his return, 'have I seen such rubbish presented in such ornate surroundings.' Immediately he set the architect Cecil Masey to work turning the Bernstein cinema empire into buildings worthy of the name picture palaces. The most imposing of these was the great neo-Gothic edifice he built at Tooting, a monument to the era and to Bernstein's own artistic visions.

Sidney opened the cinema in September 1931 with a fanfare sounded by the Grenadier Guards. As Ian Nairn, the self-appointed arbiter of London's splendour, has written:

> Ninety-nine cinemas may be a shoddy counterfeit and so may
> ninety-nine films, but this is the hundredth. Gothic arches are all .
> around the auditorium, dimly lit by the reflections on the screen.
> When the lights go up there is Aladdin's cave; if you walk to the
> front for a choc ice or orange squash and turn suddenly, the view
> may literally make you gasp. Pinnacle after gilded pinnacle to the
> back of the gallery; one of the sights of London. Miss the Tower
> of London if you have to, but don't miss this.

And as if this praise was not enough to convey the cathedral-like
scale of the cinema's grandeur, the *Sunday Times Colour Supplement* was to describe it thirty years later as 'one of the two great
originals in Britain'. It could justly claim to be one of the wonders of
the age, with its flamboyant baroque wall decorations, its delicately
lit stained-glass windows, its 150-foot long hall of mirrors, and, of
course, the Mighty Wurlitzer organ, without which no leading
cinema of the day was complete.

Around the same time Sidney was also presiding over the building
of the equally impressive Phoenix Theatre in the Charing Cross
Road (in a flat above which, by another neat coincidence, this book
came to be written). Though the Phoenix quickly passed out of
Sidney's business interests and much of the Italianate magnificence
in the auditorium that the great designer Komisarjevsky conceived
has disappeared, the gilded and marbled foyers have been lovingly
restored and preserved by its present owners, Gerald and Veronica
Flint-Shipman. It remains one of the finest of London's theatres,
and its main entrance foyer and staircase were recently turned into
a permanent memorial to Sir Noël Coward in commemoration of
the first, glamorous offering with which Sidney Bernstein welcomed
the public to his latest theatre: Coward's *Private Lives*. With Coward
himself co-starring alongside Gertrude Lawrence in the two leading
roles, and the young Laurence Olivier partnering Adrienne Allen
as their unfortunate stool-pigeons, Bernstein was again demonstrating an artistic integrity, innate taste and shrewd business
acumen at work. Here indeed was a personality with whom leading
showmen like C. B. Cochran were happy to deal.

The battles Bernstein waged to ensure the Phoenix's rising in
Charing Cross Road in the splendour he had envisaged certainly
justified its name. No detail was too mundane to fire his passions.
At one point he was discovered standing forlornly outside on the
pavement, as disconsolate as a St George who has lost the maiden

to a dragon and been badly singed in the process. 'Come and see what they want to do to my beautiful staircase,' he wailed to the son of his old partner, Maurice King. 'They want to ruin it!' *They*, the dragons, turned out to be the London County Council, and the desecration they wrought was their insistence on a safety handrail. To a man of Sidney's perfectionist taste, it was a rape on the marble virginity of his sweeping stairway. Memorabilia of his first great triumph now take the eye away from the offending handrail. I must confess that, though the Phoenix is practically my home (living above the shop, as it were), I have never even noticed the cause of this sensitive man's artistic outrage.

Sidney built this theatre on a plot almost as unpromising as the rubbish tip at Edmonton, though it did have slightly more theatrical history attached to it. Besides the decidedly tatty properties on the site abutting Phoenix Street (after which the theatre was named), had been a building that was once a factory. Later it had been turned into an odd form of variety theatre called the Alcazar, but with nothing like the chic of its namesake in Paris. The greatest novelty of its all day and half the night non-stop entertainment was its three performance platforms and a perambulating audience – the customers simply strolled from one stage to the next once a turn was over.

The Bernstein replacement was not about to perpetuate the old Alcazar's far from high-class image. In its issue of 25 September 1930, *The Stage* reported glowingly on the edifice which C. B. Cochran opened with due ceremony (Bernard Shaw having regretfully declined the honour):

> The distinguished columns here are blues and pinks on a cream ground and the whole is lavishly picked out with modelling in gold. Large windows in the adjacent promenade allow late-comers and others who might for some reason or other be prevented from getting to their seats to view the stalls level and the stage. The circle appears to have come far forward and has a commodious upper circle above it. Care has been taken in the comfort of the seating. Each seat has sufficient body and leg room and is provided with its own hat rack [those were the days when no gentleman was dressed without a hat and ladies were being constantly requested to remove theirs when they blocked the view]. There are six roomy private boxes. The upholstery has a touch of the medieval and is in a rare shade of dark pink with a touch of heliotrope or light purple in its pattern. In the front of the house rich reds, blues and gold appear to be the prime colours. Bars and cloakrooms are well-appointed but no attempt

has been made here in the shape of elaborate decoration. A striking feature in the interior decoration will be found in the fine reproductions of works by old masters. Here we have well-executed copies of pictures by Titian, Giorgione, Tintoretto, and Pinturicchio. The safety curtain carries Jacopo del Salaio's 'The Triumph of Love', the original of which can be seen in the Oratorio de S. Ansano, Fiesole. These reproductions are the work of Vladimir Polunin.

A man who would pay good money to have Titian, Giorgione, Tintoretto, and Pinturicchio lovingly recreated on the walls of his theatre would clearly also be capable of dreaming of making Manchester a rival to Essen, Duisburg and Krefeld, even if most Mancunians had never heard of them. He was, however, careful also to follow his father's commercial dictates by providing his theatre with a parade of shops along its Charing Cross Road frontage.

It becomes less surprising that someone with his inherent concern in housing his ventures in a suitably stimulating architectural environment should eventually bequeath to Manchester the sleek, green edifice with its spiralling watch-tower which rises out of the grey drabness beside the River Irwell as a symbol of the city's new television age. The impact of Bernstein's Granada TV on that grimed Gothic city has been every bit as startling as the arrival of Komisarjevsky's Gothic flight of fantasy in Tooting three decades before.

Not, it must be added, that everything which led to Granada's arrival was subject to such lofty idealism. In comparing Sidney Bernstein's taste for aesthetic perfection with Lew Grade's more peasant preoccupations, it must not be forgotten that the high-minded young Tsarevitch of the Empire circuit was himself not above a few short cuts to boost profits. When he was managing the affairs at the old Edmonton music hall, he hit on a scheme for numbering the programmes and using them as a kind of lottery. A member of the audience was invited to go on stage and pick the winning number. It would, Bernstein assured his partner, be a big boost to the revenue, with the programmes selling at threepence each and the prizes presented by the shops situated so conveniently close through the foresight of old Alexander. And so it was, until Sidney was summoned for conducting an illegal lottery.

Nothing daunted, he appeared before the local magistrates and informed them that, before embarking on the enterprise, he had been careful to take counsel's advice. The Bench was impressed by

90

his prudence. Indeed, they told him, were it not for the fact that he had taken the precaution of counsel's advice, an extremely heavy fine would have been imposed. As it was, Sidney was let off with costs. What the magistrates were *not* told by the young repentant who stood before them was that, having duly taken counsel's advice, he had promptly ignored it; counsel's advice had been exactly the same as the magistrate's verdict: that Sidney's lottery was illegal.

Elsewhere, however, his handling of the ever-widening spread of his circuit owed a great deal to his father's branch of matching social responsibility with self-interest. He introduced the first children's matinées. He inaugurated the first detailed market research on the industry with detailed questionnaires distributed regularly to his customers and to 'prominent persons in various walks of life'. The resulting findings were then conscientiously reported in *The Times* and the trade press.

The 'imaginative champion of "Variety Presentation" in cinema programmes' – as the *Bioscope* (the trade journal of the industry) was to describe him – could not fail to see the practical advantage of such innovations. The cut-price matinées, besides keeping the children off the streets and introducing a little educational propaganda in their programmes of 'suitable material', were also doing a fine job of initiating the next generation into the cinema-going habit. The questionnaires, with the rather shaky basis of their random research, might not satisfy today's meticulously monitored market researches or opinion polls, but at least they gained Bernstein's cinemas some welcome free publicity of the most impeccable kind.

His personal blend of pragmatism and cultural ideology was developed to a fine art by the time he came to move in on Manchester. Moreover, he alighted on Manchester as a base for his new enterprise in much the same way he had come to build the very first Granada Cinema at Dover. For it was at Dover that the name Granada was launched.

Bernstein's habit was to make forays around the country looking for places which were ill-served by cinemas but with populations sizeable enough to support one if he provided it. He sold off a major part of his interest in the chain his father had founded (keeping just under 50 per cent of the shares in the family), and while he remained their programme adviser, he was restless for new outlets. For the first time he decided to look outside the London area, and Dover answered all his requirements so far as potential was concerned (just as Manchester was to do later).

With a new building, the beginning of a new chain, he wanted a new name. Others had used 'Alhambra', 'Palace', 'Majesty' or 'Rialto' in their endeavours to conjure up an exciting brand image; Bernstein was after something different.

There are many apocryphal stories about how he chose the name. But it was the memory of a holiday visit to Spain's old Moorish town, with its Alhambra palace and its exotic architecture, which prompted him to opt for Granada. It had just the flavour of adventure, excitement and exotica he was looking for.

In the weeks before the cinema was due to open, a publicity tease campaign was launched. All around the town were plastered posters which bore nothing but the command: 'START SAYING GRANADA'.

14

By the time the Independent Television Authority came to place their advertisements inviting applications from would-be contractors, a great many people had stopped saying Granada. There could be no mistaking the signs for a wily operator like Bernstein. Television had knocked cinema audiences for six. The generation of customers he had so carefully nurtured with his cut-price children's matinées had grown up, gone to war, and come back to enjoy the novelty of entertainment brought to their own firesides. Whereas at the height of his expansion the Granada circuit could boast fifty-seven houses, Sidney found himself, after the war, retrenching in his cinema chain and pouring more cash into his live theatres – which could at least offer as competition the one thing television could not: 'Flesh and blood theatre' as the immortal Dame Edna Everage has dubbed it. The cinema boom was over; television was the coming medium for the masses.

Unlike Lew Grade, who had largely ignored the growth of television, except as yet another profitable outlet for his agency's clients, Sidney was quick to grasp both its potential and its dangers. His constant trips to the United States were enough to warn him well in advance of what his cinema returns back home were already beginning to hint.

Yet, as we have seen, he was among the most ardent advocates of keeping television's influence under the firm control of a public body. The idea of giving private enterprise the right to communicate directly into the homes of the public instinctively repelled him. On the other hand, Sidney's brand of socialism had always been of a light pink hue. Just as Lord Woolton found himself chairman of a new breed of 'practical' Conservatives in the House of Commons, so the future Lord Bernstein practised a 'practical' sort of socialism: a kind which definitely did not disdain the making of large profits by individual effort. He might fight shy of businessmen taking television into the home, but he did not propose to sit back and let it knock the bottom out of his cinemas. Nor did he intend denying himself a slice of the action.

Bernstein's first answer was to set about mounting a strangely eccentric scheme, conceived to obtain a licence to operate a large-screen public television service in his cinemas. Though he nobly insisted that 'the right of access to domestic sound and television receivers of millions of people carries with it such great propaganda power that it cannot be entrusted to any persons or bodies other than a public corporation or a number of public corporations', he nevertheless argued that 'this public monopoly of broadcasting to the home should not be artificially shielded from the competition of forms of entertainment which are made available outside the home'.

He was determined to see that his Granada cinemas would be among the first to provide that competition. Exactly why he should find this a more acceptable face of capitalism is difficult to understand. Are people more susceptible to the powers of propaganda if they sit knitting in front of the telly at home instead of getting dressed up to go out and pay money for it? However off-balance the logic, Bernstein was something of a public figure by then. During the war he had been films adviser to the Ministry of Information, chief of Film Selection at Allied Forces Headquarters in North Africa and chief of Film Selection at SHAEF (Supreme Headquarters, Allied Expeditionary Force). When he spoke about the powers of propaganda, he knew what he was talking about. And he persisted with his campaign to operate a private television system for screening in his cinemas.

His petitions to the Paymaster General's office for a licence were, more often than not, treated with discouragingly formal official stonewalling – 'Dear Sir, I am instructed by the Paymaster General to acknowledge your letter and to say that its contents have been noted...' But he never let it rest. It was, he claimed, the only way the film industry could fight back against the competition of the new medium. The film industry 'has a right to expect that it shall not be required to fight this duel with a shorter sword than its opponents' was the swashbuckling phrase he used to make his point. As quid pro quo, he volunteered, the film industry would make their first-feature films more readily available to the BBC. The advantages of his notion were that 'it would safeguard the position of the BBC vis-à-vis its licence-holders; it would give yet another stimulus to the film industry's efforts to evolve new and higher standards of showmanship and of entertainment and artistic values; it would encourage the most beneficial co-operation in television between the BBC and the film industry; and it would give the consumer the advantages which flow from competition for his time and attention'.

Interestingly enough, the arguments he used here for the private consideration of the Beveridge Committee were very different from the ones he was to employ later as the new franchise holder for the North. By then, his high-minded concern for safeguarding the BBC's position had given way to public pronouncements such as, 'We would be most dishonest if we did not say at this point that we expect our programmes to be different from the BBC's and from those of our fellow contractors chiefly by being better.' And his eagerness to make first-feature films available to the BBC soon evaporated once he had been given a commercial franchise of his own.

'We are not in favour of showing films designed for the cinema screens. Not even old films,' he declared shortly before Granada TV started transmission. What he proposed instead was a production partnership with Alfred Hitchcock to make movies for television only. The boast about disdaining old films had, however, acquired a very cracked ring by the time Lord Annan was to complain, as the franchise came up yet again for redistribution, 'Independent Television's choice of films from the American market shown in peak viewing hours is at times deplorable.' Annan was not, of course, directing his criticism directly at Lord Bernstein or Granada TV, but as members of the Network Programme Committee, on which each jealously protects his place in the sun but the basic principles of working together 'have long been worked out', (in Granada's own words), they could not be absolved from the general disgrace. Yet some parts of the promise were prophetic. Gradually, over the twenty-five years of its existence, some signs emerged that films made specially for television were propping up the ailing movie industry, especially in America. Bernstein's collaboration with Hitchcock was extremely popular for a while.

And though he himself had long retired from active control by the time his dream of an impressive production alliance with a cultural heavyweight was developed further, it was Granada, through their executive producer, Derek Granger, who lured the elusive Laurence Olivier to the small screen to co-produce and star in a filmed series of classic modern plays.

Lord Bernstein has a reputation among his associates for being a man whose left hand is totally unaware of what his right hand is doing – a man of total contradictions. But there is little doubt that, whatever the reasons why he went back on his earlier insistence that independent television should not be handed over to commercial interests, his vision for his station was never lacking in artistic inspiration or level-headed practicability. His second letter to the Independent Television Authority, after making the initial brief bid, was far more detailed and extremely illuminating.

> We wish to become exclusive Programme contractors for the Manchester–Liverpool Station for seven days a week [it informed them]. We also desire that for two consecutive weekdays each week the programmes we put out from this station should be televised from all other stations under your authority.

That took care of networking. It was Viscount Swinton, in the later stages of the parliamentary debate, who had crystallized the economic advantages of competing regional contractors sharing air-time between them. 'It is the only way in which any of the programmes would reach a big listening public and command a large price,' his lordship explained succinctly. And Sidney Bernstein, with his careful study of American television over the years, was not about to disagree.

As to his company's ambitions for programme planning and regional involvement, he was equally brief and to the point:

> We appreciate that there may be interests in the Manchester–Liverpool area who would wish to be associated and, should we be appointed, we would welcome their proposals.
>
> It would be our purpose, equipped with our experience in presenting ballet, symphony concerts, opera, stage plays, pantomimes, variety shows and, of course, films, to provide programmes of high quality and wide scope which would attract the public at all levels.
>
> Our programmes would be devised to appeal to the public

most likely to be available for viewing at the time of the broadcast taking into account what alternative programmes are being offered. The exact proportion of time devoted to any class of programme cannot be specified definitely at present.

This last statement is, of course, exactly what Lord Hill was to complain about when, as chairman of the television authority, he lamented that it was comparatively simple to assess which group had the strongest finances when it came to shelling out the contracts; the greatest difficulty was to judge between their promise and performance. The authority, as Granada's initial application so cockily assured them, had only to pick up the phone and speak to Barclays Bank to satisfy themselves that the company could lay their hands on the necessary £3 million. But how were they to judge the promise?

On paper, Bernstein's claim for a contract could not have looked more impressive. Certainly Lew Grade's consortium would have had some difficulty, even with the combined interests of Parnell, Littler and Lord Renwick, in billing their experience in ballet, symphony concerts, opera and stage shows above their knowledge of variety. But the get-out clause had been cleverly inserted in this initial draft of Granada's aspirations. Bernstein had not been in the business for thirty-seven years without knowing how to cover his options. That the 'exact proportion of time devoted to any class of programme' could not indeed be specified definitely was what London Weekend Television was to find when the next batch of contracts came on offer.

Bernstein himself was the first to admit that he had not the slightest notion of how he came to be awarded the contract. Nor is he alone. No one save the committee who awards the contracts knows precisely how they come to be handed out. Among the most invidious of the many inherent weaknesses in both the ITA and its successor, the IBA, is this same obsessive secrecy. No one outside Bernstein's headquarters in Soho's Golden Square and the cabal at the ITA knew exactly how Granada proposed to run their station if they were given the licence. And not even Granada knew why *their* proposals had been accepted against other claimants when that licence was given. This is surely iniquitous in a body officially empowered to entrust access to such overwhelming influence and such colossal wealth. That the two go hand in hand we can take for granted.

Even Bernstein, with his insistence on the finer things in life distinguishing his attitude to showmanship, is forced to admit that, where ITV is concerned, the two are inextricably linked. 'I would be a damned hypocrite if I said I wasn't interested in money,' he once told George Scott in answer to the question: 'What is your chief reason for being in television?'

In making these complaints against the way the IBA operates, it is not intended to accuse them of taking their applicants' assurances at face value. When it came to asking that their hours of broadcast time should be no fewer than the BBC's, and that their first contract should run ten years, the Granada bidders were not allowed to be as entirely unspecific about their scheduling as they had hoped in their letter. The questionnaire sent out to interested parties by the ITA was definitely aimed at weeding out the boys from the men. Its contents were wide-ranging. And since we are allowed to know so little of the debate that resolves the granting of a franchise, I take the opportunity to reproduce them here in full, if only to bring the merest chink of light into this dark area. What the ITA wanted to know from its original applicants was:

1: Who will be your Directors and chief officers?
2: Are you aware that your company must not be under the control of disqualified persons?
3: (a) What will be your financial resources?
   (b) Are you prepared to produce a Banker's reference if necessary?
4: What is the experience of your directors and officers in –
   (a) entertainment in general;
   (b) television?
5: What are your resources or plans in respect of studios and equipment?
6: (a) What are your plans with regard to the contents of your programmes?
   (b) Can you give us specimen schedules of your programmes?
7: How many hours of programmes a day would you be able and ready to produce?
8: (a) How do you think news should be handled?
   (b) If you would propose to do it yourself what are your plans?
9: (a) Do you plan to 'stockpile' programmes?
   (b) How many hours of programmes would you have on hand by the time broadcasting commenced? (i.e. say August 1955).
10: (a) How much would you propose to sub-contract?
    (b) With whom?

11: Would you be prepared to combine with other contractors if the authority wished?

12: (a) What are your ideas on organization? Do you favour (i) a system of one contractor per station; (ii) a system of time-sharing by days of the weeks; (iii) a system of time-sharing by hours of the day; (iv) any other system?

(b) If (i) which station are you interested in?

(c) If (ii) or (iii) which days or hours would you prefer?

(d) Whichever system you favour, how do you envisage the network arrangements would work?

As we have seen already, this highly detailed document did exactly what it was intended to do. Of the twenty-five hopefuls who responded to the original invitation to turn up at the feast, twenty rapidly melted away as soon as they felt the heat from the kitchen. Bernstein stayed to gather the pickings. But still he fought shy of elaborating on his open-ended assurances regarding programme content. Question 6 was left unanswered. Presumably the ITA looked into their crystal ball to assess just what percentage of Granada's programmes would reflect the company's boasted interests in ballet, symphony concerts, opera, plays and even pantomimes, and what would be governed by the calls of Mammon.

15

The meeting at which the ITA vetted their prospective contractor elicited no more specific proposals on the balance of their programmes. Sidney Bernstein led the delegation, along with his brother Cecil. They were accompanied by Victor Peers, their close associate in their film operations, and Granada's company secretary, Joseph Warton. The authority made its presence felt in the not insubstantial shape of its chairman, Sir Kenneth Clark (later Lord Clark of television *Civilization* fame, but then better known for his work as director of the National Gallery), his deputy, Sir Charles Colson, the authority's vociferous director-general, Sir Robert Fraser (an Australian journalist of the blunderbuss school who had risen to become director-general of the Central Office of Information), and one of its founder-members, Sir Henry Hinchcliffe.

They were given to understand from the Bernsteins that everything concerning content would depend on the manner in which the programmes were transmitted. If it were based on a regional system, Granada would place a heavy emphasis on the local tastes and interests, including sport – and, of course, on 'culture'. National and world affairs would be dealt with, the ITA were informed, as they made themselves felt in the region. As for networked programmes, these would reflect the wide scope of Granada's experience in the entertainment field.

If Sidney was not hypocrite enough to deny his interest in the profits to be made out of commercial television, he was also idealist

100

enough not to forget the obligations which went hand-in-hand with his source of revenue. When Granada eventually won through and made its belated début on the coat-tails of its three competitors, its viewers and advertisers alike must have been somewhat taken aback by the little finger-wagging lecture to which they were treated on that first night.

An announcer materialized, presumably to reassure the public that they were not about to be brainwashed into a ruinous spending orgy, as some had feared with the advent of the new means to subliminal suggestion. 'For most of you Independent Television has been a new experience,' the viewers were informed in the tones of the friendly kindergarten schoolteacher which television tended to adopt at that time. 'We have brought advertisements to your television screens at home. We think you will like them, no* only because they are entertaining but because they are info. native. Products and services, whose names you will be seeing, are a guide to sensible buying and will help you to get value for your money. Television advertisers have faith and pride in what they offer. Granada stands behind them and their statements. We hope their names will become as familiar to you as the names of your friends and neighbours. You can use Granada advertisements as a trust-worthy guide to wise spending. Wise spending eventually saves money. And savings can help deal with one aspect of our country's economic problems.

'So, before we shop, let us say to ourselves "is it essential?". If it is, let us buy the best we can afford. If it is not essential, can we save? Save not only for a rainy day but also to make sure that tomorrow and the day after will be sunny.'

If this thick helping of golden syrup before bed-time d .n't send the audience off up their little wooden st' .s with bellyache, then they were probably strong enough to st-.nach anything the commercials had to offer. But it must have i .ed at least some of the advertisers to have potential customers warned, in that are you sitting comfortably then I'll begin fashion, that they must only spend on essentials. The whole art of advertising is to implant seeds which will, with luck, burst forth into the fruits of impulse-buying.

It did, however, demonstrate Sidney's flair for imbuing everything he did with the aura of a good deed well done. Those sugar-coated sentiments at the end of Granada's first evening's commercials made the whole operation sound as if Lord Reith himself had invented the commercial break. Lord Reith, of course, had done no such thing. In fact, when he came to chair a Commission of Enquiry into advertising which the Labour Party set up in 1964, his findings put the objections to advertising in language which Moses might have used after carrying the tablets all the way down from the mount only to find his followers prancing about in front of graven images. 'For the past thirty-five years or over,' thundered Reith's report, 'advertising has been under sustained attack as an undesirable type of propaganda which cons the public, creates anti-social wants, promotes materialism, feeds off fears of sickness and of social envy, degrades the use of the English language and presents a stiflingly banal view of life.'

No one heeding Granada's little homily could possibly have suspected that what they had just seen could ever produce Lord Reith's catalogue of contagious social diseases. Far from undermining the health of the nation's moral fibre, Granada were assuring their viewers that the £14,215 revenue the company earned from the twenty-seven advertisements shown that night was more in the nature of a social welfare fund set up on their behalf.

It was also typical of the Bernstein touch that, at the opening-night party held in the Midland Hotel – and attended by the advertising fraternity, both paid-up and potential clients of the company – the centre-piece was a four-foot-high, shell-shaped flower arrangement. The shell was open and inside was a pearl: the symbol of the programmes which Sidney and his executives had kept so carefully concealed.

Bernstein was too shrewd a businessman to cast any pearl before swine. As ever, he had done his market research well. In bidding for the northern franchise and settling in the city he had even taken into account Manchester's high rainfall, he declared later and only half in jest. Combined with the density of its population, this meant only one thing to Bernstein: that Manchester had a great mass of people staying in at nights – in other words, a captive audience.

It was in a paper he gave at the London School of Economics that he rationalized his reasons for moving north in typical Bernsteinian fashion, blending idealism with the nitty-gritty of showmanship. 'The North is a closely knit, indigenous industrial society,' he informed them, painting Manchester in the glowing colours in which he perceived it, 'a homogenous cultural group with a good record for music, theatre, literature and newspapers not found

102

anywhere else in this island, except perhaps in Scotland.' Then he went on to coin the famous phrase with which he dismissed the area in which his family's fortunes had been founded. 'Compare this with London and its suburbs – full of displaced persons,' declared the man whose cinemas stretched from Tooting to Bow and beyond. 'And, of course, if you look at the map of the concentration of population in the North, and a rainfall map, you will see that the North is an ideal place for television,' he added smilingly.

A man who could talk so persuasively of his chosen area must have appealed strongly both to Sir Kenneth Clark, with his unrivalled expertise in the arts, and to Sir Robert Fraser, with his swashbuckling crusade waged on behalf of the aspirations of independent television. This was the calibre of man they wanted to pioneer the new stations. It was also very likely why Bernstein and Collins were preferred above Grade, Parnell and Littler in the ITA's first deal. Lew may have ruefully reflected that they were the only unlucky ticket-holders in the initial hand-out because their publicity made them sound as though they owned the world. But Sidney's winning number lay in his presenting himself as someone capable of making the world a better place if he should come to own it.

Not that his claims on the authority's favour were all so altruistic. He had presented them with an abundance of evidence to prove his business acumen and his ready grasp of commercial television's profitability. He did not believe it would be economically viable to produce television films for British consumption if they did not have an eventual sale elsewhere. Granada's films would be aimed also at US and Commonwealth audiences, he informed them, pre-empting the premise on which Lew Grade was to build so much of ATV's vast revenue in later years.

He could also back up his promise to produce current affairs and fact behind the news programmes by calling on the resources of three of the five national newsreel companies. His previous dealings abroad had also brought him into close association with Ed Murrow, then the doyen of American television presenters. Murrow would provide him with a weekly review of US news and reviews, he promised.

If only he could have been more specific about the balance of his programmes, the ITA could not have wanted for more. The members of the ITA admitted candidly that they had absolutely no precedent to help them make their choice. This took as its 'main criterion ... the ability of the various applicants, so far as this can be judged, to produce as a long-term and continuing operation, balanced programmes of high quality'. Even without that balance being produced, Granada was among the first three bidders to be offered a contract, as we have seen. It was not exactly the one they had asked for. Instead of the full seven days a week and no fewer hours than the BBC, it was given the northern area on a Monday to Friday basis.

But it was, even by the ITA's own admission, one of the two juiciest plums in the pie. They did not express themselves quite like that, of course. 'The London weekday concession, followed closely by the Northern weekdays, clearly dominated the other four in value measured in terms of time on the air and popular coverage,' was how they recorded it in their first annual report.

Asked what he wanted to do with television now he had the licence to operate his own station, Bernstein was eagerly forth-coming. 'It's so hard not to sound pompous,' he told the journalist and broadcaster George Scott. 'But I felt that sociologically and politically the British people were under-privileged in having just one television company. There are so many things I want to put over. In the cinema business I could only put them over to groups of people. Now I'm able to do that for millions at the same time. That's the attraction for me.'

It was also, of course, the very thing which he had told Beveridge he wished to avoid in the days when he was playing Cassandra and warning against the powers of propaganda passing out of public control. Hey-ho, another piece of pie-crust broken.

He was, however, more than careful to pay due respect to the public body whose monopoly he had breached. 'I have a great admiration for what the BBC has done and I think that what it does is much better than traducers imply. The BBC is much maligned. It may not get the highest rating but that doesn't mean it is not doing good work.'

He could afford to be magnanimous, and he was. On the night when Granada took the air, Bernstein included a fulsome tribute not only to, but also by, the BBC as part of the pearl he set before his public. Aidan Crawley hosted the programme dedicated to saluting the pioneers of Alexandra Palace who had first brought television to Britain. Familiar BBC favourites paraded before Granada's cameras. It was, however, an astute as well as a generous gesture to have such figures as the first ever television 'personality', Gilbert Harding (who had become famous for his temper, and then simply for being famous), the medium's resident egg-head, Sir Mortimer Wheeler, and its first home-grown star comic, Benny Hill. All this lent a reassurance and a sense of continuity to the viewers of the new channel. Attila the Hun could hardly be at the gates if Gilbert, Mortimer and Benny were in the corner to dignify the proceedings with their cosy familiarity.

To the generation which has grown sophisticated on a diet of television from the cradle onwards, such precautions must seem as faded and unreal as the shadowy figures who haunted the sets then, with their pristine vowels and their formal dress for every evening event, be it a Sunday session of the *What's My Line?* parlour game or a live transmission of a symphony concert. Sidney's instinct for what the public wanted was every bit as well tuned as Lew's in certain areas, though his estimation of what they would accept was always higher. From early commercial television they wanted the excitement of something new without being frightened off by a sudden withdrawal of all they were already addicted to. Granada's opening night's entertainment could not have struck that balance more reassuringly.

A brief ceremonial half-hour in which the Lord Mayor and Lady Mayoress of Manchester, together with Sir Kenneth Clark, were dutifully quizzed on the benefits Granada would bring by Quentin Reynolds, the American war correspondent who had endeared himself to British audiences by his warmly encouraging broadcasts when the tides of war were at their most ominous. Reynolds also introduced some of the men who had helped to build the new station, thus fulfilling the northerner's deep-rooted respect for those who labour manually for their living rather than indulging themselves in arty-crafty ephemera. 'Where there's muck there's money' is the true northerner's favourite saying.

Sidney might come to regard them as 'a homogenous cultural group with a good record for music, theatre, literature and news-papers not found anywhere else in this island'. What he gave them on that first night, following the brief opening introductions, was Lena Horne, Arthur Askey, Jack Hylton, Bob Monkhouse, Denis Goodwin, Pat Kirkwood and Gracie Fields (filmed in Texas wearing a stetson). The programme was called *London Salutes Lancashire*, and was as good as its title, since it was produced by Val Parnell and networked by ATV. A featherweight boxing match was beamed from Liverpool, and Douglas Fairbanks Jnr added a transatlantic touch to the evening's viewing, presenting the first of a series called

Blue Murder. Taken with the tribute to the BBC as well as the announcer's and-so-to-bed proselytism on behalf of the commercials, the evening was calculated to make the viewer feel nicely tucked up and safe in the comfort of his own home. Even Lew Grade, with his policy of offending no one and selling to all, could not have faulted its populist appeal.

No sooner had the first contract been signed than Sidney made a show of looking at other places for his studios. With a group of his executives, he set off on a tour of the North. But the unspoken feeling was that the boss had already decided. They began in Liverpool and took a car as far as Leeds. That was as far into Yorkshire as they ventured, and they did not even spend a night there.

'We eventually settled on Manchester,' Victor Peers, Bernstein's right-hand man in the formation of Granada TV, recalled. 'I say "eventually", but I had always felt Manchester was the chosen place even before we started the tour. I think it is significant that although we went to Leeds we didn't do much in Yorkshire and we didn't even stay the night in Leeds. Yorkshire, I think, somehow even at that very early stage, was regarded as a slightly less populated area and was therefore not first in our considerations.' Bernstein's obvious lack of interest in the land beyond the Pennines was to lose him half his empire when the contracts came up for renewal.

Bernstein also had strong preconceived ideas of his own so far as television planning was concerned. The boxing match relayed from the Liverpool stadium was just a foretaste of his station's interest in outside broadcast. 'I want to see us free ourselves from the bondage of technicalities so that we can take our cameras anywhere at any time,' Bernstein was to inform his public not long afterwards. 'I want more live television, putting on people who have got something to say and can say it accurately and simply. I want television to be more immediate with our reporters throughout the world.'

It was exactly this vision of highly mobile discussions of current events which eventually encouraged the David Frost consortium to wrest the London Weekend franchise from ATV and Alan Whicker to throw in his lot with Ward Thomas's Yorkshire TV company which took such a huge slice of Granada's empire in the wake of Sir Harry Pilkington's disparaging report on the gulf between the promise of commercial television and its performance.

106

It is, of course, true that not all of Sidney's grandiose dreams of making Manchester a cultural Mecca came to pass. But the station had, from the outset, a distinct and individual voice; and most of the timbre and resonance in that voice sprang directly from Sidney, though he is always quick to give credit elsewhere. Once he was asked if he regarded himself as dictatorial in operating his station. He was by no means as wounded as Lew Grade would have been by such a suggestion; though Lew's paternal insistence that all ATV is one big family and he merely its father-figure with 1,000 managing directors on the board is not so far removed from Sidney's notions of a Granada collective, and just as misleading.

'Dictatorial? Do they say that? No, I don't think I'm dictatorial. I think I'm quite the opposite because we run our station at Manchester on a co-operative basis.' With the Co-operative Society movement having been founded in near-by Rochdale, this was indeed an astute assertion. The real truth of the matter, however, is contained in what followed. 'The only dictatorial thing we've done is to impose our standards of taste and behaviour on the people who work for us.'

The tastes and standards which Bernstein confesses he imposed on the people who worked for him also imposed something very different on Manchester. Into the clogs-and-shawl, muck-and-brass grittyness of Lancashire's heritage moved a svelte new brand of communicator. The men and women who gathered around Granada's new studios stuck out from the indigenous industrial society, as Sidney described it, like a well-manicured index finger on a hand full of sore thumbs. The influence and affluence which their jobs with Granada brought them created, in the words of the *New Statesman*'s drama critic, Benedict Nightingale, 'a tiny potted Chelsea just a few yards up the Irwell'.

By the time Granadaland, as Sidney named it, with the touch of calculated flamboyance which marked his style, established itself in Manchester, it had indeed all the outward trappings of a separate state within a state. It was not Disneyland exactly, but it was decidedly different. The new breed of adoptive Mancunian dressed differently, thought differently, and, more often than not, talked differently. They viewed their new region with a sharp cosmopolitan eye; Sidney Bernstein's eye.

The most celebrated soap-opera in television history, *Coronation Street*, is the perfect example of Granadaland's work at its most practical. Faced with the need to satisfy their advertisers by producing a popular early-evening audience catcher (statistics having shown that once the majority of viewers tune into a certain channel in the evening, they tend to stick with it all night), and their pledge to the ITA to reflect the tastes of the area, they produced a serial whose audience appeal is matched only by its remarkably sustained artistic and production values.

Tony Warren, whose original conception *Coronation Street* was, could not have been more typical of Granadaland's bright and brittle creative team, or less like anything to be found in the rest of Manchester. Born in near-by Eccles, he had acquired a precocious theatrical sophistication as a child actor. A highly articulate dynamo of restless energy, he simply looked out of his office windows one day, gazed down on the serried rows of grey-slate roofs of the back-to-back houses and said: 'Why don't we write about the people who live there?'

The BBC had turned down flat one of his previous attempts to portray life around the cobblestones of Manchester, but since he had tried to make that into a slapstick sit-com, he doesn't blame them too much for not using it. Granada, however, wanted the real thing once the idea was sold to them.

The characters who have, since then, drifted in and out of the Rover's Return and the corner shop may not – and do not – please all northerners as a mirror image of their existence. But they do have the authentic appeal of real people going about real lives, and this has continued to distinguish the series from most of its competitors. Compare it, for example, with Lew Grade's answer to the problem of providing a top-rated soap opera, *Crossroads*. Far from suffering the indignity of being cut down to size for its inefficiency and ineptitude, as has it Midland counterpart, *Coronation Street* is still winning honours from its peers. Rightly so, for Annie Walker and Hilda Ogden rank as high as Mrs Malaprop, Lady Teazle or Lady Bracknell in being splendidly observed repositories of social comment; their creation puts them alongside the great female comedy figures of popular English culture. In 1979, BAFTA gave Doris Speed a special award for her portrayal of the frozen-faced landlady of the Rover's Return, whose basilisk eye has been directed on her customers with faintly disguised disapproval and condescension for nigh on twenty years. It was no more than she, or the series, deserved.

It is, perhaps, not how the North would willingly have portrayed itself without the Bernstein régime, but it does show that a silk purse can be made from a sow's ear, even when it comes to the commercial cut-and-thrust of the ratings battle. 'I am proud of *Coronation Street*,' said Lord Bernstein when he stepped down as chairman of Granada in 1971.

Criss-Cross Quiz was a less successful attempt to marry the dilemma of giving the public what it clamoured for to a company policy of intellectual respectability. To meet the demands of the give-away quiz-show craze, which Associated Rediffusion had begun with Hughie Green egging a greedy public to *Double Your Money* and appalling the sensibilities of the Pilkington Committee in the process, Granada replied with a game which at least married the competitors' skills at noughts and crosses to a background of general knowledge. While it proffered the promise of instant riches, it at least had some pretence to educate the public.

In drama, too, in those early days, Granada's output surpassed its rivals. The reputation still clings to Granadaland, long after they have abdicated all claim to it. The most adventurous new drama on television, as any director or actor will tell you, comes today from across the Pennines in Yorkshire, which highlights another strange phenomenon. It is one of the most fascinating aspects in the history of independent television that a reputation, once made, lasts at least double its own life-span. Granada earned their spurs as purveyors of fine drama through Sidney's own personal interest in the arts in general and good writing in particular. He gathered together a fine team, wooing, besides Tony Warren, such talents as Derek Granger, the former drama critic of the *Financial Times*, a man with a reputation for the most refined and uncompromising taste in drama.

Bernstein began by promising Manchester a brand-new theatre, a hot-house of talent where writers, directors and artists could perfect their art while keeping Granada readily supplied with the fruits of their labours. In 1962, he was writing to the Pilkington Committee, assuring them that Granada was wholly involved 'helping to work out ways and means of improving the amenities and cultural life of the city so that the centre of Manchester may become an attractive place where young people can live and enjoy themselves'. But, by 1965, no 'suitable site' for his project had been found, though just a glance outside his headquarters might have yielded him as promising a little acre for his proposal as either the refuse dump on which his father had built the old Edmonton Empire or the former factory on which he had raised the Phoenix.

By that year, Manchester at last decided to give itself the arts centre he had been advocating for so long – to put it alongside Essen, Duisburg and Krefeld. The building would incorporate a theatre, and Granada would shoulder the financial responsibility of running it. The scheme eventually became tied up in red tape and bureaucracy. What became of Granada's promises was a short-lived experiment with resident theatre artists called 'The Stables'. Alas, it produced few winners. It was quietly disbanded with none of the ballyhoo that had saluted its arrival.

'The Stables' venture reflected little credit indeed on Bernstein's much-vaunted promotion of the arts. It was created out of some disused stables – hence its name – beside the Granada headquarters in 1969, and Granada gave it a subsidy to recruit a resident company. Under its artistic director, Gordon McDougall, they introduced a string of experimental plays; Mr McDougall let it be known that the grant they received from Granada was being amply repaid by the artistic heat thus generated in the theatre and fed back into television. But, before the experiment had time to find its feet, the ground was cut from under it. In 1970 the grant was withdrawn. Many within the organization as well as outside commentators felt that this action had been taken by no less a culture lover than Sidney himself.

He was known to have been upset by the rather raw nature of some of the *avant-garde* productions mounted there. Though one critic had hailed the new venture as 'the best theatre outside London' (a phrase not calculated to endear its cause to such a northophile), there was little evidence to back up McDougall's hopes of flooding Granada's studies with home-grown work from 'The Stables'. But, having been given little more than eighteen months to prove themselves, the theatre company were deeply offended by the abrupt withdrawal of funds. 'I am sick at heart,' its leading lady, Maureen Pryor, confessed when the news was broken. 'I intend to seek a meeting with Lord Bernstein and ask him how he can do this.' He could do it quite easily. Simply by getting one of his spokesmen to issue a statement, saying: 'It had become too difficult to be worth while.'

The following year Bernstein made an inadequate gesture towards revitalizing the arts in his favourite city by leasing the theatre to the Manchester Polytechnic. And Granada's reputation as a nursery of new talent and an innovator of television drama has lingered on with hardly a shred of evidence to justify it. A

110

star-packed co-production with Laurence Olivier may have been a prestigious *coup*, but can hardly be counted as anything more than an impressive rarity. Moreover, the disruption its production caused within the studios made many of the old hands at Granada wonder aloud if the ends matched the means. *Coronation Street*, the favourite rumour of the day had it, was being filmed in a store cupboard because the Olivier–Granger venture had taken up all the rest of the studio time and space.

Never mind. The disruption may well have extended the life of Granada's artistic reputation long enough to carry them through the next franchise gold-rush.

16

From the comparative obscurity of a handful of suburban London cinemas and some speculative property developments, Sidney Bernstein thus rose to become one of the main single forces who were to shape independent television in Britain. 'Well, I couldn't let the big boys get away with it,' is his own explanation for his entry into the arena of commercial television. His origins, though far from humble, could not be described as anything more than well-to-do. But, by the time he had left his mark on the face of British television, he was rich in the true meaning of the word. When he retired from active participation in Granada at the age of seventy-two, his life-style ranged over his tastefully appointed apartment suite above Granada's gleaming studios in his adoptive city of Manchester, the rural retreat of his 160 acres of rolling farmlands in Kent, and a home in London's Mayfair. He had acquired an art collection even a connoisseur like Lord Clark might admire. His taste in painting ranged from his Gauguin to Matthew Smith and Eugène Boudin. He commuted between his offices in Golden Square and Manchester by plane, and his staff stood by on anxious tip-toe for each regular arrival. Weekends, however, were always reserved for family life unless he was abroad on business. They were spent on his farm outside Sevenoaks with his second wife, Sandra, a Canadian (his first marriage ended in divorce) who is twenty-three years his junior. She provided him with a young son and daughter at a time in life when most men are expecting only to acquire grandchildren.

Not that his mode of living in any way ever matched the true spending power of his income. The cars he drove during the height of his power at Granada were as often as not nothing more grand than a Ford Zephyr or, in London, a Rover. If he had a radio telephone fitted in one, it was certainly not to out-do Lew Grade, but to spread his twelve-hour-a-day work-load more efficiently. Nor had the office he used in the heart of Granadaland any of the gilded furniture or plush trappings you would find in the managing director's suite at ATV House. The desk at which he worked was no more impressive than the average typist's; the modesty of the office was brightened only by a small but significant engraving of Phineas T. Barnum. Barnum, the innovator of the fabulous three-ring circus, is, it transpires, Bernstein's hero. A copy of the engraving at one time hung in every executive's office in Granada headquarters, and another paradox in Bernstein's nature is revealed. The sober-suited gangling man, whose predilection for art and culture could cause him to strike terror in employees whose work did not match his own high standards, was at heart a ring-master with a taste for the splendours of the sawdust arena. The squashed boxer's nose is the only outward sign of this aspect of Sidney's showmanship – that, and his inclination towards the calculatedly flamboyant charade, be it the Grenadier Guards blowing fanfares outside his Tooting cinema, recording C. B. Cochran's speech on a new 'talking machine' at the opening of the Phoenix, or putting a pearl in a shell of flowers when Granada took the air.

There are those among his employees who will testify bitterly to his reluctance to part unnecessarily with a brass farthing; the bright young men he brought to launch Granada could often have earned more elsewhere. But he offered them quality material and scope to develop their talents, and to the dedicated artist, in whatever field, this is more than gold.

Along with frugality there also went his undeniable generosity, to pose yet another paradox. Not least among the benefits he brought to Manchester was the £300,000 he and his brother Cecil found from their personal fortunes to set up a foundation to encourage the development of arts and science in the North. The company itself supports chairs of drama at the local university, sponsors concerts, television research and public lectures. And if all this is not exactly philanthropy on a Rockefeller or Gulbenkian scale, then Sidney will argue that he is not Rockefeller or Gulbenkian; he even denies the title 'socialist millionaire' – objecting to the noun not to the adjective. But, with Granada's profits and assets counted in millions every year, and – as we shall see – their business enterprises ranging in every direction from publishing to those dreadful motorway waterholes, he must for once be a little slow in his arithmetic.

He did not achieve everything he had promised, or, indeed, everything he had hoped, for independent television. 'I have been slightly embarrassed by some programmes which could have been better,' he confessed on his retirement. 'But at Granada we were able to develop a kind of immediacy. We were able to introduce over the years many cultural things and widen horizons. And one thing I have never done is underestimate the intellectual capacity of the audience.

'I'm about to become the most involved critic of Granada's many critics,' he added by way of farewell. Those who knew him best and had worked with him longest might have been forgiven for wondering what difference his going would mean. If this was the new role he was assuming at Granada, it was exactly the same as the one he had always played. He had always been his own station's severest critic. Woe betide the employee whose work failed to measure up to the Bernstein standards; his apprenticeship under his father's exacting tutelage had left its mark. Unlike Lew Grade, who felt himself disadvantaged in any area other than light entertainment – and therefore allowed a rather dangerous degree of empire-building to go on within the ATV hierarchy – Sidney made his authority felt in every facet, even in the cutting rooms. His judgement was final, though, if he felt so inclined, he would make a show of co-operative decision-making, just as he had when he toured the North, perfunctorily pretending to search with an open mind for an ideal spot to settle. If he was genuinely displeased, a cold 'this is not the way Granada does things' was sufficient to freeze even the hottest of young bloods.

From the outset, it was his remorseless task-driving and energy which transformed in only six months the drab, nondescript site (a recurring theme in the Bernstein saga), containing a single prefabricated office, into the country's first custom-built television headquarters. 'Only SLB could have done it,' said one of his staff, half-admiringly, half-grudgingly. 'You've got to admire the bastard.'

Technicians at Granada came to entertain the same mixture of admiring awe and irritation for the man who made it his business to know as much about their jobs as they did, and to make his presence felt if he didn't like the way they were doing theirs. 'Very little gets by him that he doesn't approve of. He'll always tell you if he thinks you could have done something better. And when he does, you stay told,' said one employee. 'The trouble is, ninety-nine times out of a hundred, he's right.'

There was nothing about the running of Granada that this mild-spoken man missed. An ashtray moved in his office, a mistake in the French on the restaurant menu were in his eyes as heinous offences as a breakdown in a production schedule or a programme exceeding its budget. A solitary scrap of paper left in the courtyard would be pounced on and described with outrage as making it 'a shambles'. Every penny spent had to be accounted for, and he had a nose for waste that could sniff it out wherever it was perpetrated. Yet those who stayed did so because they genuinely found the work there more stimulating than anywhere else.

Among the innovations he brought with him was his station's robust irreverence for party politicians. The young team he assembled at Granada were with him all the way in bringing something of the hurly-burly of the hustings into television parliamentary debate. David Frost much later created public furore with his early television interrogations. But it was Bernstein who paved the way for him. 'Patball Politics' was the contemptuous heading to an article he wrote in the *Guardian* attacking television's reticence when it came to bringing the big political issues to the viewer.

> Such meagre progress as has been made so far has been achieved by a slow and painful war of attrition in the teeth of official obstruction [he told the *Guardian* readers with characteristic directness]. Granada pioneered the process when it decided to televise the Rochdale by-election. They said it couldn't be done under the regulations; but it *was* done, and it turned out to be a major breakthrough on a small front.

In the 1959 General Election, as he was not slow to point out, Granada had introduced a programme called *Marathon*, which was just what its name suggested; it invited every parliamentary candidate in Granadaland (Sidney's own use of the word to denote the boundaries of the constituencies covered) to put his or her point of view to the public. Again there was tiresome official opposition. If one candidate chose not to appear, then, under parliamentary rules, none must appear. The balance between all parties had to be maintained. It was a stupid rule, and Sidney fought vigorously to breach the impasse. 'In politics as in the theatre an exclusively "star" system is unhealthy,' he reasoned. 'Why should the outstanding backbencher or even the run-of-the-mill candidate, be denied access to the electorate via the television screen?'

He was justly proud of the new ground *Marathon* trod, and for once his admiration of the BBC's high standards of presentation gave way to a public sneer.

> By contrast [he wrote], the BBC's three programmes in which electors put questions (sent in by post and subject to the Corporation selection) to the three Party leaders seemed like a timid game of pat-ball. Easy lobs are dropped on to the racquets of the Party champions.

You would never have found Lew Grade writing in such contempt of establishment figures like party leaders. But where Lord Grade proved himself entirely a showman, there was always something of the reformer in Bernstein's approach to television, despite his affection for Phineas Barnum. 'We at Granada are not asking that television should be employed to turn the election into a circus,' he wrote. 'We do not want to alter the existing democratic process but to enlarge it.'

Interestingly enough, his desire not to put politicians through performing hoops and turn the British elections into an American presidential-style campaign led him to add that he was opposed to exposing the incumbent Prime Minister and Leader of the Opposition to a television confrontation. How remote such a precaution seemed by the time when Margaret Thatcher shocked the electorate and worried her staunchest supporters by refusing to meet James Callaghan face to face before the cameras on the election eve of 1979; so established has the practice become, that her campaign was dogged by taunts of cowardice – not least from Callaghan as incumbent Prime Minister. If she had the last laugh on that occasion, Lord Bernstein could share it, if not entirely wholeheartedly, given his Labour Party affiliations.

The style of interrogation in which Frost was to specialize later, putting such subjects as the wheeler-dealing Dr Savundra under remorseless fire, was in fact pioneered at Granada by Tim Hewat, a brash Australian journalist. Hewat liked nothing better than to bring some public figure to the microphone and, without much ceremony, demand to know: 'What makes you such a crook?' Granada's live black and white transmissions often left only the colour to which his interviewees turned to the viewers' imagination. But the

116

programme Bernstein devised for him, *Searchlight*, managed to make his approach a trifle more delicate. Even so, he often fell foul of the authority's tenet forbidding any editorializing. If Hewat was persuaded not to ask outright what made someone a crook, he nevertheless left no doubt about his own opinion in the matter. The ITA went into a state of shock.

It was to do so with tiresome regularity during Hewat's ten years at Granada. During that time, they stopped him interviewing Malcolm Muggeridge after Bernstein had tried to resuscitate Muggeridge's television career in the wake of a rather mild attack on the monarchy which had been treated by the BBC and the establishment as tantamount to planting a republican's bomb. They stopped the showing of a Hewat *World in Action* programme which proved, on factual evidence supplied by the Institute of Strategic Studies, that a sizeable amount of Britain's defence budget might as well have been spent buying toffee apples for all the use it had been put to. So incensed by the ITA ban was Paul Fox, then editing BBC's rival *Panorama*, that he used part of Granada's *World in Action* war on war-waste in his own programme. For all the cries against censorship and the dangers of the BBC monopoly which brought the ITA into being in the first place, the corporation remained totally independent from the sort of government pressures which the authority regularly succumbed to.

In such issues Bernstein, having chosen his ground, would fight to the last drop of blood, himself campaigning in the thick of the fray. Support like this from the general kept his troops at Granada in tip-top battle trim at all times, even if their pay might not match that of some other brigades, and it probably explains why a seasoned campaigner like Hewat stayed for a decade at Granada, suffering the repeated agonies of the ITA's autocratic interference.

The recurring bouts of cold feet and shifting stances that have afflicted the ITA and IBA in their administration of their contract will be dealt with later. We will also see how, when the whim took him, the fearless Bernstein could be just as blue-pencil happy as the cringing Grade when it came to imposing censorship within his own organization and on his own creative talents. Suffice to say here that even as there is an inherent hit-and-miss element in the procedure which brings men like Lew Grade or Sidney Bernstein to power, so it is an even more hit-and-miss method which monitors their activities.

When he retired to become 'Granada's severest critic', Lord

Bernstein left behind his brother Cecil and his nephew Alex to carry on the family firm. I wrote to him, as I wrote to Lord Grade, asking for their co-operation and some clarification with this book. Amazingly for two men with so little in common except the driving will to succeed, they sent back polite and virtually identical answers. They could not, they said, assist me, since they were both about to write their own autobiographies. I trust as they do so that they will at least touch on some of the questions I have raised.

17

Before leaving commercial television's most influential founder-fathers, the name of Howard Thomas must rank alongside the most fertile and lasting. Thomas may not appear at first glance to have the dynastic charisma of a Grade or the crusading zeal of a Bernstein, but, in reality, he combines both in equal measure. And if the stamp of Lew's personality was indelibly set on ATV and Sidney's on Granadaland, then Howard Thomas can claim a double first. He was there at the outset to launch ABC, if admittedly in the wake of the other three pilgrim fathers of the Big Four after the original Winnick–Kemsley enterprise foundered. And he was there with the new captains who jumped aboard in Lord Hill's 1958 refit: when ABC and Rediffusion were compelled to join forces, it was Thomas who remained at the helm of Thames TV. Neither Adorian nor Wills from Rediffusion's salvaged cargo chose to throw in their lot with the new crew, and thus left the bridge entirely free for Thomas to establish his own imaginative brand of command within the company which would now supply London with its lucrative franchise for four and a half days each week.

Unlike either Grade or Bernstein, Thomas's roots were buried deep into the very soil of mass broadcasting itself. Moreover, he was part of its earliest form of popular commercialization: Radio Luxembourg. Wherever he went, he brought a unique flair for combining intellectual aspiration with popular appeal. He combined the journalist's sense of immediacy with the impresario's appreciation of talent. His taste was broad and his judgement often uncanny.

It is fruitless, of course, to speculate on what the shape of commercial television would be now if Thomas had been its first director-general instead of Sir Robert Fraser, the Australian socialist pamphleteer. He seems to have been as well equipped as anyone in the country to take on the task when the job was first advertised. Sir Robert was given the job, as we know, because the only other serious contender from the 332 hopefuls who applied was Sir Gerald Barry (the former director-general of the hugely successful Festival of Britain), and he was not considered to have sufficient drive. The terms of the appointment stipulated that candidates must have some experience in television, a condition which, given the infancy of the industry, would seem to have limited the choice to applicants from the BBC, America or Canada.

Howard Thomas did not even bother to apply. Yet his experience embraced all the media necessary to understand the nature of the new channel. He had begun his career in the radio department of an advertising agency; therefore he had a grass-roots grasp of the basic principles on which the new industry would flourish. From there he moved into script writing; an invaluable insight to the programme content of the medium. But the real measure of his mettle as a broadcaster came when he moved to the BBC. Any man who can invent the *Brains Trust* as well as Vera Lynn to meet the wartime needs of a listening public must be credited with an uncommonly wide breadth of vision.

The *Brains Trust* was one of radio's unique institutions (as, of course, was Vera Lynn). It combined as never before a highly articulate level of intellectual debate with a compulsive popularity. It made overnight stars of such donnish figures as Professor Joad, whose catch-phrases and speech mannerisms might have remained locked among the minor cults in the grove of Academe if Howard Thomas had not unleashed him on the nation and made him as instantly recognizable a character as Winston Churchill.

It was Thomas's instinct for matching exactly the most suitable personality to the most suitable slot at the most suitable moment that made Vera Lynn 'The Forces' Sweetheart'. She was introduced to him as a teenaged bandsinger who was being groomed with no small success by a music publisher called Wally Ridley. Ridley had come across her as a seventeen-year-old Cockney girl who had got

120

together a routine pub act and who made all her own clothes. She had brought him some songs, and the direct, true quality of the voice, which never wavered or missed a note over the next forty years, caused him to see beyond the considerable limitations of her presentation. He set to work ironing out her vowels and sprucing up her wardrobe, and by the time he introduced her to the young up-and-coming producer Thomas, she was singing with the Joe Loss Big Band.

In those days, however, fronting a band was no guarantee of individual stardom. You had to make your impact on radio. Many successful careers are the result of happy timing, and none more than Vera Lynn's. Thomas was pondering the problems of directing a show at the forces; he needed an identity to make it as instantly recognizable and familiar as Professor Joad on the *Brains Trust*. The moment he heard Vera Lynn's voice, with its instantly recognizable throb of sincerity, its English-rose freshness and its direct strength, he knew he had just what he was looking for. The show he devised was called *Sincerely Yours*, and radio voices did not come more sincere or become more personally the listeners' own than that of Vera Lynn. Over thirty years later, the three were brought together again, not having met in most of the interim. The occasion was Thames TV's *World at War* series. Thomas was chairman at Thames and Vera Lynn a Dame of the British Empire.

Thomas's innate sensitivity to the demands of the times allied to an instinct for good taste and an appreciation of fine music was to make a wine which, miraculously, travelled well. When he moved to Radio Luxembourg, doyen of the popular commercial stations, it remained unshaken. Among the clamour of the station's commercial demands, Howard Thomas introduced *The Cadbury Hour* on Sunday afternoons – possibly the Cadbury family's first initiation into the benefits of broadcast advertisements (the firm's heir, Peter, was later to start up his own station, Westward, and thus to reverse the pattern somewhat). The programme was a sponsored concert by the London Philharmonic Orchestra, with the virtues of the Cadbury product suitably packaged between pieces. It was, of its kind, a brave and innovative move.

From the cut and thrust of the commercial station, Thomas moved on to the visual immediacy of *Pathé News*. This prepared his visual capabilities in preparation for the advent of ITV. By the time the Coronation came about in 1953, it was Howard Thomas who, as documentary head of the Associated British Picture Corporation, contributed the definitive record of the spectacle with his film *Elizabeth is Queen*. As the contenders for the new stations lined up, Thomas was inundated with offers to throw in his lot with the various consortia. Among the many who begged his services as their general manager was the Kemsley–Winnick group. But he remained with ABC, desperately trying to arouse their interest in the pot of gold waiting at the end of the rainbowed legislation hazing its way through Parliament.

Among the many chance falls of the dice which won the day at the outset of ITV, few were more fortunate than Thomas's decision not to be lured across to the seemingly invincible Winnick–Kemsley camp. For, with Lord Kemsley's inglorious back-down seven months before ITV was due to take the air – despite the pleadings of his step-daughter Ghislaine Alexander, herself a shareholder and a BBC television personality through her decoration of the *What's My Line?* panel – the weekend Midland franchise was literally going begging.

In the early days, Associated British had vehemently opposed commercial television in company with other vested cinema interests, not least among whom, as we know, was Sidney Bernstein. They were, however, much slower to realize its inevitability and to change direction with sufficient conviction. Thomas had, at long last, persuaded them to put in a bid. But until the arrival of their American chairman, C. J. Latta (who represented Warner Brothers' interests in the operation), it was an uphill struggle. Latta, like Thomas, firmly believed that, if cinema couldn't beat television, it should lose no time in joining it. With his backing, the British board were convinced of the realities of the situation and set up ABC Television with Howard Thomas as its very first managing director. The ITA breathed a sigh of relief and the contract was signed on the very eve of the new channel's London opening. The ITA may have lost its ideal director-general by his own default, but ABC had gained the very man for the job. It was to reward both of them richly.

Thomas was handed a £1 million guarantee to launch the company. This was also the cost of the equipment ABC bought from the defunct Kemsley–Winnick group. In its first years, the company made a loss of £87,000, which was less than the calculated risk, and from then on it never looked back or dipped into the red. Occasionally the embittered Winnick would call on the man who had, through the fault of neither, usurped his place in the hierarchy of the original

122

Big Four and inquire about ABC's progress. The burgeoning graph of its success could have been no balm to his broodings on what might have been. The station's strongest points were Thomas's strongest points; his viewpoint was ABC's viewpoint.

Because of the nature of his operation, however, his journalist's appreciation of television's potential had to find outlets other than current affairs. The weekends were not thought fit times to bring the problems of the world into the viewers' parlours. The Lew Grade axis was the one on which Saturday and Sunday spun so far as the Network Programme Committee was concerned. But Howard Thomas saw to it that ABC made its mark both in the popularity ratings and in programme content. He came up with the ideal Sunday-evening audience boost in *Armchair Theatre*, which, almost single-handedly, established television drama as something new, topical and stimulating.

Sydney Newman is quite rightly given credit for the all-round excellence of the series and the boldness of the choice of individual plays. But, basically, it was yet again Thomas's ability to translate art to the medium which gave the venture its impetus. He brought Newman over from Canada where he had established a formidable reputation as head of drama with the Canadian Broadcasting Corporation. Until then, Dennis Vance, a gifted director in his own right, had run ABC's drama department. But the company's chief executive was keenly aware of the fact that, until this time, plays on television had been mostly small-screen stage presentations or, at best, scaled-down cinema. He wanted something that was unique to television; with his journalist's gifts, he sensed that its plays should be as immediate as the morning headlines – even if they turned out at times to be as redundant the next week.

The appointment of Newman to the task was inspired. Above all his other gifts, he brought the freshness of a stranger's eye to the British scene. As such he was able to see more quickly than most that a great surge of change was already taking place on the drama front. One of the first plays he saw on coming to London was John Osborne's *Look Back in Anger* at the Royal Court Theatre. This, of course, helped to change the face of English writing on the stage. Newman grasped its exciting New Wave possibilities for television too. He was among the first to fill the screens with the new naturalism in what some reactionaries dubbed the 'Kitchen Sink' school of drama. But ABC's plays made both news and the ratings.

The team of directors Newman inherited at ABC were more

than sufficient to establish the station's supremacy over their rivals at the BBC. Ted Kotcheff, Philip Saville, John Moxey, Wilfred Eades and Dennis Vance himself, all contributed to Newman's vision of what television drama should be. Backed by Thomas, whose views were so similar to his own on the subject, he knew that, where the small screen is concerned, there is no such thing as a captive audience. You are a switch's flick away from oblivion if you do not capture the viewers' attention in the first few moments. It is, once again, the journalists' oldest maxim: establish what you want to say in the first paragraph and elaborate on it later. Newman's techniques gave the adage a new life, and soon the BBC, which had thought its supremacy in this field unrivalled, found itself out-played and out-rated. The debt television owed to the talents wooed away from the theatre and the inspiration it found there was repaid in fine measure when Thomas announced the establishment of a £16,000 a year grant to enable regional theatres to employ their own writers-in-residence and so keep the flow of original writing coming on to the stage.

Even so, *Armchair Theatre*'s popularity and solid achievement were by no means a guarantee of safe-conduct. The issues touched on by many of the plays aroused their share of controversy outside the industry (those were innocent days), and vested interests created the threat from within. Not least of *Armchair Theatre*'s detractors was the all-powerful Lew Grade at ATV. His personality dominated the Network Programme Committee, as we have seen, and in order to keep their weekend drama slot safe from competition from within the ITV companies themselves, ABC had to make several concessions, the greatest being the shifting of their prime product from Sunday to Saturday for the reasons stated (page 73) in the rise and rise of Lew Grade section of this book.

Perhaps the surest measure of ABC's success in this area, however, was, ironically, Sydney Newman's eventual departure. The BBC had become so stricken by his success that, in desperation, they decided to play ITV at its own game and go in for some professional poaching. Newman's defection to the BBC was the very first change in direction of the flood-tide of talent flowing from the corporation to the commercial companies.

Insiders suspect that personalities played as much a part as did performance in the reshuffling of ITV franchises. Certainly Lord

Derby had never bothered to conceal his feelings for Charles Hill. There was little love or respect lost between them, and several people have suggested that Lord Derby's loss of the TWW franchise had as much to do with this as with the company's Olympian stance on maintaining their headquarters in their imposing Sloane Street edifice in London or the quality of their programming.

As for the demise of Rediffusion, John Spencer Wills's relationship with ITA had none of Lew Grade's subtle appeasement or Bernstein's self-aggrandizement. When it became clear that Grade was going to opt for the entire Midland franchise (it having been made clear to him that ATV could no longer take two bites at the network cherry every week), ABC took the lion's share of what remained of Wills's company. Thomas's reputation as a programme manipulator and medium man stood high enough for ABC to survive in all but name. Yet, basically, it all boiled down to a glorified public-relations exercise as to who retained what and where. It cannot have helped Rediffusion's cause to have its achievements summed up by its retiring general manager with the words: 'Some call us doggedly decent. I say we are reliably good.' Captain Tom Brownrigg, the man in question, was hardly as good as his swashbuckling name when it came to captivating the ITA.

Indeed such a statement, for all its commendable honesty, scarcely trumpeted the impressive array of innovations they brought about through their reliable goodness. ABC may have scaled new heights in television drama with *Armchair Theatre*, but it was Rediffusion who first introduced Pinter to the viewing public, cast Benny Hill as Bottom and screened *Electra* in the original Greek. ATV may have ruled the light entertainment area, but it was Rediffusion who unleashed Peter Sellers and Spike Milligan in a memorably lunatic series, *Cool for Cats*.

There was, too, a bravura quality about the way Paul Adorian introduced schools broadcasting when Rediffusion's profits were sinking slowly down the drain – a venture the public service in the shape of the BBC had been too cowardly to tackle. And there was courageous foresight in the manner with which the company pioneered the Ampex video system that revolutionized the programming of television at a time when the rest of the Big Four were anxious only to expand the expectations of their shareholders.

In the event, all this counted for nothing so far as Rediffusion was concerned. Thomas and his ABC company won the day and he became managing director of the newly formed Thames Television.

At least justice was done in the face of his achievement. In some quarters, however, his victory was looked on misguidedly as merely pyrrhic. Although the giant British Electric Traction Company retained a substantial holding in the new station, shares plummeted. For a brief spell there was the chance of a lifetime to acquire a slice of Thames at January sale prices.

It was not long before the City realized its foolishness in failing to recognize the golden-egg possibilities in a franchise covering four and a half days of the country's most lucrative area. Within ten years, Thames's revenue had reached a record £56.2 million, a trading profit of £22.3 million; and even after handing over its levy of £13.6 million, there still remained £8.6 million in pre-tax profit to cheer Howard Thomas on his way. After a decade's reign he had reached the compulsory retirement age of seventy, and though his influence on the day-to-day running of the station's programmes had passed into other, more cavalier hands when he stepped up to the post of chairman in 1974, his standing as a force within the industry remained remarkably undiminished and commendably untarnished.

With a force like Howard Thomas as its chief executive, Thames might have been expected to be particularly strong in its current affairs department, and it did indeed corner the main midweek slot with the admirable *This Week*. Its managing director's entire approach to all aspects of television was that of a journalist. He even went so far as to describe ITV as 'the *Daily Express* of television' and suggested that the Fourth Channel would be its *Daily Telegraph* if handed over to the existing ITV companies. Mr Thomas was ever the powerful advocate of extending the scope (not to mention the profits) of the independents. As far back as 1971, he distributed a news letter to his staff at Thames, putting his case with subtle persuasion. 'It is essential that ITV2 should be granted to the existing contractors,' he wrote airily in his news letter.

A completely new group of contractors could only inflate ITV costs to an impossibly high level and, in the process, debase programme standards to the lowest common denominator. ITV2 would offer a full evening and weekend service, using existing contractors' studios and equipment with increased manpower. The regions would produce more networked programmes. Thames would operate a seven-day week to produce additional peak programmes.

126

The arguments in favour of keeping the Fourth Channel in the independent family were not, of course, peculiar to Thomas or Thames; it has been the constant battle-cry of them all, and a great deal of time and trouble as well as finance has been extended towards this end. But the implications of Mr Thomas's seemingly simple statement were not lost on that admirable television journalist Chris Dunkley. Writing in *The Times* of 31 July 1971, he pointed to the bait being dangled to the industry by Thames's then managing director.

Mr Howard's [*sic*] carrots are contained in the phrases 'increased manpower' and 'seven day week' – both promises being almost irresistible to the television unions in general and the Association of Cinematographic Television and Allied Technicians in particular, since more than half their members are out of work. This high unemployment figure is currently playing a major part in forming the attitudes of the ACTT – the most important of the television unions – and also in the psychological battle between the union and managements.

It was a psychological battle which was to go on for many more years at Thames and elsewhere before the vexed issues of the Fourth Channel were sorted out – and even then not entirely to the satisfaction of men like Howard Thomas. He was committed from the outset to a solidly commercial approach to broadcasting. In fact he led the clamour for the abandonment of the £24 million levy on profits with the rather ingenious reasoning 'ITV is not seeking any government subsidy, but simply to keep the revenue it earns.' Such psychology, given the huge revenues involved, has been fundamental in ITV technicians' battle for an ever-growing stake in the cornucopia. In one of many confrontations which ITV management have had over pay claims, it was revealed that several cameramen at Thames were actually earning more than the Prime Minister's salary, which then stood at £25,000. And still they wanted more.

The biggest outside broadcast ever planned by commercial television, the Queen's Silver Jubilee celebrations, in fact came to nought as a result of an industrial dispute involving thirty-four girl production assistants at Thames's Teddington studios. Here was to have been Thames's moment of journalistic glory, with more than thirty cameras all set to line the route of the Queen's procession from Buckingham Palace to St Paul's, transmission starting at 10.15 and riding the nation's crest of patriotic fervour through to the evening's spectacular firework display. But in place of the greatest London spectacle to be screened since the Coronation, ITV were ignominiously forced to see the day through with a succession of sporting events; victory went instead to the BBC.

The row had been sparked off by the then Labour government's Pay Code, which Thames company chief, George Cooper, refused to break, despite his assurance that he was 'happy to pay' the extra £800 a year the girls were demanding as the cost for introducing new editing techniques at the studios. Since the Pay Code had been enforced to combat the country's economic malaise, the whole sorry saga could hardly be said to have reflected the chauvinistic mood of the moment.

The reasons for this cruel disappointment cannot, of course, be laid at Howard Thomas's door. For the man who had taken over as chairman of Independent Television News from Sir Robert Fraser, and who had succeeded the then Sir Lew Grade as chairman of the all-powerful Network Programme Committee, the humiliation was, however, doubly keen. His autobiography, *With an Independent Air*, published only a month before these doleful wranglings, hinted pointedly that the man who had participated so creatively in the development of ITV was swiftly becoming disenchanted with the medium in which he was such a past master. 'I have deliberately organized myself to gaze less and less on screens of any size,' he wrote somewhat surprisingly.

The cinema has lost its enchantment for me and my television watching has diminished. Perhaps my eyes and my senses have developed a form of claustrophobia against the confinement of such small areas of vision. More and more I have the compulsion to go out into the open...to glory in vistas which refuse to be encompassed within the eye of a camera. When I come upon a panorama of grandeur I am grateful films and television can never reproduce this.

There is about these words, and others in his book, the tone of a man who has lost enthusiasm for his own creation. 'As one who has been responsible for filling so many screens for so many hours, I sometimes brood over the consequences of the commitment of so much of our precious life to watching electronic signals take shape,' he says. And goes on to paint a bleak vision of British family life becoming devoted to video gazing, a profusion of television sets scattered through the home to facilitate individual preferences within the household. 'Rooms will be lined with shelves containing video discs grouped into performances of ballet and music – visual

128

encyclopedias,' he prophesies, and adds, in case anyone might run away with the notion that this would not be an altogether bad innovation, at least so far as keeping the family focus within the home:

> How many hours of every day will father, mother and children spend gazing at electronic pictures? How many teachers will want to import the outside world into the classroom? How many businessmen will be making decisions motivated by a screen image? To look across the bay to the Golden Gate bridge at San Francisco, to sail between the Greek Islands at sunset, to climb a Welsh mountain – all this is seeing and believing. Television, you are wonderful. But there are other things.

The gradual growth of Thomas's pessimism at the outcome of the video revolution engulfing the industry had already been established back in 1971 when he addressed the Cannes International Television Market. To his peers, assembled from all over the world, he gloomily forecast floodtides of pornography and crude ideological persuasion flowing from the small screen. 'The home will be exposed to everything from the most vicious propaganda to the bluest film,' he warned the gathering. 'We must decide which of the world's organizations should set up rules to preserve the standards of conduct which will be acceptable by most of the world's broadcasting services.'

It would be quite wrong to say, however, that Howard Thomas's unease at certain developments within the industry was born of boredom or lack of care. It was rather that the higher he climbed the more Olympian became his view of the scene. He was always a campaigner for more airtime, even if he also urged viewers not to rely exclusively on the camera to bring them all the richness of a full life. He was, for example, among the first to see the possibilities of breakfast time television, which, as the competing companies lined up for the 1980 franchise distribution, was the licence to attract some of the liveliest bidding. David Frost, not surprisingly, was there among the most eager contenders, in the formidable company of the giant Robert Stigwood organization, Paul Hamlyn's publishing firm and – more discreetly – the BBC's own golden girl, Angela Rippon. Miss Rippon had travelled a long distance since presenting a midday woman's programme for Peter Cadbury's Westward TV. By way of the BBC's news team, she quickly established herself as a

129

marketable woman and, like David Frost before her, became astutely aware that television appearances can open the door to many a boardroom.

But it was Thomas as much as anyone who had been tirelessly arguing for the opportunities which brought such a diverse array of interests into the arena on this occasion. 'I am asking for freedom of the air,' he once declared, back in 1966. 'Let the public say when and where it wants us. Let's open at breakfast time and compete with the morning paper.' It took fifteen years for the dream to become a commercial possibility, a brief experiment by his name-sake, Ward Thomas, at Yorkshire having in the meantime tested the temperature.

The variety of the 1980 competitors wanting the freedom to take the air on 1 January 1982 also reflected Thomas's unshakeable belief in the benefits of regional broadcasting. He would often urge local cinemas and newspapers to combine interests to provide a commercial newspaper-of-the-air service for their areas. It all suggests a man whose breadth of vision has broadened rather than narrowed with the passing of time. Yet, by the time he came to write the words, 'Television, you are wonderful. But there are other things,' into his autobiography, he had moved aside from the creative hot seat at Thames.

For many years he had let it be known that he intended to retire the moment he reached the age of sixty-five, presumably the better to scale those Welsh hills, sail around the Greek Islands and gaze raptly at San Francisco's Golden Gate bridge. The facts of life were not to be quite so idyllic. The company managed to retain his services directly for a further five years by offering him the chairmanship. And, by the time he had reached seventy, the compulsory age of retirement, other totally dissimilar figures had set the boardroom at Thames resounding to the clash of personalities. When Howard Thomas stepped down in favour of the powerful one-time press baron, Lord Barnetson, Thames was a hive of high-salary hirings and one major quitting. Bryan Cowgill, a former copy boy from Clitheroe, had become the station's new image-maker; and Jeremy Isaacs, the talented programme controller he inherited from Howard Thomas, was the man who departed, describing his own going as 'somewhere between resignation and the sack'.

18

Bryan Cowgill arrived at Thames Television in a flurry of sensation and publicity. Only two months after being appointed BBC TV's director of News and Current Affairs – in their astonished gratitude for the ruthless skill he had shown in trouncing ITV in the battle of the ratings – he accepted the post of managing director of their arch mid-week rival. The fact that Thames were paying him around £2,000 a year more than the BBC were paying their own director-general only further inflamed the bitterness which his defection caused along the executive corridors of Television Centre. Cowgill was the man on whom the BBC hierarchy had been pinning all their faith, despite the fact that, for the twenty years before being made controller of BBC1, his entire television experience was confined either to sport or outside broadcasts. They had seen the havoc his cavalier brand of programme planning had caused among the ITV opposition. Once they had accepted the fact that BBC television could actually be more popular than ITV without the wrath of Lord Reith sending thunderbolts of lightning to strike the culprits down, the corporation decided to promote the man who had wrought this phenomenon post haste. There were, in fact, four or five rungs left in the ladder for Bryan Cowgill to climb before he absolutely reached the top. But he decided not to wait.

'Howard Thomas made me a very good offer both professionally and financially,' the fifty-year-old Cowgill told the press with a bluntness that has come to be recognized as characteristic of his style. 'I can't bear the thought of retiring at sixty, which is obligatory at the BBC.'

This candour in no way mitigated the enormity of his cheek in taking on the task of re-vamping the BBC's entire current affairs schedule and then, barely sixty days later, sweeping out with all his privileged inside information to the very station against whom Auntie's strategies were directed. But then the BBC had not groomed this ex-marine lieutenant commando for power in recognition of his sense of fair play. The new ruthlessness in the corporation's competitive zeal, of which Lord Annan had spoken with something approaching admiration, was almost solely attributable to the man the media had begun to dub the 'Clitheroe Kid', for want of an instant image. Cowgill's sudden emergence as a force to be reckoned with in the BBC had caught most commentators by surprise. Until he took over the running of BBC1 he had been known, if at all, only as David Coleman's boss in the Sports Department or as the sturdy man with carefully combed gingery hair who occasionally stepped in front of the camera to receive an award on behalf of the unit.

Cowgill was, in fact, born in Clitheroe. Given the fact that everyone has to be born somewhere, the 'Clitheroe Kid' nickname unfortunately diminishes his achievement. Its roots belong in popular imagination to a particularly juvenile radio comedy series from some years ago featuring the diminutive Jimmy Clitheroe. Taken out of that context, it suggests a provincial cowboy. Neither captures the whole truth about Cowgill.

It is true to say that he did not fit easily into the typical BBC mould. He had left school – the Royal Grammar School, Clitheroe – to train as a copy boy on the local newspaper. This humble fact conceals the reality of the situation: the Cowgill family had warmed the editorial chair of the *Clitheroe Times* for many years. Their son and heir was, however, to continue that tradition for only two years. At the age of twenty-eight he was travelling to a meeting by train and happened to read through a discarded copy of the *Daily Telegraph*. In the situations vacant column (odd matter for a young editor to be reading if he was entirely content with the direction of his life) he saw that the BBC were inviting applications for the post of stage manager for their Outside Broadcast Department. To the amazement of his family and friends he applied, and accepted the post at what was even then the modest salary of £750 a year.

He joined the BBC on the very day ITV came into being, but the job was far too lowly for any auguries to be read into the coincidence. If there were comets in the sky that night, they were not for Bryan Cowgill. Among his fellow programme assistants, however, was Paul Fox, the man who was to bring a similar combat zeal to Yorkshire TV and to fly the BBC nest leaving similarly ruffled feathers. Like Fox, Cowgill's competitive toughness took him speedily to a position of influence; in his case to the Sports Department, which thereupon felt the full effects of his skills. Perhaps the fighting instincts and lightning reflexes instilled into commandos is ideal training for the rough and tumble of a television producer's world. Certainly he admitted no sense of inferiority in his total lack of university education, which was in those days, as it is now, almost a primary requirement for any aspiring personnel. What affected him far more keenly than the BBC's Civil Service attitude to promotion was the day-to-day task of beating the opposition to the draw. He literally saw ITV as a deadly enemy. But not as a dangerous one, to judge from his notorious contempt for their achievements.

As BBC head of sport, and later as head of the Sports and Outside Broadcasts Group, he consistently scored bull's-eye ratings. 'I don't believe they [ITV] take their work seriously,' he told the *Observer* back in 1972 when his BBC empire had established itself sufficiently for him to be written about as a serious influence on the medium. 'To them it's just another commercial proposition and I suppose the mark of success is that the advertisers go on paying for it.'

The advertisers did go on paying for it, but they couldn't have been too happy in doing so in view of Cowgill's showing on the opposite channel. His earliest impact was on *Sportsview*, which became a model for informed and exciting coverage. And, by the time of the Munich Olympics, ITV had all but thrown in the towel and decided to cover only the odd event.

Their carping complaints that sports coverage should be equally shared received a snarling lack of sympathy from Cowgill, who was busy flooding the BBC's screens with blanket coverage. 'Look at the 10,000 metres,' he sneered at one of ITV's few attempts to rival him. 'We had eighteen million viewers, they had two million. It's all very well for them to go on about sharing sport and alternating coverage of the big events with us. I daresay I should try the same thing if I were in their shoes. Share with them? What? Eighteen million to two?' he added, managing to make it sound like a winning score in some Cup Final fantasia.

133

His achievements within the Sports Department were far more impressive than mere audience catching. Twice he won the annual award of the Guild of Television Producers and Directors, his peers' tribute first for his coverage of the 1966 World Cup series and then for the Mexico Olympics. Before he moved on to higher things, he had bequeathed to the British public two television sporting institutions: the programme *Match of the Day* and the technique of the 'slow action replay' – a device which the BBC was once told it could scrap only over his dead contract. To satisfy the Football League that his pet innovation would not be used to hound officials for erroneous decisions, however, he had a strict code of practice drawn up, pledging that this slowed-down videoed evidence would not be used to expose league members to ridicule. 'But that doesn't mean we would pretend not to notice when a mistake has been made,' he added, serving due notice that, while he would not sanction trial-by-television techniques, neither would he flinch from withholding evidence when he saw fit.

Yet not even Cowgill's celebrated taste for unconditional victory could overcome the Football League's traditional nervousness about jeopardizing match attendances by transmitting live midweek games, though he had somehow bullied or cajoled £1 million from his usually parsimonious pay-masters specifically for this purpose. He remained rattled by this setback for long after he left the corporation. 'I cannot believe we will go to our graves without ever having seen our national game televised live on some regular basis,' he was still lamenting as Thames went into battle to retain its franchise.

Here, then, was the sort of man who, against all the formbook calculations, became Controller of BBC1 and, in doing so, acquired the nickname 'Ginger' as much for his combative nature as for the colour of his hair. Here was the man who beat ITV at its own game and on its home pitch: that of popularity. It was often said with some sarcasm when Cowgill was in charge that, if anything could kick, bat, bowl, run, jump, catch or swim, BBC1 would screen it. And it is true that there was always a strong emphasis on sport at peak viewing times; but this was only one of the things which his channel did better than its opposition. The viewing figures proved it time and again.

In achieving such remarkable boosts to the corporation's ratings he had shown few scruples. His most telling talent lay in programme

134

planning. Where ITV were strongest he would hit hardest. He pitched mass-appeal shows into the entrenched schedules of his foe as he would fling grenades into enemy strongholds in his old commando days; and do it with deadly accuracy. Nothing was sacred. *Omnibus*, worthy as its standards always were, was plucked from its peak Sunday-night spot and Esther Rantzen's irritating, audience-pandering *That's Life* was commandeered to blast holes in his rivals' ratings. *Kojak*, with its millions of fans, was trundled to whichever spot it could inflict most damage; the term faithful follower was never more aptly applied to its devotees as Cowgill deftly switched this hit series from Saturday to Monday and on to Thursday. The Tuesday documentary, always a weak spot on the viewing graph, was scrapped completely; *Play for Today* was accommodated elsewhere.

'It has always seemed to me that the genius of the BBC is to find a wavelength which reaches the popular culture of the country. You feel most successful in the end when you know you're grabbing the interests of the housing estates of Glasgow and the East End and the living rooms of Surrey and Dorset. You only achieve this by aiming at the best of any kind of programme,' said the BBC's star tactician in the days before he was wreaking havoc on the corporation from his headquarters at Thames. However, 'the best of any kind of programme' is a sufficiently imprecise phrase to defy critical definition. The fact of the matter was that the council estates of Glasgow and the East End did join forces with the living rooms of Surrey and Dorset to swell viewing figures for such BBC1 winners as the *Miss World Contest*, the *Eurovision Song Contest* and Bruce Forsyth's *Generation Game*. They also lapped up such award-winning series as *Porridge* and *Monty Python*.

Whenever he had a hit on his hands, Cowgill's policy was always to exploit it till its last round of ammunition had been fired in the ratings battle; he would always screen repeats of old successes at prime times. The habit appalled purists within the BBC (and even shocked that other hardened campaigner, Paul Fox), but always boosted his chart showing. Once he even transmitted two repeats consecutively to keep the mass audience tuned into his channel. It had never been done before, but it was part of his style that he should be the first to break the unwritten rules of the game if it was the rules which threatened to lose the day.

*

When they set out to recruit Bryan Cowgill, Thames were in trouble and in desperate need of a trouble-shooter. The feeling within the company was that despite, or because of, their huge profits, the IBA would not consider enough had been done to earn them. A clear case of pre-franchising nervousness had set in, and Cowgill was the man who had done most to smash their confidence.

The guiding spirit of Thames, Howard Thomas, had made it clear when he succeeded Lord Shawcross as chairman that he would not be content as merely a figurehead, that he would insist on being a participating member of the team. Nevertheless, he was no longer the force he once had been. The day-to-day operation of the largest company in ITV's Big Four had been taken on by their former sales director, George Cooper. As a seller of advertising space Cooper had been brilliantly successful; didn't the soaring profits show it? But he had no taste for the cut and thrust world of programme planning or production. This was a field he was only too happy to leave largely to his director of programmes, the gifted Jeremy Isaacs.

Isaacs had scored some fine successes for Thames, not least his epic *World at War* series. He had inherited from Brian Tesler, who left Thames to become managing director at London Weekend, the task of filling 1,000 viewing hours every year on what was now a £10 million budget. Intellectually and by training Isaacs was ideally suited to the task of keeping standards high. At Oxford he had been president of the Union, an honour which carries with it an almost certain guarantee of eminence when the holder spreads his wings in the world outside. Sidney Bernstein, with his penchant for filling Granada with young eagles, snapped him up as a current affairs producer immediately his Oxford days were over. From then on his career was a rapid climb upwards. At Rediffusion he produced *This Week*; at the BBC he edited *Panorama*. He then returned to Rediffusion to raise the quality of their children's programmes. Thames, when it was formed from the ashes of Rediffusion, were eager to secure his talents and made him controller of features and current affairs programmes, a vital area for the mid-week franchise. He was promoted to director of programmes in 1974, the year in which Howard Thomas was due to move over into the chairman's seat.

The appointment was just reward for the talent and flair which had marked him out as something very special in broadcasting. There had never been any doubt in anyone's mind that Isaacs was destined for the top in television; moreover, he had proved himself to be a tireless champion of quality and independence among the producers who worked for him. He would defend their judgement to the last ditch if he thought they had justice on their side. A long article which appeared in *The Times* just before his appointment demonstrated conclusively that he was not a man who feared his masters.

'ITV – where I work – is in chaos worse confounded,' wrote Isaacs, pointing boldly to the Gilbertian situation which renders the IBA judge, jury and Lord High Everything Else in its own court. It was an elegantly argued case to unchain ITV from the fetters of its own ambiguities. 'The Act may need to be changed again. But at the moment the IBA's regulatory function is too often in conflict with its duty to inform. A publisher is not a censor. The roles should be separated,' he told the readers of *The Times*, adding that, as a journalist, if he made the same mistake on three occasions he would expect his boss to fire him. The trouble with Independent Television was in deciding the identity of the real boss.

He would have cause to ponder those brave words on a more personal level during his next five years at Thames. In George Cooper he had a managing director who was only too pleased to leave matters of programme planning to him, and in Howard Thomas a chairman who was increasingly given to the morbid speculation about there being better things in life than watching electronic impulses form themselves into images in cathode ray tubes. Brian Tesler, the man most widely tipped for the managing director's chair at Thames, would have been a more formidable force by far; he was, after all, Isaacs's own immediate predecessor as programme controller of the station. Indeed, it was Tesler's chagrin at Cooper's appointment over his head that prompted him to throw in his lot with John Freeman at LWT and thus to form the kind of strong working partnership which was unfortunately soon found to be lacking at the top in Thames.

Howard Thomas came to see the need for a more powerful deputy to himself as chairman. He was witnessing the BBC wiping the floor with the ratings and he knew who was responsible. Thus Cowgill was wooed and won. From the moment the contract was signed, Isaacs's future at Thames was at best uneasy.

What Howard Thomas had bought himself so expensively was in effect a second programme controller. He had also precipitated an impossible situation for Isaacs. No station can function with two men in the driver's seat steering in different directions, and Bryan Cowgill was not a man known either for tempering his judgement or for caring too much about how he made his presence felt. At the BBC he was reputed to have told one of his drama producers in so many words that, as long as he was in charge, he was 'fucked if he would allow any of that fucking language on his fucking channel'. It was hardly a style to endear himself to the intellectually fastidious Isaacs.

The inevitable clash of temperament may have been heightened by Isaacs's lack of newspaper experience. This is in itself unusual among current affairs producers, who tend to be recruited from Fleet Street – or, in Cowgill's case, from Clitheroe. Nor can Cowgill's lack of a university education (again an exception to the rule) have made their association exactly a meeting of like minds. At all events, the shopping trip which Cowgill now embarked upon to recruit new talent showed, only too ominously, what he himself thought of Thames's programme strength, especially in the current affairs department.

Isaacs was himself known not to be happy with the lamentable slough into which their prime-time programme *Today* had fallen, and there is said to exist a pirate videoed record of one particular tirade which he mounted on the studio floor in his frustration at the poor showing it continued to make. The crunch, as the current affairs media men used to be so fond of saying, eventually came about through Isaacs's fearless championing of his employees' causes when he felt they had been wronged. In this case it was over the IBA's banning of Thames's documentary, *The Amnesty Report*, which alleged brutality by British troops in Northern Ireland. Isaacs felt so strongly that the evidence amassed by his team should be shown in the interest of public information, that he handed the censored footage to the BBC, who used it on their *Nationwide* programme.

Isaacs's new superior was livid. To Cowgill, the highest principle was the winning one. Fierce as his contempt had been for ITV in his days at the BBC, his entire energies were now directed to doing the BBC down. To hand them on a plate a scoop like *The Amnesty Report* film was, to him, an act of treason. Isaacs's arguments – that if the IBA refused to screen something which the public ought to be shown, then the only responsible alternative was to hand it to the only other outlet available – were as irrelevant to him as if they had been an opinion expressed in a tribal dialect of Outer Mongolia.

When Jeremy Isaacs described his departure as 'something between resignation and the sack' he was probably speaking the entire truth. Cowgill announced the parting as 'a resignation', and Isaacs had spoken of his 'real sense of regret' at going. There was also a real sense of regret among the people he left behind. 'No station can be happy to lose the services of someone with Jeremy's unique talents,' said one executive, who prudently wished to remain anonymous in the atmosphere of hiring and firing which prevailed. It says a great deal for the esteem in which his talents were held at Thames that Isaacs returned there on an independent basis only three months later to assist in their prestigious *Hollywood* series. Mike Wooller, one of Bryan Cowgill's new signings, was responsible for the production of the series as newly appointed head of a treasure chest of profits that had never been so full. He had a record £20 million in the kitty, and he set about using it in ways which he was uniquely qualified to know would score best.

'I always have to spend the first six months of every new job trying to live down my "Look-out-here-comes-Ginger" reputation,' Cowgill explained when he first went to Thames. 'It may have been true years ago when I was known to raise my voice now and again in the director's gallery. But you do not survive twenty-two years in this business merely by raising your voice. If you don't carry your people with you, then you're not going anywhere.'

Events showed only too well how Cowgill could carry people with him when he decided to go somewhere. 'On my long drive home I would often wonder after putting together a BBC Christmas what I would do if I were competing for ITV,' he said as his plans for Thames began to materialize. 'Now I'm here I'd back money on my chances. We shall certainly be celebrating Christmas properly on ITV this year.' And they did. For not only did he bring over the corporation's top executives like Michael Townson and Wooller, he also commandeered their entire traditional Christmas format: the *Billy Smart Circus* and the *Morecambe and Wise Show*. The BBC's Christmas was as unthinkable without these two long-serving institutions as Santa without a present in his sack. But the corporation simply had to think about it. Cowgill had bought both, though he showed self-righteous indignation at the BBC's claim that he had paid £1 million for the Smart Circus alone. 'Whoever thought up those prices shouldn't be televising circuses; he should be in one,' he snapped, giving it out that the price was 'eighty per cent wrong', but not saying in which direction.

Thames also launched their biggest ever season of star-lined entertainment for the autumn schedules, buying up such perennial favourites as Ken Dodd, Tommy Cooper, Max Bygraves, Vera Lynn and Harry Secombe; hardly innovative stuff, but in Cowgill's popularist view it was what the public wanted. So was the return of such low-brow favourites as *George and Mildred* and *Robin's Nest*. For those who believe that the public cannot know what it wants until it has seen something of everything, Cowgill's brand of programme planning makes dismal reading. Most critics – and the public too – were also often disappointed by the transition when their idols turned up on ITV. Something of their old warmth disappeared with Cowgill's determination to prove that Thames could do what the BBC did, only better. The *Morecambe and Wise Christmas Show* was slick and lavish, but the team's essential intimacy seemed to be missing. Michael Crawford, still at the time the BBC's top draw with his series *Some Mothers Do 'Ave 'Em*, did a deal with Thames in the hope of widening the range of his popularity. The series never caught on and, if anything, dented his reputation as an unfailing audience puller.

One of the few bold experiments to creep into Thames's block-busting tactics, however, was the *Kenny Everett Video Show*, a wild, anarchic collage of television techniques which began as something of a cult for afficionados until it grew into a major attraction. Everett was one of the few radio DJs with enough individual flair and personality to make the transition to television (another being Noel Edmonds). And this bizarre, often brilliant, new show was built up entirely around and by his personality. It broke most of the tired rules of television light entertainment while managing to remain pure television. It was anything but a videoed variety show, and had no hint of being a warmed-up BBC left-over.

If Cowgill's brand of competition was calculated to produce little that was not aimed straight at the mass audience, his style of programming showed he had lost none of his cunning when it came to keeping viewers tuned to a single channel for an entire evening. He would fire his big guns early in the evening. Where, on a typical Tuesday, the BBC would follow their ramshackle *Nationwide* current affairs round-up with a repeat of *The Wonderful World of Disney*, he would counter with a screening of David Attenborough's widely acclaimed and compulsively popular *Survival* series. Where the BBC began the evening with Robert Robinson's sedate and somewhat parochial *Ask the Family* quiz show, he came up with the brash brain-and-brawn competition *The Krypton Factor*. And so it went on.

But whatever the IBA thought of the hard-headed competitiveness at Thames, they did not smile on Cowgill's failure to replace Jeremy Isaacs with a fresh programme planner. For over a year Cowgill combined the duties of chief executive with that of overall programmer, a consolidation of power which the IBA were far from anxious to encourage. With the franchise approaching, no one at Thames, least of all Cowgill himself, was in a mood to risk giving offence in that quarter. Annan's Report had urged ITV to 'show some steel and wield the axe', but this the IBA considered to be too much steel and too much axe. So, when a new programme controller was finally announced, it was one whose reputation made it generally clear that the brief one-man band theme at Thames was over. Whether or not there would now be harmony remained to be seen.

Nigel Ryan came in with as spectacular a reputation for success as Cowgill's. Over the previous two years he had been earning an annual salary in the region of £76,000 as vice-president of the top-rated *NBC News* in New York. And American television has enough lions in the television news game not to need to import one unless his roar is quite exceptional. Ryan's was. NBC had bought him after his years as editor and chief executive of ITN, the totally independent news section of Independent Television which has long been one of the brightest jewels in the commercial crown. When Ryan was appointed editor of *News at Ten* shortly after its inception, he faced the daunting task of providing a viable rival to the BBC's long-established and revered news service, considered by many to be among the best in the world. This he accomplished in the most conclusive fashion. During the nine years of his editorship, *News at Ten* completely overtook the opposition in style, content and popularity. Constantly in the top ratings, it established itself as a first-rate gatherer and disseminator of news and information. It showed none of the BBC's unctuousness in presentation, nor did it in any sense trivialize its material. And with Ryan promoted to editor and chief executive of the whole ITN network, its standards never flagged.

Rumours had been finding their way into print for some time

141

that Ryan was being wooed back to Britain. Many speculated that he might be holding out for the offer of the post of programme controller of ITV-2. Certainly Thames could in no way match his stupendous American salary. In fact he took a £45,000 pay cut to take on the job so long vacated by Isaacs. It may therefore safely be assumed that he was being offered inducements beyond the prospect of becoming a Cowgill side-kick. Certainly Thames were proving to the world that they were taking their responsibilities as competitive presenters of news and views as seriously as they took their audience figures. How the Ryan–Cowgill axis will resolve itself will become clear with time. But with the top executives almost totally changed, and with such strong personalities in key positions, Thames entered the race for the licence renewals with a zest born of confidence.

Among all these fascinating games of musical chairs, no development at Thames is more calculated to bring an unknown X factor to the face of the station than the arrival as chairman of Lord Barnetson, a baron every bit as grandiose in his sphere of influence as Lord Thomson was in his own day. Bill Barnetson began in journalism in his native Scotland. Eventually becoming editor of the *Edinburgh Evening News*, he rose quickly through the ranks of executive power until he headed a conglomeration of newspapers and magazines which stretched around the world. Although his power has rivalled, and in some ways surpassed, that of the old press lords like Beaverbrook, Northcliffe, Kemsley or Thomson, and his appearance is a cartoonist's dream of how a typical baron should be, his persona is hardly known to the public at large. Yet, as chairman and managing director of United Newspapers, Lord Barnetson's empire has acquired over the years not only the *Observer* but also *Punch*, the *Yorkshire Post* and the pioneering *Sheffield Telegraph* as well as a host of other lucrative provincial publications and such esoteric specialist journals as *Dairy Farmer* and the *Farmers' Guardian*.

His experience is international, and his views are expressed with the vigour of an accomplished after-dinner speaker. His rise to eminence may seem to have the conventional stamp of the traditional press magnate. But, as with most of his predecessors, there is more than a touch of the unconventional adventurer about his beginnings. He began to write professionally as his university correspondent for the *Sunday Times* while still at Edinburgh, but did not follow this up with the move to Fleet Street which might have been expected; instead he travelled to Spain and set up as a freelance writer during the Civil War. After the Second World War he went to Germany to assist with reshaping the shattered German newspaper industry. His instinct for news, his flair for business (he is a member of the London Board of the Bank of Scotland) and his broad view of world affairs manifested themselves when he became chairman of Reuters. Of his ability there can be no doubt. But the range of his vested interests and sphere of his influence might, on past form, seem to mark him as a man the IBA would rest uneasy to find in the chairman's office of their largest independent television company. They had, after all, forced Lord Thomson to reduce his interest in Scottish TV when they became jittery at the returns in money and power his holdings were reaping. They had vetoed Rupert Murdoch's sideways attempt to move into a similar position with LWT.

But to trace any thread of sustained logic in the decisions of the authority is as perplexing as reassembling a Chinese box. Why, for instance, should they decide to hand back to their companies £3.3 million of their levy on profits in the very year which followed record incomes? The windfall was, in fact, the result of a change in the accounting system, and the IBA took legal advice to confirm that the refund was 'not improper'. But the Commons Committee on Public Accounts considered it highly improper and said so. In their 1979–80 Report, they declared that they considered the IBA to have been 'generous' in back-dating some of the ITV companies' refunds to 1974, and in this the Commons Committee can only be judged guilty of gross understatement. They also expressed their concern that, in deciding to hand over such a staggering amount to companies whose coffers were groaning under the weight of their revenue, the IBA did not consult either the Home Office or the Treasury about the change in accounting. The question must again be asked: if the IBA are responsible only to the government, when does that responsibility begin and where does it end?

Such riddle-me-rees make it impossible to calculate why an ambitious man like Rupert Murdoch should be deemed unsuitable for power within a company and a man like Lord Barnetson considered eminently acceptable.

Thames, however, felt confident enough in their possession of Lord Barnetson to face the franchise distribution with him as a long-term figurehead. He was, at the time of taking office, only sixty-one, which leaves nine years before the compulsory retiring age. So the appointment cannot be seen as a mere stop-gap. Lord Barnetson has arrived upon the commercial television scene with every intention of staying. Whether or not his will be the personality which eventually makes its mark on Thames only time and the regranting of their licence will tell. But he is plainly not reticent in conveying his point. Nor is he limited in his choice of where and when to make his views known. The New Zealand Parliament, for example, were deeply offended by a cable Lord Barnetson sent them. It urged them against passing legislation that would withhold the names of accused persons in court cases until either the accused is found guilty or the court directs the name to be published.

The cable brought forth an indignant speech from New Zealand's Minister of Justice, accusing Lord Barnetson of 'nineteenth century diplomacy that is best forgotten' and telling the British press to put its own house in order before its barons started 'preaching to us about a free press'. Lord Barnetson had sent the message in his capacity as chairman of the Council of the Commonwealth Press Union – another arrow in his impressive quiver. His argument with a law that would withhold the identity of an accused person unless found guilty was a mute one. Given the suppression of information all around the world, he told the Minister of Justice in his communication, the legislation in New Zealand seemed 'certain to cloister justice and curtail the right of the citizen to see justice done'. 'With full regard for the intentions you seek for the legislation,' the cable ran, 'we also share the anxiety of our New Zealand colleagues that the formula for restricting news of the courts must so complicate reporting that effective and comprehensive coverage will become virtually impossible.'

It was not exactly a reactionary or irresponsible view to take, especially for a man who had dedicated his life to collecting and publishing information in a free press. But it mortally offended the New Zealand government of the day, who described the telegram as 'a sour note'. And it provoked a counter-attack on the British press which Lord Barnetson himself must have found slightly embarrassing. 'Before preaching to us about a free press,' retorted the angry Minister of Justice, 'I suggest that the CPU and its chairman take a look at the standards of their own papers such as the *Sun* and the *Mirror*. Our press in New Zealand clearly does not stoop to the standards and prurience of them.'

A man prepared to take on a government in the cause of press

144

freedom cannot be expected to remain a rubber-stamp chairman. He will, however, have equally forceful executives, including his deputy Cowgill and his programme controller Ryan, to preside over. Whichever of them eventually stamps his style on the station, Thames cannot remain the exact product which Howard Thomas created.

19

Before moving on from the impact the early pioneers have made on popular taste, it is worth taking a passing glance at the ways they have been allowed to husband the fortunes made. It is true to say that, prior to being nudged sideways by the redistribution of the areas and the tightening up of regulations, the original Big Four had things very much their own way; and Lords Grade and Bernstein, by nature of their own dominant personalities, manipulated the Big Four much their own way in their turn. The ITA's introduction of a host of regional operators to supplement their output did little to curb their hold. 'It will operate in the great press tradition of this country,' trumpeted Sir Robert Fraser in his neo-Churchillian style, 'with the major companies acting as national papers and the rest filling the local needs.' Unlike their counterparts, the national press, whose losses over the years are only offset by clever diversification into more profitable areas, the Big Four continued to take up about 80 per cent of network air time.

Their profits outstripped even their wildest hopes. In ten years, their net revenue, before paying the levy, was £82.6 million. About this time ATV were going public with the Grade's investment of £15,000 apiece transformed into a £615,000 holding. And when EMI bought themselves an £8 million stake in the company, those original £15,000 investments had put an estimated £1.3 million into the personal coffers of the brothers.

Bernstein's Granada, late on the scene, had missed the worst of independent television's cold first winter when money seemed to be pouring out of the companies' coffers like water through a sieve. By 1959, when ATV and Associated Rediffusion's profits were already soaring to £2.7 million, Bernstein was sufficiently stung by the comments made about Granada's comparatively modest showing to retort: 'Granada seems to be involved in a hullabaloo when they are doing well. I may be old fashioned but I think that over a million pounds' profits last year, when our capital equity was only £350,000, is very good indeed.' Most of us are old fashioned enough to agree with him. He went on to add: 'We have always considered the first charge of the company is our responsibility to the public.'

By his responsibility to the public, of course, Bernstein meant utilizing his profits to raise the standards of programmes; in other words, ploughing them back into the industry and not hiving them off for further enrichment. In an industry which risks no overseas competition, a secure and ready home market and no other medium capable of competing on equal terms, this may seem to be little enough to expect. It is not. When Lord Bernstein stepped down as chairman, the complex companies Granada covered were spread over book publishing, theatres, property, receiver rentals and separate television broadcasting as well as catering, which can scarcely be counted as an allied industry, unless the Bernsteins were taking an extreme view of the old socialist adage that if you feed a man's belly you allow his mind to soar to loftier heights. Personal experience of Granada catering has hardly borne out the theory.

But, besides raising the same vexed questions at ATV's monolithic control of theatre agencies, record companies, music publishing firms and the like, we should wonder, along with many of the people who gave evidence to Lord Annan, just why such heavy diversification is necessary in this low-risk enterprise.

It was a constant refrain in evidence given to the Annan Committee that any profits over a reasonable rate of return to the shareholder should be ploughed back into the industry, either in re-equipment, better working conditions, more programmes or higher quality. The ACTT, the Writers' Guild, Equity, and the Association of Directors and Producers were all vehemently against any diversification, except to improve the industry. They demanded that the companies should be compelled by law to plough a fixed portion of their profits back into making programmes – which is what they were given their licences for in the first place.

Some members of the Annan Committee were alarmed by the evidence they had been given of the companies, created specifically to bring television programmes to the public, expanding into quite separate fields. They considered, according to the Report, that such diversification should be prevented or severely curtailed. 'Diversification safeguards shareholders at the expense of the services and the employees,' they added, and went on to reiterate the complaints of the artists, writers and directors that television companies 'hold a public right to make television programmes, not to be absorbed into Media conglomerates which can easily be dominated by investment decisions in quite unrelated fields of real estate, catering, amusement, etc.'

This, of course, is the great worry about the vacuum left when the real showmen like Grade and Bernstein drop out, as drop out they have done and must do. The next great mogul who dominates the scene may be no light-entertainment expert or art buff, but a faceless financier who cares not a fig what goes on to the screens so long as it keeps the profits pumping into his conglomerate.

The Independent Television Companies' Association, which naturally and justifiably fights any move to clip its wings, came back with a whole list of reasons why they should not have more restrictions placed on their expansion into other territories. Why, they exclaimed, the very industry itself was founded on diversification by other interests: theatre, cinema, newspapers and the like. In claiming this historical respectability for their actions, of course, they tell no lies. But it is rather like saying that, because Boot Hill was outlaw territory, the sheriff shouldn't ride in.

With more justification, they can point to the levy, which, as we have seen, ties up a sizeable amount of excessive profits and is based on their yearly revenue. Lord Annan's reply to this was that the levy should be stretched even tauter than it is. 'The remedy is in the Government's hands,' added the Report.

Why should not ITV enjoy the same freedoms as other industries? demanded the ITCA. Because they don't run any of the risks of other industries, is the dusty answer.

The tack was then altered to make diversification seem to be television's knight in shining armour, rescuing it from more perils than Pauline ever encountered. It eliminated the liquidity problem in the short term, and helped to spread the heavy load of television's

148

overheads in the long term. What is more, they argued, the stock market approved of diversification, it kept their shares stable. No one expected them to agree that diversification deprived programme budgets of extra and often much-needed cash. And they didn't.

What they did do, as a final flourish, having laid hold of every other argument, was to tell the Annan Committee that, if high profits were injected back into the industry to raise its programme standards in good years (of which there have been many), this could lead to 'over-programming' and 'over-manning', for which they would pay dearly in the lean years (of which there have been but few). Such a catastrophe could create in the bad years exactly those problems of redundancies and cut-backs which the unions wanted to avoid, they claimed. By these clever 'Catch 22' arguments, they painted themselves not only as the champions of the stock market but also as the saviours of the trade unions. In other words, by not creating any more work they would avoid having to sack anyone when there wasn't as much work as there used to be. 'Diversification protects jobs,' was the extraordinary conclusion they sought to sell to Lord Annan. They might have more accurately said, 'Diversification protects jobs that aren't there.'

Mildly the Annan Committee inquired why, instead of rushing out and buying up bread factories, salt-mines or oil fields, the companies didn't set the huge profits in the years of plenty against their hypothetical losses in the years of famine by making use of bank investment facilities or even the Stock Exchange. Such a measure would make their assets far more liquid, since they could be drawn upon at all times and thus prevent cut-backs in programmes on rainy days. It was, after all, more difficult to sell off a business enterprise to raise cash than to sell shares or sign a cheque.

The ITCA's answer was one of monumental arrogance. 'We are good businessmen,' they retorted. 'We trust ourselves to make our business grow. Why should we hand it over to someone else who will not have our over-riding interest in it?'

Annan, eventually worn down by the ITCA's double-tracking, supported some diversification as 'a valuable hedge against a recession in television revenue', despite the voices to the contrary within his committee. The committee was, however, unanimous in recommending that the companies should be required to 'distinguish clearly in their published accounts between their UK television operations and their other activities'.

*

The IBA, and their predecessors, the ITA, have fought a long battle against secret deals, both by individual companies with outsiders and between the companies themselves. It all began when the four original contracts were handed out, and the businessmen among the new franchise holders began horse-trading with air-time so as to spread the costs. Peter Black long ago exposed the deal Sidney Bernstein made with the shrewd operators at Associated Rediffusion. In *The Mirror in the Corner,* among the many fascinating facts he alights on is the one that, because of the back-stairs agreement, Associated Rediffusion was taking up to 85 per cent of Granada's trading surplus.

Bernstein had entered into this agreement with John Spencer Wills, chairman at Associated Rediffusion, in 1956. Granada, according to the two foolscap sheets of the secret contract, would make 15 per cent of the programmes it was required to produce under its ITA contract, while Rediffusion would 'produce or procure' for Granada the remaining 85 per cent. For shouldering the bulk of Granada's operational risks, Rediffusion was to receive all its surplus net advertising revenue after operational costs, less an agreed amount. In the four years while the agreement was in effect, says Black, the deal cost Granada a total of £8,044,238. This no doubt accounted for Granada's programmes not always living up to the lofty aspirations which Bernstein boasted, and was also why Granada's initial profits were so slow to catch up with the rest. In his chairman's address for 1959, Bernstein did allude to the agreement, but managed to put the best possible construction on it. Granada, he said, had 'a working agreement with another contractor for exchanging programmes and networking. It was made in 1956 when we went on the air and protected our television subsidiary from heavy losses. We think the agreement was in the best interests of the company and of Independent Television.'

Mr Black and many others who sniffed out the details thought that it looked more in the best interests of the Bernstein family.

Faced with the possibility of running out of money, and of having to part with family control as a price for getting more, at a time when the money was flowing out in thousands of pounds a day, an agreement that, as has been said, protected their television subsidiary from heavy losses was in Granada's interests. It was a shrewd stroke that put the company on a fortune to nothing.

Rediffusion, it was true, backed by the seemingly bottomless resources of British Electric Traction, took all the risk while

150

Bernstein collected the credit. But they were made of different stuff from Bernstein, who was as much a visionary as he was a businessman. Harley Drayton of British Electric Traction, who had bought out Lord Rothermere's early *Daily Mail* interests in the Rediffusion consortium, was a buccaneering financier whose investments took in railways in Chile as well as laundries in suburbia. Wills had come into television via a number of omnibus companies in Yorkshire. No one at Rediffusion, except perhaps Paul Adorian, the managing director, had sufficient interest in the stuff of television to stamp their personality on anything at Rediffusion except the account books. Their manoeuvres precisely fitted the description which Peter Black borrowed so aptly from Robert Louis Stevenson: 'All this epical turmoil was conducted by gentlemen in frock coats and with a view to nothing more extraordinary than a fortune.'

Rediffusion's gentlemen in frock coats made their fortune before they lost their franchise. Bernstein's artistic endeavours cost him plenty but kept alive the goose that laid his golden eggs. But, by the time he was renewed, the authority had smelled a rat and the rules which left such loopholes were quickly mended. There are always, however, plenty more men in frock coats willing to follow the pioneers into business.

PART FOUR
New Faces, Old Hats

20

New faces were waiting in the wings by the time Lord Hill had taken his seat as chairman of the ITA and decided on a drastic reshuffle among the companies. There was no shortage of eager takers when the offers of the franchises were handed out for the second time, and behind the ignominious sacrifice of Associated Rediffusion's lease on the public airwaves could be detected the direction in which Lord Hill hoped to steer the channel. If Peter Black described the men behind the boardroom table at Associated Rediffusion as gentlemen in frock coats, Sir Kenneth Clark had coined a similar image of them long before: 'Gents in pinstripe trousers.' He meant, of course, businessmen who looked no higher than their profit margins and audience ratings.

Perennial Associated Rediffusion stand-bys, like *Double Your Money* and the late Michael Miles's weekly exercise in victim humiliation, *Take Your Pick,* did nothing to dispel this image. Their chairman, Sir John Spencer Wills, could not have helped their cause either, back in 1956, when he nailed his company's colours firmly to the mast of the *Good Ship Lollipop* by publicly denying that television had any duty whatsoever to foist educative programmes on to the public. 'That I cannot accept,' he rashly told his shareholders. 'If an adult has the intelligence to elect a Member of Parliament to rule him in peace and war he has the intelligence to elect what programme he wishes to see during his hours of leisure.' No great fault can be found in the logic of this argument, except that it begs the vital question of a suitably varied choice for the intelligent adult. But it does not sit so prettily in the ears of those anxious to create an acceptable image for ITV.

In actual performance, Associated Rediffusion had not lagged too far behind Bernstein's northern outpost. As we have seen, the highbrow lord of Granadaland had been only too happy to accept such programmes as *Double Your Money* and *Take Your Pick* at peak hours in his secret agreement with the London company. But Sidney had the knack of saying all the right things and getting them heard in all the right places. It was a trick the gentlemen in frock coats ignored to their cost. Sir John Spencer Wills was a trustee of the London Symphony Orchestra, and, as such, his company began to subsidize orchestras and concerts within its area. In this their influence on the culture of region was much more effective than Bernstein's later dismal experiment with the Stables Theatre. But, worthy as the gesture might have been in winning friends and influencing people at the ITA, it went for nothing. The gents in pinstripe trousers had not learned Bernstein's showman's gift for self-promotion. While they were openly admitting as unabashed businessmen that they had tried to bring classical music to their screens and that it was 'virtually impossible', Bernstein was making a great public clamour as a guardian of good taste that Manchester should have the arts centre its heritage deserved. That he did little or nothing else to bring this about probably prompted the *Guardian* to inquire impolitely what, 'in terms of what one sees on the screen', he had achieved to enrich the culture of the North?

Whatever else they had not done by the time they were disenfranchised, however, the men at Associated Rediffusion had played their part in creating the next generation of television mogul. They had hired, fired, and hired again a young man called David Frost.

It was Kitty Muggeridge, wife of Malcolm, who minted the cruel description of David Frost's burgeoning fame: 'He has risen without trace.' Her phrase is not without a certain glib aptness. He would indeed appear to have floated into the big league from cloud Number Nine. But this is to deny him the qualities he has in common with all the men, like Bernstein and Grade, who made their mark at the top of television. Each possesses a boundless drive, an innate showman's flair and a nimble grasp of the medium. Their presence is felt wherever they choose to make it. 'He is like an internal combustion engine that burns 99 per cent of its gases,' is how one friend describes Frost.

As a Cambridge undergraduate, Frost may not have appeared to be ideal television material. He was untidy, his accent was scarcely microphone tuned and his features were certainly not in the matinée idol mould. But he had applied his energies to the university's showcase *Footlights Revue,* edited an eye-catching magazine and somehow found himself invited to Rediffusion's headquarters in Kingsway as a possible candidate for a training contract after graduation. He was given the contract – there were only two on offer – and might well have *sunk* without trace as a result of it. For, apart from an undistinguished pop item called 'Let's Twist on the Riviera...' his presence was not much required before the cameras.

It was a dogged determination to persevere with the cabaret act, following very much in the swathe cut by the *Beyond the Fringe* team, that changed his fortune in his chosen medium. His agent, Richard Armitage, caused an advertisement to be placed in *The Stage* – the theatre's trade paper – congratulating the 'brilliant young comedian David Frost' on his cabaret début, while the paper's anonymous club critic, 'Nightbeat', found a few kind words to say on his behalf. Ned Sherrin, then a forceful current affairs producer at the BBC, saw the issue. He was scouting for talent for a new satire show which he intended to launch and decided to go to the Blue Angel club to check out the new act. The rest, as they say, is history. But at least the story gives the lie to the bowdlerized version of the old theatre joke: 'What are the three most useless things in the world? – The Pope's testicles, a eunuch in a nunnery and a rave review in *The Stage.'*

Ned Sherrin maintains, with the wicked twinkle and sincere smile which are the hallmark of his style, that the act he saw that night did not go well. 'But there was something about David's delivery which made me feel instinctively that he was right for the show, despite his reception.' The note he sent to Donald Baverstock, the BBC's brilliant Welsh firecracker producer, was slightly more charitable: 'Ex-Footlights (Cambridge), looks promising. Have seen him conducting Press Conference as cabaret turn at night club where he was limited by the stupidity of the customers.' He could think on his feet, was Sherrin's assessment of his technique. And he thought himself straight out of any obligations to Rediffusion.

The television show which followed was, of course, BBC's *That*

Was The Week That Was (or TW3 for short), which revolutionized not only television humour in the short run, but David Frost's long-run career. 'Before David no one in Britain understood that appearing on the television screen unlocks boardroom doors,' his former mentor and lasting friend Ned Sherrin says. 'David always intended to use television in every way possible right from the beginning.'

The way he has used it from his earliest appearances has been little short of astonishing, even by the ready access to instant fame and, sometimes, fortune which the medium offers. Sherrin, as is so often told, had decided on John Bird as the anchor man for the new satire show. But John Bird flew the nest, following Peter Cook and the success of *Beyond the Fringe,* to New York. Frost was in the right place at the right time. Given the role of link man, he was soon Sherrin's right-hand man. It can and has been argued that, of all the team of flashy young talent which TW3 projected on to our screens, Frost's was the least original or prepossessing. But talent is only at best a third-part ingredient in any success story. The other two thirds are luck and temperament, and not necessarily in that order. It is a fruitless exercise to maintain that Sir Laurence Olivier, say, is the most talented actor of his age. He can be said to be the most talented actor whose luck brought him to the public's notice and whose temperament has sustained him there. Somewhere there must be some mute, inglorious, but equally talented Olivier. It is difficult to imagine that there could be a mute, inglorious Frost, however; or a Grade; or a Bernstein.

It takes a special kind of temperament, for example, to walk out at the end of a training contract with the words, 'Get out and never come back!' ringing in your ears; then to have a prodigious success like *TW3* and *Not So Much A Programme More A Way Of Life;* and then to return to your former training ground with all the confidence of one who really has taught his grandmother to suck eggs.

Sherrin describes him as the only man he knows who learns by his mistakes. And, in a career that has gone ever-upward, there is little evidence of the same mistake being made twice, although his detractors like to say that Frost himself is not ready to admit that a mistake is ever made once.

Nevertheless, back to Rediffusion he went, and it was from there that he launched himself into the really big league of tele-politics and tele-business. With the BBC he had gained notoriety, both from *TW3* and from *Not So Much A Programme.* He had also gained a foothold in America, land of opportunity but also, more important to him, home of commercial television. *That Was The Week That Was* had become a focus of reactionary attack during the last stages of its irreverent life, not all of it uninvited. But, on the assassination of President Kennedy, Sherrin's team produced a programme which has probably never been surpassed for its spontaneous response to the emotions of the moment. This was television at its most immediate and its most impressive. And, it has to be added, it was television that you would not then find outside the BBC, for all Sidney Bernstein's protestations that he wished to broaden the basis of current affairs.

The TW3 team were invited to the United States to repeat their exceptional tribute to the fallen President. Its vitality, its sincerity and its sensitive comprehension of what every viewer was feeling had made it a *cause célèbre* over there: the home of commercial television was also quite unaccustomed to programmes of this high standard. It was screened twice and voted the best documentary of the year. As the son of a preacher – a Methodist minister – Frost was entirely at home in this admirable requiem to a dead hero. By the time the TW3 artists and writers were flown out to give a live performance of the eulogy at Madison Square Garden, Frost had more than made his presence felt. He was the only one of that clever and talented group to join the Americanized carbon copy of TW3. It gave him even wider horizons.

Though his British follow-up, *Not So Much A Programme More A Way Of Life,* brought about the end of the Sherrin–Frost professional collaboration and left the young maestro with his increasingly celebrated face somewhat covered in egg, he was already poised to move on to bigger and better things. Satire was a spent force and on this occasion David was not about to be around when the funeral orations were made.

'The Marketable Man', as he was described rather pejoratively in the *Sunday Mirror,* he bounced right back and sold himself to his old masters at Rediffusion for a £25,000 contract to make a twenty-six part series of *The Frost Programme.* This remarkable *coup* was effected on the strength of his final two-year fling with the BBC, *The Frost Report,* to launch which he had also effectively sold himself to almost everyone who was anyone in London at a memorable breakfast reception in London's elegant Connaught Hotel. He did nothing by halves once his mind was made up and he had a new objective in sight.

159

In his unremittingly admiring biography, *David Frost,* the late Willi Frischauer records how even the Prime Minister, Harold Wilson, turned up promptly at 9.30 a.m. for 'the intimate breakfast party' Frost was giving for 'some of his friends in high places'. What Mr Frischauer tactfully omits to mention is that the breakfast was not nearly so intimate as most of those friends in high places had been led to believe. When they accepted the invitation, many were no more than mere acquaintances and arrived under the impression that they would be sharing bacon-and-eggs tête-a-tête with the twenty-six-year-old *Wunderkind* of the television screen.

However, it served its purpose admirably. *The Frost Report* made news because he had seen to it that he had access to people in the news. Shyness has never held back his career; his style of self-introduction would amount to brazenness in anyone less personable. The film producer Bryan Forbes, for example, became a firm friend after bumping into him in a top people's store in London and finding a box of chocolates Frost just happened to have handy thrust upon him by the man whose face he only knew from his television screen until that moment; they have collaborated profitably and in perfect harmony ever since their opportune brief encounter.

Nor, as Sherrin has indicated, was he ever a person to repeat misjudgements. The key people with whom he surrounded himself while putting together *The Frost Report* included the one person who had been least impressed by his abilities in his earliest days at Rediffusion, the late Cyril Bennett. Bennett was the man who had kept Frost simmering with unrequited self-expression during his trainee days at the station. And Bennett it was who paved the way for his return there. They were to become the closest business associates in his sprawling entertainment empire. One of David Frost's most admirable qualities is his ability to spot talent in others and harness it to his own drive; this is not merely plagiarism, as the more mean-minded of his detractors have suggested. It takes both a confident and humble man to surround himself with creative ability he genuinely admires and not feel threatened by it. Frost encourages others, just as he himself was once encouraged. It is a gift more rare than is commonly suspected.

For the show he assembled a cross-fertilization of comedy talent, lively, inventive and individual enough to make the programme itself resemble a golden age of television. He brought in the likes of John Cleese, Marty Feldman, Dick Vosburgh and John Wells – a satirist who had in the past made Frost himself a prime target for his ridicule. The two Ronnies, Corbett and Barker, were teamed in front of the cameras for the first time to bring their appealingly off-beat humour to such British institutions as voting, loving, education and nudism. It was far and away a more popularly innovative form of television journalism than Hewat's rugged investigations had been at Granada. And, though the BBC's executive producers had decided that Frost's brand of satire was played out, he had already read the writing on the wall and covered his tracks with well-laid plans to return to his former employers at Rediffusion. He came back to the fold not as a penitent, but in the grand manner of a conquering hero bringing home the spoils of war.

The Frost Programme was one more step in a career in which few if any of its steps have been backward. Antony Jay, the producer who had first spotted Frost's potential at Rediffusion, was among his chief mentors for *The Frost Programme,* as was Cyril Bennett, the producer who hadn't. They returned to the origins of Donald Baverstock's scintilating *Tonight* programmes for their inspiration, and it was here that Frost's image as the public's pet grand inquisitor was first launched. At first, however, the executives at Rediffusion began to suspect they had bought themselves an expensive pup instead of a star watchdog. The pilot programmes which were to launch their latest signing on the choppy waters of the TV chat show were frankly disastrous; so much so that one of the programme's earliest participants, Denis Norden, introduced his host with the cryptic comment: 'Ladies and gentlemen, let me introduce David Frost, the man who has made more pilots than a randy air hostess.'

Mercifully, the format worked out by Jay and Frost to add audience participation to the topic under discussion, worked on the public's imagination better than the appalling pilots had led anyone to hope. Of course it had the sure-fire ingredient of Robert Morley as its chief guest; and since chat shows might have been designed specifically with Morley in mind, Frost was not exactly taking any chance of sinking like a lead balloon, even if his main attraction was designed to resemble one.

The subject, too, was tailor-made to raise the blood pressure to an acceptably watchable level: education. There can hardly be a man, woman or child in the land whose views on how and what to teach are disinterested. A good sprinkling of teachers among the audience ensured that the ensuing debate was at least lively and informed. Mr. Morley, who can be counted on to produce a stream of anecdotes on any subject under the sun, brought his usual highly personalized brand of humour to bear on his own public schooldays, and the show was deemed a success, though including singer Sandie Shaw on a programme devoted to education perhaps indicates something about its pretentions to serious intent. Frost may profess unswerving admiration for the early television interviewing techniques of his friend and associate John Freeman, but he himself was to cling to the knockabout level of his entertainment origins when formulating his own approach.

Still employing the comedy talents he had gathered in *The Frost Report* – most memorably John Cleese – did not shame him from introducing a running series of excruciating gags based on the theme of cross-fertilization. Few of them managed to rise above the standard of: 'Cross a kangaroo with a ball of wool and what do you get?...A woolly jumper.' It had to be explained to any visiting Americans among the audience that jumper was the English word for a sweater, but no one could explain to anyone what such jokes were doing on the air in the first place on a programme which took it upon itself to inquire into such vexed topics as corporal punishment, Rhodesian UDI, democracy, education, mercenaries and the notorious execution of Timothy Evans for murder.

Clive Irving, Neil Shand, a witty and ambitious Fleet Street journalist, and Peter Baker, also from the street, had joined the Frost back-scene entourage, and the programme gradually evolved a greater sense of purpose; with it, Frost's weight as an interviewer also increased. His confrontation with Dr Emil Savundra, a morally bankrupt financier whose insurance company went into liquidation eight months or so after he shed his controlling interest in its debts of over £1 million, was the stuff of which television journalism is made. It had the lot: an arch-villain condemning himself with every callous chuckle, widowed victims protesting their hardships brought on by his calumnies and – not least – David Frost in the role of 'Knight in Shining Armour' growing visibly more angry and outraged by every statement his guest made.

A selection from *The Frost Programme,* collectively called *Frost Over England,* walked away with two Golden Rose awards at the international television festival of Montreux. By now it was Frost all over the world. And when Lord Hill was ready to reshuffle the pack, the Joker Frost was holding an unbeatable hand and only too ready to play an ace of his own. In doing so he unsentimentally trumped his former partner, Rediffusion Television. And Cyril

Bennett, among many Frost faithfuls, was also in the game with more than one ace up his sleeve. If Rediffusion lost its licence, it was part of LWT's deal with the ITA that he would join them after a suitable three-month period.

The notion of applying for a London ITV licence ironically enough occurred to the by now popular and prosperous Frost at a party held by London's resident contract holders, Rediffusion. Everyone had by then scented Lord Hill's wind of change. Yorkshire was the favourite area for most. It was, after all, the largest county in the country, and it had no incumbent franchise holder, being freshly carved out of the Bernstein empire.

But Frost was among the first to perceive that the day of the men in frock coats and pinstripe trousers was over. Lord Hill was set to improve ITV's creative impact in the face of the mounting criticism it was attracting because of its high profits, mediocre output and low risks. So it was to creative men that Frost went first. Clive Irving was his earliest confidant. Peter Hall, later to take over the running of the National Theatre from Sir Laurence Olivier, lent the not inconsiderable weight of his reputation to the venture. 'Count me in,' said Hall, never slow himself to be counted in on a good thing.

Frost's scheme gathered momentum. And then he went for even bigger fish in much the same style he had launched himself with his celebrity breakfast. He contacted Sir Arnold Weinstock, managing director of the enormous GEC company. Sir Arnold's company was involved in the manufacture of television hardware, and he was a natural to bring into the proposed consortium on this consideration alone. The fact that Frost had never met Sir Arnold was by now no hindrance to a meeting. 'I simply picked up the telephone and called him,' he says. The fact that Sir Arnold responded so readily to the call says an awful lot for the Frost telephone manner and television reputation.

For other financial backing he went to David Montagu, a merchant banker. Not unexpectedly, Montagu was delighted to be included in the proposal. By this stage in the history of commercial television, any banker worth his seat on the board would have surrendered the combination of his numbered account in Switzerland to be allowed to back a successful franchise bid. And, of course, if the bid were to be unsuccessful, the losses would be negligible. Even my own inordinately cautious bank manager would not shrink from guaranteeing substantial capital if he thought I might attract a contract from the IBA. He would lose little but face if I failed, and think of the clover his branch would be in if I won! Backing was not difficult to find in 1967. Arrangements were readily agreed for a bank overdraft of £2 million.

Frost went on to consolidate the broad base of his own bid by jetting out to Delhi and dropping in on the British High Commissioner, John Freeman. Freeman would add considerable weight to the enterprise with his reputation as a fearless television interviewer (he had reduced Gilbert Harding to tears in one of his impressive *Face to Face* confrontations on BBC). Humphrey Burton, Aidan Crawley, and, not least, Michael Peacock, the man who had spiked the guns of satire at the BBC, were all brought in.

Only John Freeman was missing when the Frost consortium lined up to put in its £6 million bid for the lucrative London Weekend contract. Freeman remained firmly with his diplomatic career for the time being.

Besides the £2 million overdraft from his friendly bankers, Frost and Crawley each staked £75,000 (5 per cent of the holding), while their other financial backers put £1 million up front and guaranteed £3 million more should it become necessary. It was an impressive array of business interests which they had attracted: the publishers Weidenfeld & Nicolson, the paper firm of Bowaters, Lombard Bankers, the Imperial Tobacco Pension Fund, Pearl Assurance and even Magdalen College. Even before the ITA requested that they take aboard magazine and newspaper interests (part of Lord Hill's pet scheme to spread the jam across the media), they were over-subscribed by half a million.

Frost's own position as a television performer disqualified him, under ITA rules, from being an executive on the board. It was and is their belief that, to control a station and star in its programmes, is altogether too great an embarrassment of riches not to invite abuse. Frost's experience was to prove that you are as vulnerable in front of the cameras as you are behind a desk, and perhaps more so. Once again Lord Hill was going to reflect bitterly on the gulf that lies between promise and performance. The London Weekend experience was to become one of the authority's least shining hours.

The Frost report which went before the ITA, laying claim to the London Weekend franchise, ran to eighty foolscap pages, beautifully bound in morocco leather. It was a more fulsome document by far than Granada's comparatively modest table of intentions had been back in 1954. More or less the same pin-sticking procedures were adopted as before for picking the winners. The applicants trouped before the chairman and his twelve committee members, and submitted themselves to close interrogation on their claims. Strictest secrecy, as ever, was maintained. And while the various contenders awaited a decision from on high, Frost went out on the road again with his one-man show, presumably in the American presidential electioneering spirit of shaking hands with the people. 'Surprisingly, but prophetically,' says Frischauer in his book, 'one local critic remarked that David was in danger of getting too nice and clamoured for more of the old rough stuff.' I suspect I was that offending local critic, for about this time I reviewed Frost's stage act at the Adeline Genée Theatre in East Grinstead, Sussex, for the *Brighton Evening Argus,* and remember being singularly unimpressed by either its bite or its freshness.

The gnat-bite inflicted by this chance observation did not in any way affect the outcome of events. When Frost, Montagu, Crawley and their partner, Tom Margerison, arrived at the authority's headquarters on the fateful Sunday morning when the deliberations of the members were made known, they fared far better than either the delegation who preceded them into the inner sanctum, or the one which followed. Going in, they came face to face with a glowering Lord Derby, whose TWW had just been axed for its hapless showing in Wales in favour of the Burton–Taylor Harlech consortium. When they came out, 'dazed' by the news that they had been awarded the contract, they were confronted by the luckless Paul Adorian, managing director of Associated Rediffusion, about to enter and face the guillotine.

A wild celebratory lunch at the Ritz was the next item on the company's agenda. However, in the course of his studies for the second-class honours degree he obtained at Cambridge, the youngest franchise holder in ITV may well have come across the Elizabethan poet Richard Barnfield's lines: 'nothing more certain than incertainties; Fortune is full of fresh variety: Constant in nothing but inconstancy.' He would have done well to remember them when, in the full flood of his own good fortune, he proclaimed that LWT would be bringing the viewers fresh variety instead of old variety with a capital V.

The fresh variety which Frost's company produced was certainly constant in nothing but its inconstancy. And Lew Grade, the King of Variety with a capital V, was to see to that.

21

The sudden débâcle of the London Weekend Television's régime's hopes is also the story of the IBA's own built-in weakness. They make their appointments with all the secrecy of the confessional and yet, when their flock go out and sin, the only penance they extract is a Hail Mary or two. They interfere shamelessly in what are virtually family affairs, and then offer sanctuary when one of their parishioners is in trouble.

London Weekend soon found itself on the run. Something went badly wrong from the start. A technicians' go-slow was the least of their problems. Either Frost over-estimated the public's taste for change, or he was over-optimistic about his own popularity in bringing it to them. In its first few weeks of operation, the screens were practically blanketed with Frost and more Frost. On Friday they had 'Frost the Inquisitor'; on Saturday they had 'Frost the Laughing Ombudsman'; and on Sunday they had 'Frost the Celebrity's Friend'. They soon switched over to the opposition, and the unthinkable had happened. The BBC was taking up to 61 per cent of the ratings. Never had ITV's viewing figures dropped so far behind since it began in 1955.

What came next I have already touched on in demonstrating the power of the single personality within the Network Programme Committee. Lew Grade, in theory now merely a Midland weekday franchise holder, was in practice to prove himself still the Mr Big of the Big Five. Hand in glove with the newcomers at Yorkshire,

ATV dropped Frost's major Saturday slot altogether and replaced him with Dave Allen. The other two network companies closed ranks and relegated the show to late evening. In television terms, it was like sending it to Siberia.

The effect was to create a strategic breach in LWT's scheduling and to sabotage their morale. The entire edifice of their programming began to crumble. The shareholders developed severe nervous reactions which sent shock waves through the boardrooms. And by the time the year was out, the very foundations on which their franchise rested had disappeared. Michael Peacock, Frost's chief architect in the new-deal television, was ousted for sticking to the principles of their contract with the ITA. As LWT's managing director, and an honourable as well as a brilliant man, he felt his position untenable when panic measures were advocated to bring back viewers.

He found small comfort in the ITA, from whence cometh no help. Lord Hill, having set the pigeon among the cats, had departed for the BBC by the time the feathers began to fly. His successor, Lord Aylestone, was left to sort things out as best he could. The fact that, with the departure of Peacock, Margerison and several other of the original creative talents, London Weekend were hardly fulfilling any part of their promise to bring a new look to weekend viewing, seems to have figured little in the subsequent precautions the ITA took to see that it continued to hold its franchise and pay its way. As Sir Robert Fraser had remarked so early in the ITA's history, its only real moment of authority was when the contract was handed out. And that moment had passed.

Peacock's fate was sealed from the moment when the £6.5 million so eagerly subscribed or promised began to drain away almost faster than the viewers. In the general panic and horse-trading that followed, the General Electric Company withdrew financial backing and sold 8 per cent of the shares to Rupert Murdoch's *News of the World* group. Murdoch's company went on, unchecked, to raise their stake first to 16 per cent of the holding, then to a massive 36 per cent of the voting shares. Murdoch himself joined the board, and anyone less likely to maintain the adventurous and imaginative formula worked out by Peacock and his creative team would be difficult to imagine. This ambitious young publisher had already taken British journalism back thirty years with his bum-and-titillation brand of newspaper salesmanship in launching the *Sun*. It was inconceivable that, as a controlling shareholder on the board of LWT, his notions could avoid a direct clash with Peacock's. This is exactly what happened.

The IBA stood meekly by and allowed Peacock, his assistant managing director and his programme controller to leave before deciding that something should be done. London Weekend's franchise had effectively fallen into the hands of a man who had proved himself as strong and ambitious as any Grade or Bernstein, yet who had never been given any legal contract to own a station. Even taking into consideration the undemocratic basis at work in operating ITV for such huge stakes, this was absolutely indefensible. Lord Annan's committee were uncharacteristically swingeing in their indictment of the board's pusillanimous conduct in the affair. It was, indeed, a scandal by any standards.

The company had no chief executive and no programme controller to answer for its actions. No one save Murdoch, was at the helm, and he certainly had no authority to be there, having bought himself in by the back door with a £500,000 infusion of capital. Even by their own hit-and-miss standards of secret appointments, the IBA could hardly tolerate this kind of take-over. The contract they had given to the London Weekend consortium was by now flagrantly breached in almost every detail. Yet still the board did not withdraw it. Instead, they issued a stern warning that the franchise was 'in question'. They gave LWT time to draw up a list of new proposals for managerial responsibilities and programme policy, and they let it be known that the name of Rupert Murdoch would not be acceptable at the top of that list. In short, they did the least they could possibly do under the circumstances.

It was just sufficient a shot across the Murdoch bows to warn him that his future in British commercial television was limited. He shortly moved the main centre of his burgeoning media empire across the Atlantic, where there is less obsession with such few niceties as the IBA impose.

What to do to hold on to the franchise at LWT did not occupy David Frost's quick mind overlong. As Frost's luck would have it, and it usually did, John Freeman was by now free from his ambassadorial responsibilities. The timing could not have been more opportune, either for Freeman, looking for a post to match his diplomatic eminence, or for Frost, searching for an acceptable solution to the vacuum left at LWT. The two men had become extremely friendly over the years, with Frost paying the Freemans several visits during their Washington posting, and the ambassador himself with his family spending a vacation at Frost's Bridgeport home.

Thus the threat to the franchise was staved off and control kept within the family. Frost's former Rediffusion boss, Cyril Bennett, completed the neatness of the transition by agreeing to become programme controller. Like Freeman, he possessed exactly the qualities needed to steady the ship in its present stormy waters and to steer it back on course. A practical as well as a gifted man, his comment on the station's responsibilities was unequivocal. 'Our duty is to survive,' he said. He could have been spelling out the entire philosophy of ITV.

With the unimpeachable respectability of Freeman, both as a public figure and broadcaster, and with Bennett's recognized experience ready to save the day, the IBA announced in April 1971 that London Weekend 'was secure in its contract', as were the other companies. None the less, the Parliamentary Select Committee on Broadcasting were gravely troubled by the whole affair, though not nearly so scathing in their verdict as the Annan Committee would be when they came to look into the matter.

'We refuse to accept the arguments of the Independent Broadcasting Authority', reported Annan. Nearly three years of upheaval and inadequate programme planning were as much a criticism of the authority as of London Weekend. The wind-up of the current affairs unit, the mainstay of their original programme proposals, and the removal of Michael Peacock were, in Annan's view, as they must be to any impartial mind, irrefutable evidence that London Weekend 'was incapable of maintaining its franchise undertaking'.

The most damning indictment of the IBA's chicken-hearted role in the protracted cock-fight came in the Annan Report's finding that:

> The Authority ... was not prepared to support a programme company against the short-run fears of its boardroom. The IBA had sanctions available. They chose not to use them until the chaotic situation which occurred after Mr Murdoch acquired his interest in the company compelled them to do so.

Like Mr Micawber, the authority were hoping that something would turn up. Only when it did, and when it turned out to be Rupert Murdoch, did they start to squawk.

David Frost's interests in the company were hardly damaged by any of this. He had no executive role to play. He was, throughout, an entrepreneur; the 5 per cent holding he held in the company was a mere fraction of his business interests. The stronghold of his empire is David Paradine Ltd, of which at the time when LWT was tottering, he owned 99 per cent of the shares with his mother owning the remaining other odd one. While Murdoch made his inroads on LWT, David Paradine Productions supplied television films for the United Kingdom and the United States. David Paradine Films made feature films for the cinema. David Paradine Plays had interests in West End productions. David Frost Enterprises handled his television appearances ... The list of Frost's financial investments spread on into property and into publishing until it rivalled Lord Grade's. In one publishing agreement alone, he is paid a yearly sum of £150,000. His homes are in the two continents to suit his much-publicized Concorde-hopping across the Atlantic. In London, his house is furnished with the expensive good taste of a man who isn't home much.

As Ned Sherrin has said, he is someone who realized that television unlocks the doors to many boardrooms.

John Freeman's emergence as a power within commercial television was not, however, merely another manifestation of David Frost's proven facility to place the right man in the right job at the right time – often including himself. While it was indeed Frost who effected the ticklish negotiations (he had been flying a 'Freeman-for-chairman' kite off and on for the past five years), others played equally important if less creditable roles. Rupert Murdoch himself had no small hand in the final outcome, as did the top brass of the remaining Big Four, Granada, Yorkshire, ATV and Thames.

The companies had been appalled by the warfare at LWT, and dispatched Ward Thomas, then managing director of new-formed Yorkshire TV, to meet face to face (Freeman fashion) with the hapless Brian Young. Only four months into his director-generalship of the ITA, Young probably mistook the Big Five's alarmed self-interest for altruistic concern at his own board's embarrassment. If this was so, he was soon disabused. He was told bluntly that unless something was resolved, and quickly, he would face a far more public delegation of vocal ITV chief executives. Somewhat implausibly Ward Thomas was assured at the highly confidential meeting that 'all would be well'. What Young did not know when he gave his absurdly bland assurance was that his visitor was the first harbinger from a gathering flock of vultures, each anxious to scavenge as much from the carcass of LWT as he could grab. Thames – according to an authoritative *Sunday Times* 'Insight' report of the back-stage pecking order – wanted to swallow London Weekend whole, and thus to dominate the lucrative London area seven days a week.

Lew Grade, having lost his own hold on London's weekend franchise, was only too well aware of what was at stake and was ready to ally himself with anyone who would prevent Thames's audacious opportunism, eventually proposing a consortium which would throw Thames a tempting scrap (the difficult Friday-night slot) and keep the real feast (Saturday and Sunday) in the clutches of the remaining three: himself, Ward Thomas and Sidney Bernstein. Outraged, several of the smaller regional outposts, notably John Davis's Southern TV, argued that, if Rupert Murdoch could buy his way into the network for half a million, so could they. In the following weeks after his meeting with Ward Thomas, Young was to meet each and every one of the big chiefs concerned in the power struggle.

Fortunately for Young, and probably for ITV in general, Frost and Murdoch were in touch and in accord. Freeman was their man: 'Mr Clean', who would stamp his brand image on all the dirty linen which had been laundered at LWT. Aidan Crawley, the sorely tried chairman at the company throughout Murdoch's firings, conveniently stepped down in Freeman's favour, thus saving Murdoch from an even closer comparison with Macbeth. It looked as if this Duncan had abdicated.

So, in the home of a neutral LWT director, Freeman and Frost clinched the agreement. Murdoch and the IBA later added their blessing, both with considerable relief. Freeman had consented to lend his considerable reputation to bail out LWT on the clear understanding that Rupert Murdoch was in full accord and that he himself would have over-all powers at the company. That Murdoch freely acceded to this may account for the new chairman's extra-ordinary tribute to the man whose advent at London Weekend had provoked the furore. It was part of his conditions in coming to LWT that Murdoch stayed on, he announced. 'He is a man who is near genius in financial matters,' said Freeman on his arrival at his new headquarters. 'And extremely experienced in the field of communications. I had confidence in joining the company at a time when he had been prepared to invest £500,000. I scarcely knew him. It wasn't a personal thing. It was his track record, not his personality.'

172

Freeman's own track record needed no Rupert Murdoch to plead his cause. It spoke for itself. Probably he first imposed his considerable if oddly chilly presence on the general public when television was in the first flush of its own innocent youth. He was its first grand inquisitor. More formidable by far than David Frost, Freeman demonstrated his skills in his still famed *Face to Face* confrontations. With assorted celebrities of the day, he showed himself to be a tough interrogator who gave no quarter and showed small mercy. His style was deliberately unobtrusive so far as the viewers were concerned. He would position himself in deep shadow, back half-turned to the camera, while his subject faced the full glare of its baleful scrutiny and his remorseless questioning. The technique is not unfamiliar in NKVD inquisitions and Freeman always managed to impart an atmosphere charged with tension and a sense of occasion.

The most notorious of his *Face to Face* sessions was, of course, the one with Gilbert Harding, the irascible tele-celebrity who Freeman reduced to tears with his relentless probing about the death of Harding's mother. Freeman has always maintained that he took the calculated risk of wounding his guest in order to show that there was a sympathetic, softer side to Harding's noted ill-temper. The public professed outrage that their hero with the lion's head had been forced to reveal the heart of a deer. But they clamoured for more.

Said Kingsley Martin of Freeman at that time: 'John needs power but hates publicity. He is the only man who made himself famous by showing the public his backside.'

He had, however, been marked out for power and enjoyed some fame long before he began to show 'the public his backside' on *Face to Face*. His social and academic pedigrees were impeccable: Westminster and Brasenose. His fascination with the media led him, curiously enough, to take at first a post with an advertising consultancy. It was obviously intended to be just an initial step to much higher things. 'Journalism,' he once said, 'is what I have always wanted since I was seven years old.'

It was a very short stay on the periphery of his chosen profession. The war arrived and Freeman was the calibre of man the army needed. He had, as they say, a good war, and returned not to journalism but to politics. Though the two are often allied trades, this change of hats is typical of the restless search for a fresh challenge which has always marked out his brand of ambition.

There is nothing more single-minded about him than his determination to do better and aim higher.

'A delightful man to have in a crew,' said an anonymous rowing report on Freeman in the 1931 school magazine for Westminster. 'A tremendously hard worker. At present rows rather like a village blacksmith – next year his aim must be "Maximum power with maximum ease".' It was a lesson he learned with consummate success.

He captured the supposedly safe Tory seat of Watford for Labour in the 1945 socialist landslide, as much to his own surprise, he says, as to everybody else's. 'If I seriously thought I was going to win I might not have allowed my name to go forward,' he confessed long after. But the myth and the persona were gathering momentum. There is a story that the first time Churchill saw the tall, blond, young backbencher in the Commons' Smoking Room, still sporting his uniform with the Desert Rat flashes on his shoulders and battle-ribbons on his chest, he burst into tears. The tears may have been a genuine tribute to the successful maiden speech Freeman had just made to the new Parliament, but it was more likely chagrin that so promising a new recruit was sitting with Attlee's interlopers instead of among his own ranks.

The very fact that Attlee's choice had alighted on this untried newcomer to rise in answer to the King's Speech on behalf of the government says something of the impression his presence and his intellect have on all who meet him for the first time. The Prime Minister's faith was not misplaced, as Winston's tears were to prove. Freeman had rounded off his stirring reply with the battle-cry that rang out with the patriotic rhetoric Churchill himself would have found difficult to surpass. 'We have before us a battle for the peace no less arduous and momentous than the battle we have lived through in the past six years. Today we go into action and it may rightly be regarded as D-Day in the battle for the new Britain,' he told the war-weary house; and they received the news with clamorous applause.

After such an introduction, his star continued to rise. Immediately he was appointed private parliamentary secretary to the Minister of War, then financial secretary at the War Office, whence he led the UK Defence Mission to Burma. Finally he became a parliamentary secretary at the vital Ministry of Supply. In all this he stood well to the left of the party's centre, with such as Harold Wilson, Michael Foot and the late Aneurin Bevan. It was Bevan who remarked:

'John is the most dangerous of us all.'

In 1951 he resigned from the government on a matter of socialist principle in company (significantly enough, in view of his later career) with Harold Wilson. Together with Aneurin Bevan, they quite in protest against the introduction of National Health charges, a split which helped to erode confidence in the Attlee administration and indirectly paved the way for commercial television by hastening the downfall of the Labour government. Out of office, Freeman returned to his first enthusiasm, journalism, joining the *New Statesman* under Kingsley Martin and eventually replacing him as editor when he retired. It was at this time that Freeman's public persona began to impose itself on the man-in-the-street. He was a celebrity; a man whose television appearances were looked forward to beforehand and talked about avidly afterwards.

Yet his interviewing technique was so perfected as to expose everything there was to know about his subject and nothing at all about the man himself. Though he was voted the 'Best Dressed Man of the Year' by the *Tailor and Cutter* at a time when it still mattered how one dressed and did the rounds of public speaking, fête-opening and the like, the man himself remained an enigma. Ivan Rowan, writing in the *Sunday Telegraph*, has declared that everyone who ever met Freeman always felt on the verge of discovering who he really is. 'The moment when it comes,' added Rowan, 'is like arriving at his house for a long deferred appointment and being greeted by a tall, sandy-haired man with flat blue eyes and a smile and voice as delicate and precise as a vicar's: "I'm afraid the *real* Mr Freeman was called away five minutes ago. I know he would have been delighted to see you. Is there any message?"'

Perhaps the aloofness stemmed from his upper-middle-class childhood. A nanny and a succession of governesses saw to his upbringing, while the household itself was dominated by his disturbingly eccentric father, a barrister who Freeman himself has described as: 'A stern man. No, I would say *formidable*.' Freeman Senior spent a great deal of his declining years devising a will designed specifically to baffle his colleagues. When he did die the document read to the effect: 'I wish my property to be treated as if I had died intestate.' It was not an easy act to follow for a son already described by a master at Westminster as 'a rather cool and detached sort of boy'. Maybe here, too, are the roots of the many contradictions in his character and history. For one who had risen so high so soon and abandoned government office on lofty socialist ideals, his editorship of the *New Statesman* was distinctly low key. He was, indeed, accused of taking it far to the right of Kingsley Martin's radical standards. As a journalist he therefore had no true claim to being a firebrand, unlike his colleague Richard Crossman (another contemporary contender for the editor's chair at the *New Statesman*). His own column in the journal was even less inspiring. Moreover, to those who have turned to his television interviewing techniques to find the key to his own psyche, he has been effectively discouraging, always denying that his questions had anything to do with psychology of any kind. Quite the opposite, he insists. His questions were based on patient research and interest.

As to his parliamentary career, he is equally dismissive. He says that he regrets all the double dealings that are an integral part of political life, and adds, with startling candour: 'Power is a disagreeable element in life. I tend to think those who like it have disagreeable elements in their personality and I include myself in that.' Which, coming from the horse's mouth, is answer enough to those who protest naive astonishment when the men to whom power is given turn out, at best, to be devious, like Sir Harold Wilson, or downright dishonest, like Richard Nixon. Freeman's career before uttering those uncharacteristically revealing words had brought him close to both these men. For it was his old rebel associate, Wilson, who chose him for the key post of High Commissioner for India when Labour was returned to office in 1964. From New Delhi, where he lived in some splendour, he was awarded the plum ambassadorial posting: Washington. It was an enormous honour, but one entirely commensurate, as was proved, to his abilities. His duties in Washington coincided almost exactly with the election of President Nixon.

Some measure of Freeman's flair for diplomacy can be gauged by his own domestic circumstances in Washington. As well as being the official intermediary between the two tricky men of the West, Wilson and Nixon, the new ambassador had a ticklish problem of protocol on his own doorstep. His third wife, the former BBC TV producer Catherine Dove, had previously been married to the BBC's distinguished Washington correspondent, Charles Wheeler. Inevitably the paths of the ambassador and his lady and Wheeler and his new wife would cross in the narrow, incestuous round of Washington's diplomatic life. All such meetings, it seems, were carried off with perfect aplomb by those concerned.

Yet, for a man reputedly cold and withdrawn, Freeman's marital

176

history is unexpectedly untidy. After presiding over the life of Britain's largest embassy at No. 3100 Massachusetts Avenue, Washington DC, with every sign of vivacious harmony for many months, and gaining for themselves the reputation of witty and elegant hosts, the Freemans announced their separation. After their divorce, and his eventual appointment as London Weekend chairman, he quietly married the women who had been Catherine Freeman's social secretary in Washington, thus adding one more puzzle to the enigma of his personality. It was said at the time that he had made up his mind to quit Washington even before the General Election and the return to office of Edward Heath's new Conservative administration made it impossible for him to continue as ambassador.

Freeman's Washington days had seen a significant change in the way he viewed his personal encounters. Back in 1964 he had described President Nixon as 'a discredited and outmoded purveyor of the irrational and the inactive' – a judgement which proved to be prophetic in every detail except the last. He was also on record as having described Nixon's 1960 election defeat as 'a victory for decency'. As an ambassador, however, he travelled a long way after making that damning indictment, and his friendships in Washington came to throw a most curious light on his judgement of men. Among his closest circle of friends were Nixon's ultra-right-wing Attorney General, Mitchell, and his grotesquely embarrassing Southern belle wife, Martha. Before Mitchell was imprisoned for his part in Nixon's corrupt administration and Martha had been incarcerated alone and hysterically embittered in a sanatorium to fight her drink problem, Freeman was quoted as saying: 'I am very fond of the Mitchells. Twenty years ago I would not have been.' Twenty years before, indeed, he had been resigning from the government on the principle of defending a true welfare state.

This, then, is the man whose reputation and abilities more than any other factor saved London Weekend in the face of dithering by the IBA and naked opportunism from its competitors. His style at the new South Bank headquarters is, like himself, impressive and remote; imperceptible yet unmistakable. He is a man full of contradictions, yet also of undoubted merit.

'He was always wonderfully loyal to his staff,' recalls one writer from his *New Statesman* editorship, testifying to Freeman's administrative ability. 'I have actually heard him tell cabinet ministers that

177

he would refuse to speak to them if they had rung to complain about a story. He could also be very snobbish. We would be in conference and suddenly he would say: "I had an excellent wine last night." Then he would lean down and grub around in his bottom drawer until he found the cork from his damned bottle and it would be solemnly passed around so we could all have a sniff and say what we thought.'

For someone whose achievements have taken him to the hub of power, both in politics and the media, Freeman is extraordinarily self-deprecating. 'I have never seen life as being a career in which you start at the beginning and work on until someone pensions you off at the end,' he says of his own restlessness. 'I have always thought opportunities come along and you just take them. I am far from satisfied with life in the sense of what I have achieved. I think I have achieved very little. If I died today no one would remember what I have done. But I have been rather more content than most with my lot.'

22

In Yorkshire, the vast, virgin county which all David Frost's friends and associates had recommended as the fruit most ripe for picking, a very different tale unfolded. It was LWT in reverse. Out of the least likely seeds, and with many false starts, bloomed at last a rose worthy of Yorkshire. We have already seen something of Yorkshire's impressive achievements over the years: the strong drama department which Peter Willes inherited, the current affairs department which John Fairley carved out of Yorkshire's raw clay, the often fearless crusading spirit. Yet, curiously enough, when the 1980 franchises went again on offer (with fifty serious contenders as compared with those original far-sighted five back in 1954), the top man's position was reckoned by many informed insiders to be more precarious than most.

How did this come about? The answer again seems to be bound up inextricably with individual personality. The former pilot, Gwyn E. Ward Thomas, CBE, DFC, is an *éminence grise* among the moguls at the pinnacle of commercial television's tree. Where even the severest criticism of Lord Bernstein or Lord Grade is often tempered with reluctant admiration, Ward Thomas has his finest achievements spoken of without affection.

He it was who eventually captured the area relinquished by his former boss, Lord Bernstein, achieving this spectacular *coup* by some very neat horse-trading on his own account. Not that he was any stranger to the business side of television when he set about wresting the Yorkshire area from his competitors. He had already made his mark at Granada as one of Sidney's original team before moving ever on and upward to emerge as chairman of the diminutive Grampian TV company. Sidney may well have been as sad as he professed to be to see Ward Thomas depart Granadaland. Yet he must, even then, have been aware of the limitless ambition behind this young high-flying eagle's dealings. With Granada being very much a Bernstein family concern at the top, there could never have been any real possibility of the enigmatic ex-aviator sitting some day where Granada's real controls were manipulated: behind Sidney's deceptively modest desk.

At Grampian, however, he showed exactly how well he had learned the tricks of the new trade. Financially the company flourished, and though neither it nor its chairman made much public splash outside their own limited region, within the television industry itself Ward Thomas made waves. It was no surprise to any who knew him that, when his former mentor's domain was carved in half by the ITA, he was fastest off the mark to move into the big league. There were, of course, many other contenders for the prize. You did not have to be a resident chairman of a minor company to know by this time that the Pennine gold was there for the mining.

The advantage which Ward Thomas offered, and which set him apart from the rest of the field, was hardware. Whatever lavish programme plans the other contestants may have put forward for Yorkshire, he was one step ahead in being able to promise (at least on paper) the means of transmission. He is, as no one will deny, a smart operator; you do not start out as a pilot and wind up being ferried around in your own executive jet as head of a rich TV conglomerate by being a bone-head.

Ward Thomas did his homework thoroughly. He approached the various civic authorities in the area to scent out which would most eagerly welcome a new television station in terms of providing the acreage. Leeds, it transpired, would be only too thrilled to offer the most practical assistance in making space available on the most favourable terms, though, with the example of Granada across the Pennines, he was not short of seekers for his custom. It was a Dutch auction in which the least high bidder won the day.

Thus provided with a site and the firm promise of civic backing, he set out in search of building contractors and architects who could draw up detailed plans of studios with the costing and timing set out. This done, he recruited his team. Donald Baverstock, the Welsh dragon and fire-eater, was brought in from the BBC to lend his considerable creative reputation to the conglomerate (he was to last only six years); Stuart Wilson was welcomed aboard too (he lasted even less). An alliance was formed with the roving reporter Alan Whicker. But apart from these heavies, the production team who eventually inhabited the studios Ward Thomas built at Leeds were far wetter around the ears in terms of television fame than the glittering parade of talent David Frost was able to list in his eighty-page morocco-bound prospectus.

'I can think of no other reason for giving us the franchise than that Ward Thomas was able to show them that he could provide studios and provide them quickly,' says one of the earliest of the pioneers at Leeds. 'No one else had thought sufficiently of that. They all went to the authority with their marvellous new theories for serving the district. Ward Thomas just went and virtually said: "I've got the studios all organized and I'll see my programmes reflect what Yorkshire wants." Local programmes for local people is virtually all the programme policy we had to offer. But since hardly any of us had been further north than Watford in any meaningful way, we were hardly in a position to know what on earth the locals did want.'

The Yorkshire landowning Worsley family – who through their daughter Kate were basking in the reflected glory of being closely related to Royalty – were approached to provide some capital as well as prestige. Though by no means a wealthy family in terms of the neighbouring landed gentry (compared to the Duke of Norfolk, for instance) they managed to put up £38,000. In three years their investment had all but trebled. It was sufficient reward in itself for lending their ancient respectability to the shortly to be *nouveau riche* Yorkshire conglomerate. Most of the money put up for the new company was Yorkshire based.

This, too, may have impressed Lord Hill and his twelve apostles in favour of Ward Thomas's bid. What other explanation is there? Had they used the same yardstick for Yorkshire that they obviously used for London Weekend, his claims would have fallen far short on promise.

The moment the contract was secure, however, he lost no time at all in giving Yorkshire a more glamorous public image. Ironically, the colours which he chose for his new station were the ones it would wear with least success. The company launched a widely publicized deal with Associated London Scripts, a comedy 'factory' incorporating the creative comedy talents of Johnnie Speight, Dick Vosburgh, Dave Freeman, Eric Sykes and Frankie Howerd. This not only promised much so far as the viewers were concerned, but was also a calculated sop to Lord Hill who had expressed himself dissatisfied with the amount of original comedy shows being launched by his companies – especially as the BBC were sweeping the board in this area as part of their strategy in the rating race.

Ward Thomas also announced, with some flourish, that twenty-four top BBC and ITV executives had been recruited for the key appointments at his station, including the posts of programme planning, head of news, head of light entertainment and head of sport. It all began to look most impressive; at least, it did on paper. That Yorkshire had to wait until the advent of Leonard Rossiter's series *Rising Damp* before fulfilling its promise as a sponsor of popular comedy series, and that many of those top executives would soon be sent packing by the man who had so eagerly poached them, only serves to reiterate Lord Hill's lament: the easiest part of awarding a franchise is assessing a company's financial stability; the most difficult is calculating its subsequent performance.

We cannot know for certain the reasoning behind Lord Hill's beneficence towards Ward Thomas's consortium. It offered nothing to compare with London Weekend's ambitious programme of innovations, beyond pledging itself to reflect the interests of the district it served. It was headed by no celebrity dynamo; its board contained no figure of Sir Arnold Weinstock's standing. But everything points to the success of his bid having been for exactly the reasons his earliest recruits suggest. He emerged a confident victor by promising the ITA its first-ever custom-built colour television studios. The contractors, Richard Costain & Sons, proposed impressive 'critical path analysis' techniques to complete the first 4,500 square feet of studio space in Kirkstall Road, Leeds, on time. And an admiring article in the *Financial Times* on 13 June 1967 reported the Yorkshire network's managing director to be still bravely nailing his flag to the mast of light entertainment. 'We think it is time for a new look in this field, ' he told the newspaper. 'It is no secret that most critics would say that BBC light entertainment was better than ITV.' The words were carefully calculated to

182

bring joy to the ever-hopeful heart of Lord Hill. Thomas even invoked the aspirations of his old master, Lord Bernstein, quoting the advice he had been given while still at Granada: 'If you aim a little above people's heads they will reach up for it. If you aim for the sky they won't bother to look up.'

He was, however, rash enough to scorn any thoughts of producing a 'soap opera' in these early pre-transmission days. People would look to his station, he told the reporter, for quality. 'To get us on the hook of a day-to-day serial would be absolute death.' Before long he was going on record saying that, of course, Yorkshire TV would be taking Lord Bernstein's soap-operatic *Coronation Street* on the basis that you do not reject a winning formula; and, even later, he would preside over the daily rural ritual of *Emmerdale Farm* – the spirit of Grace Archer resurrected on television.

But all of this lay in the future. His immediate concerns were to satisfy Lord Hill and the men in the ITA headquarters opposite Harrods that their faith (for it could never be described as anything more tangible) in their franchise holder was justified. To this end, he even changed the name of his company from Telefusion Yorkshire to Yorkshire Television Network. Some quirk of reasoning persuaded Lord Hill's authority that the original title smacked too much of the commercial aspect. Telefusion, the northern-based television rentals firm, were a major share holder in Ward Thomas's conglomerate. Commercial television must not be seen to be commercial: Norman Collins's pioneer strategy in christening the authority still prevailed.

Towards the end of 1967, work began in Kirkstall Road, Leeds. Alas, it soon became evident to the two dozen or so top executives whom Ward Thomas had assembled to bring his new station into being that having building land ear-marked and blue-prints to hand are vastly different from having programmes – successful or otherwise – on the air. Compared with the smooth operation being prepared at London Weekend – give or take a technicians' labour dispute or so – matters fell little short of mayhem in the former trouser factory which served as their headquarters while Messrs Costain & Sons raced against transmission time. Sidney Bernstein's six-month miracle amid the wastelands of Manchester was not being matched in Leeds. High winds caused the collapse of the massive new aerial mast built out on the moors to serve the new empire, and many among the new recruits took it as an ill-omen for the future. For not a few of these their fears were well-founded so

183

far as personal careers were concerned. At this point, however, it was not so much a question of keeping one's job as of defining it.

The opening network transmission, it has to be said, represented a considerable *coup*: a live outside broadcast of the 1968 England–Australia Test Match from Headingley. Given not so much the Yorkshireman's love of the sport as the BBC's virtual monopoly on these hallowed occasions, then the event was not without its historic significance in television terms. It also gave some outward indication of how, among Yorkshire's faceless backers, was one Kerry Packer, the Australian tycoon who was much later to use international cricket to further his own ambitions in television empire-building. What Packer eventually did to Australian television and the sport in general by his sponsored TV matches was to make Yorkshire's foray into monopoly-busting look small beer indeed, but in its time it served its term.

Meanwhile, back at the clothing factory, all was not nearly so sunny. Whatever key posts Ward Thomas named in answer to the ITA's exhaustive questionnaire, in practice, the men who converged eventually on Leeds in effect carved out their own niches. John Fairley, who was to bring such acclaim to Yorkshire with his documentaries on vagrant teenagers and Rampton mental institution (and to be sacked for his pains at the height of his success), gradually moved in to annex the Current Affairs Department as his own without any formal appointment being made. This may explain the rather low £12,000 + annual salary he was receiving, quoted as late as 1979 when Paul Fox (of whom we shall hear much more shortly) announced the parting of the ways. Fairley had come to Yorkshire as a producer-director in Ward Thomas's early bulk-buying spree. He virtually invented his own area of responsibility.

'Occasionally he [the head of department] would issue orders which nobody heeded and John went on doing more or less what he felt inspired to do, like the rest of us,' one of the new-boy contemporaries recalls. 'Eventually the poor man took the hint; after six months or so we never saw him again. It was very like schoolboys ganging up on a chosen victim, I suppose. All very childish, looking back. But they were unreal days indeed. We just decided that the man Ward Thomas had appointed to that particular job wasn't up to it and we were, so we went about our business and ignored him.

'The only trouble was that we had become executive producers without a formal appointment and without our salaries being altered. But it was some time before anyone rocked the boat by

184

asking for their position to be formalized. I expect that Ward Thomas allowed the *laissez-faire* to continue because it was saving him so much money.'

In this way Yorkshire's programme planning evolved rather than was given shape. The man who had brought it into being did little to regularize the general haphazardness, perhaps – as is suggested – to save money. On the other hand, the situation could have been calculated to keep his people on their toes. Yorkshire has never been a station where job security is counted as a prime attraction. From the top to the bottom, heads have rolled with regularity, and the swiftness of the axe has been the hallmark of the execution.

Stuart Wilson, for example, was invited to share a short-hop business trip in his boss's flashy executive jet. He boarded the plane, a formidable lynch-pin of the organization; by the time the undercarriage was lowered for landing, he was without a job. Mr Ward Thomas, it appears, has not lost his reliance on the aeroplane as a machine for shooting down a suspected foe; not for nothing does he sport the DFC. There is something to be said for the gambit: he has the chosen victim entirely at his mercy until the plane lands, the unfortunate being hardly likely to jump out as a means of avoiding the issue (and Ward Thomas is reputedly not the sort to provide his passengers with psychological parachutes in such emergencies). Today Wilson runs a chain of extremely successful sports shops in the Yorkshire area, and is among those campaigning actively for a Fourth Channel alternative to the IBA.

In 1973, Donald Baverstock, the former BBC whizz-kid who became Yorkshire's original powerful programme controller, also departed, in greatly different circumstances but to similar public surprise. 'I had to ask myself whether I really saw myself doing the same job in three years' time, which would be the same as being there for ten years,' said the mercurial Baverstock, putting the best light possible on his resignation. He had, to say the least, become an unpredictable asset to Yorkshire, and possibly Ward Thomas was being no more than honest when he commented: 'I suppose I know better than anybody else the enormous amount of creative pressure which has been required of Donald in the past six years, and having discussed the decision with him I fully understand his reasons for wanting a change.'

By this time, however, Ward Thomas had become adept at accepting resignations in the manner of a benefactor allowing a protégé to go on to higher things. Syd Colin, brought in to master mind his pet Light Entertainment Department, had made his exit stage left even earlier. By January 1970, Mr Colin could only list such mediocre attainments as *Mr Digby Darling*, starring Sheila Hancock and Peter Jones, *Inside George Webley*, with Roy Kinnear, and an unlikely series featuring Bruce Forsyth. Reviewing his short stay at Leeds, Mr Colin charitably was moved to comment: 'It was a hard haul but I enjoyed it. Now I want to return to writing.'

The blame for the failure of Yorkshire TV's ambitions to become the light entertainment king of commercial television Colin put firmly on the networking arrangements, which, as we have seen elsewhere, proved to be the graveyard of Lord Hill's hopes to alter the image of ITV. It was the entire system which needed an overhaul, declared Colin as a parting shot. 'When we produced the Bruce Forsyth series it was scattered at different times throughout the network. I worked it out that a keen fan with a bicycle could have seen it six or seven times a week by moving from area to area. This is a state of affairs to no one's advantage and it is a serious drawback to a new company trying to make its way.

Such shows were costly to produce and were, by their nature, directed at national rather than regional viewing. They should therefore, Colin claimed, have been shown at a uniform time throughout the country. It was the old story. On the Network Programme Committee, he with the loudest voice is listened to most respectfully. And not for nothing has Lord Grade been heard to admit: 'Even when I whisper, I shout.' Syd Colin's fruitless efforts to establish Yorkshire's comedy programmes across the nation had not found favour with the man who, more than any other, put the word 'business' into 'showbusiness' where commercial television was concerned.

The departure of Syd Colin was not, however, the first indication that Lord Hill's ambitions for Yorkshire were, from the start, being kept airborne on little more than a wing and a prayer by Ward Thomas and his crew. As early as June 1969, there was gloomy talk of a deal between Anglia and his own company; Lord Thomson's oft-repeated incantation about the magical money-spinning properties in commercial television soon required more base metal before it worked at Leeds. The collapse of the 680-foot transmitter on Emley Moor, of course, was the worst of luck, an unmitigated disaster. It set them back not only in time but in cash estimated at between £500,000 and £1 million. In a desperate effort to cut costs, the board itself at Yorkshire determined all the departmental budgets – hardly a popular move with heads of departments trying to establish themselves. The discussions with Anglia were aimed at rationalizing production outgoings.

'A full-scale merger is not on the cards,' declared Ward Thomas bravely. Nevertheless, the talks, so early in the wake of the franchise redistribution, were held with 'the full knowledge of the ITA'. In other words, they had their blessing. It seems evident that there were forces afoot moving stealthily if not more actively to try to squeeze the newcomers out from the prime network hours – as they had with LWT. In their own interest, once again, the ITA was forced into the position of playing mother hen to a chick it had hatched, to protect it at all costs. Although it was a private company which therefore did not have its shares quoted, the unofficial price had taken a mighty tumble. And nothing prods the ITA into action as much as a slump in their franchise-holders' profits. As late in the day as 1980, angry questions were being asked in Parliament on this very topic when, inexplicably, the IBA calmly handed back a massive percentage of the levy on the grounds that the companies had been having a rather lean time; and this after profits had shown a 29 per cent leap to a record £320 million!

A decade earlier, in 1970, Lord Hill's successor at the ITA, Lord Aylestone, was attempting to do much the same thing, having been left holding Lord Hill's squawling babies. At that time, between £29 million and £30 million were being creamed off their advertising revenue; and with the advent of colour television staring them in the face, panic set in. Hence the ITA begging bowl and Lord Aylestone's assumption of the role of Cassandra, prophesying the end of regional television as it existed and the enforced mergers of Yorkshire and Anglia, Scottish TV and Grampian, Granada and Harlech. Privately, however, many ITA members admitted that they had cried wolf too often in the past in their attempts to keep their fledglings under control. Considering how rapidly and how high company profits were seen to soar, the government would find it very difficult to help them to feather their nests any further at this stage. In the event, Yorkshire effectively merged with neighbouring Tyne-Tees under the banner of the newly formed Trident company.

The end of any cash crisis at Leeds was effectively signalled by the spring of 1972. It was announced that the new chairman of the Trident parent company was to be Mr (later Sir) James Hanson, a man whose name in the City had become synonymous with vast and fast profit. Hanson had, ironically, just been defeated in his £38 million bid for Richard Costain when he took over the chair of the company they had supplied with its chief ammunition. Trident, again with the blessing of the ITA, controlled not only Yorkshire but the neighbouring Tyne-Tees regional station, a situation which would not be smiled upon so sweetly by the time Ward Thomas was defending his holdings.

The new chairman was cut in an altogether more flamboyant mould than was his managing director. He was a favourite figure in gossip columns through his liaisons with beautiful women, not least with Audrey Hepburn. The days of his engagement to her had been meticulously kept count of by the popular press. His money came from his family inheritance. Largely unknown outside his native Yorkshire in his earlier days, he and his father Robert ran one of the country's largest lorry-dealers. From this he moved into the new-style holding company business, which peaked during the property boom of the late 1960s. When others, like his partner John Bentley, found themselves out-stripped by their own assets, he survived spectacularly. By the time he emerged as chairman of Trident, his own company – Hanson Trust – had grown into a sprawling conglomerate, taking in property, building material concerns, construction and transport.

The City regarded him as a man with the Midas touch, and he seldom failed to live up to their expectations, despite the rather haphazard basis on which his business grew. He had inherited his father's flair for buying firms cheaply and, in the words of one City expert, 'spitting out the bits which did not fit into his operation'. His interest in commercial television was, in the first instance, merely as yet another fine investment on his own doorstep, though, as a man of the world, and having close associations with at least two of its most beautiful actresses, he was not slow to seize the ready access television gave to influence as well as money.

Less than two years after his appointment as chairman of Trident, he was announcing half-yearly pre-tax profits of £2,757,000 – an increase of almost half a million over the previous six months. On top of this, Trident could face the future with liquid assets in cash and short-term deposits of some £5,700,000. Lord Aylestone had indeed been crying wolf on behalf of his companies back in 1970, to judge by this buoyancy at Trident's headquarters. No director or

188

shareholder could complain if their tall (6-foot 4-inch) elegantly dressed captain was to be seen almost as regularly strutting the decks of his £700,000 267-ton yacht *Boule Dogue* in St Tropez with his family as he was to be found in the headquarters of Yorkshire TV.

Like his partner, Ward Thomas, he had a love of personalized executive jets and helicopters; but, socially, he aimed to fly higher. An avid fox-hunter and former master of fox hounds of the Grove and Rufford Hunt, his home life embraced a picturesque country house in Berkshire, a Belgravia apartment and a sumptuous house in Palm Springs. Like his homesteads, his business also spread across the Atlantic, some two thirds of his holdings being reckoned to be in the United States. Moreover, he had the dubious honour of inclusion in Sir Harold Wilson's notorious 'lilac' resignation honours list, though, it must be added, he was hardly acquainted with Lady Falkender, who, it was subsequently claimed, was the hand that held the pen when the list was made. Nor had Sir James ever made any bones over his unswerving devotion to capitalism; no millionaire socialist he.

Shortly before his knighthood, however, his shoulder was tapped in quite another way at Trident. In one of those surprise low-key press announcements which have pitted the history of Yorkshire Television, it was revealed that Hanson was stepping down as chairman. Into his shoes stepped his deputy chairman and managing director, Gwyn Ward Thomas. At the age of fifty-two, Ward Thomas was now in effective control of a powerful and highly successful network station and a regional station as well as a subsidiary called Tritel which dealt with 'non-TV programme matters' such as the group's rental interests in Australia.

Again the *Financial Times*, recording the change-over at the top of this multi-million pound consortium, was careful not to alarm investors. 'The change-over (Hanson is to stay on the Board and retain his substantial shareholding) is more in recognition of past policy coming to fruition than any new policy departure,' said their 'Men and Matters' column tactfully in its leading story on 17 February 1976. Thus, once again, the picture was conjured up of Ward Thomas holding open the door to allow a hard-worked colleague the freedom to go on to higher things after a job well done. The impression was further enhanced in the obsequious 'Men and Matters' column.

Although Ward Thomas regards himself more as a commerce man than a creative man it was felt, when Trident was put together, that a corporate specialist was needed in an advisory capacity. Who better therefore than James Hanson – with his Yorkshire family background, his association with the Slater Walker stable (exemplified in his build-up of Hanson Trust) and his interest in show-biz related matters.

Since his 'interest in show-biz related matters' had been largely confined to his engagement to Miss Hepburn, his friendship with Jean Simmons and his patronage of the top showbusiness tailor Dougie Hayward, one is led to assume that the piece was calculated to put everything in the best possible light.

Within Yorkshire TV itself the question has always been: did he go or was he pushed? On the face of it, such a rich and powerful man would seem to have been more than a match for someone like Ward Thomas had there ever been any question of an open boardroom power struggle. Yet one must always remember Hanson's 'free-form management' style of operating: if it left his colleagues in management freedom to manoeuvre, it also left him vulnerable to those manoeuvres.

It has also been pointed out by those with little cause to admire Ward Thomas's ambitions that a man like James Hanson has little to gain by hanging on to a post such as chairman of Trident where a man like Ward Thomas has everything to gain by aspiring to it. A multi-millionaire with multifarious business interests around the world and a lavish social life on much the same scale can afford to bow out of the cut-and-thrust of television politics with good grace and a knighthood. 'Men and Matters', on the other hand, was being less than usually bland in describing the in-coming chairman as 'a dyed in the wool TV man'. They are another breed entirely.

In the meantime, at Yorkshire TV headquarters, there had arrived an even more formidable dyed in the wool TV man, Paul Fox, a tough, blunt-speaking ex-paratrooper who had also proved himself to be a highly creative as well as an ambitious character. It was little short of a bombshell when he defected to Yorkshire to replace his former colleague, Donald Baverstock. For Fox, as controller of BBC 1, had been one of their most competitive innovators. Then he was pipped at the post as BBC director of programmes by Alasdair Milne, a former colleague and rival in his days of spearheading the BBC's best current events programmes.

His chagrin at finding his way thus blocked in the BBC's promotion stakes was no secret. He said openly that the only job worth having at the BBC was the director-general's, and that this set-back in his steady climb through the ranks had effectively put paid to his ever attaining it.

Ward Thomas must have known the mettle of the man he invited to replace the rogue genius of Baverstock: someone with ambition to match his own, plus creative energy and the experience to back it. Fox's move was described by one associate as being 'like the managing director of Ford deciding to run a filling station'. And Fox's BBC colleagues professed themselves to be astonished at his decision to bury himself in the regions, putting it about that he must be doing it for the money. Ward Thomas cannot have entertained any such delusions. Fox had seen the possibilities he himself had seen at Yorkshire: a glittering prize.

Nor was Fox long in establishing his dominance, style and flair at his new station. As the profits rose under the chairmanship of James Hanson, so its reputation increased under the programme planning of Paul Fox. And, by the time Huw Weldon's job as managing director at the BBC fell vacant and Fox's name was touted as a possible contender, he let it be known publicly that he had no intention of leaving his adoptive company. 'I am delighted to stay,' he said. 'Money was not the prime factor in deciding to take a new job. I am very happy here.'

He soon had cause to be. Eight months after he made that statement, James Hanson had stepped aside, Ward Thomas had moved up and on, and he was appointed managing director as well as retaining his post as programme controller in a spirit very different to his former colleague Cowgill's attempt at the same feat at LWT. Yorkshire at last had a readily identifiable hand shaping its image. The man who had pushed the BBC well ahead of ITV in the battle for the viewers after he first took control of BBC 1 in 1967 was now well on the way to becoming a commercial mogul in his own right. His tough, competitive methods had not always found favour with the more Reithian sensitivities still surviving at the BBC. They were, however, exactly what Yorkshire was looking for.

Fox's flair for producing good-quality television which viewers enjoy puts him alongside the Bernsteins and the Grades in terms of popular achievement. Thanks largely to his influence, the company has won almost fifty awards for their output of drama, documentaries

191

and light entertainment. Their showing in the ratings has been equally impressive. That Fox is a working television man, someone who has risen through the ranks from being a BBC script-writer, enables him to command the respect of those who do not necessarily share his viewpoint.

When John Fairley's row broke it was with Trident, the parent company, not necessarily with Fox. Fairley had been campaigning actively for a redistribution of ATV's large area to rationalize the network system – an echo of Yorkshire's own earlier pleadings before the advent of their Tyne-Tees link-up. Trident, however, wanted no rocking of the ITV boat as the franchises came up for rescrutiny. It was inevitable that Ward Thomas should eventually choose between Trident's vested interests and John Fairley's plans for a new East Midland commercial TV area. And it was inevitable what that choice would be.

Fairley was thus relieved of his responsibilities as head of news, documentaries and current affairs, the department which had reflected so much glory on Yorkshire TV. 'We never felt it was wrong to lobby for improvements to the ITV system. We felt it was something we ought to be doing; it was only a campaign at the time. But there was no blazing row and we haven't been kicked out in the streets either,' said Fairley. With him went his colleague John Wulford. And their immediate boss, Paul Fox, eschewed the usually sugared announcement that had accompanied previous departures from Yorkshire. His statement was honest enough: 'Both men have known of the possibility for some time. Sadly their future is not with ITV. That is their choice, regrettably and inevitably they will have to be replaced. I am glad that both will remain with us as long as possible and continue working on programmes.'

Fairley's going, and the reasons for it, were, however, the first public indication of the opposition Ward Thomas could expect when his franchise came up for renewal. A workers' co-operative was being planned, and Yorkshire was among those licence-holders who would find themselves having to put their past record on the line in competition with the very men who had made that record: their own employees.

Sidney Bernstein was, in his day, very fond of speaking about co-operatives. The 1980 batch of franchise-bidders demonstrated exactly what a real co-operative would mean, especially to men like Ward Thomas whose association with the business is mainly confined to its commerce. They are in the position of the restaurateur abandoned by his chef, maître d'hotel and staff who have opened up a rival establishment down the road; it is no earthly use his advertising the old menu and service when the people who made it possible have gone into business on their own account.

Yorkshire's record of industrial relations has, from the outset, been unenviable. Leaving aside the boardroom musical chairs and executives' departures, their dealings with the men and women who supply the nuts and bolts of broadcasting has left much to be desired. Back in 1971, six minutes from the end of their successful drama series *Kate*, starring Phyllis Calvert and Colin Welland, viewers were astonished to find their screens filled with a chalked message on a studio blackboard. It read: 'Yorkshire Television have threatened to sack us. We are going on strike.' And they did. Screens went blank until the scheduled advertisements were networked. The dispute was between the Ward Thomas management and the Association of Cinematograph Television and Allied Trades members who refused to work overtime in a pay row. Whatever the rights or wrongs of the union's claims, the incident pin-pointed how low labour relations had sunk at Yorkshire. There was little loyalty or love to be lost.

The management had already made itself look ludicrous in the eyes of its employees and the public in their celebrated 'trouser suit row' when a ban on female office workers turning up for work in trouser suits led to a full-scale union confrontation. What sort of management in 1970, and representing the most modern medium of the age, could allow itself to take such an autocratic, Victorian stance? They were, of course, openly defied and ridiculed, and in the end the losers. The pattern – if the expression can be forgiven in this context – was set. Television technicians are not the most easy-going of people to handle; their disputes, restrictive practices, truculence and general unwillingness to assist the industry through its various stages of technical progress have tried the patience of more flexible men than those at Trident. But, when the BBC found their vital Christmas programmes held to ransom by production staff in 1978, the only ITV company to find itself in the same boat was Yorkshire. They were blacked out for the entire Christmas period over a productivity deal at an estimated cost to the company of £100,000 a day. More than £1 million was said to be lost in revenue.

The experience did not appear to have mellowed Ward Thomas's attitude towards creative people. Trident, in a move to present itself as a patron of the arts in the old Bernstein tradition, elected to sponsor the Old Vic Theatre Company in one of its London productions as the eve of the great franchise reshuffle dawned. Toby Robertson, the then artistic director of the Old Vic, sent them the script of the play he thought most appropriate for their patronage: a historical narrative about a forgotten soldier's mutiny out in the Empire.

A gala first night was arranged for the benefactors at Trident, and Mr and Mrs Ward Thomas sat next to Toby Robertson, who had been as effusive and ebullient as ever in his gratitude to them. As the play unfolded, the Ward Thomases held a whispered conversation. Before the curtain went down, Ward Thomas turned to his host and declared audibly: 'We are withdrawing our backing.' The play and its sympathies had obviously not pleased him.

'Toby was struck dumb,' reported one of his party, close enough to hear the exchange. 'I know Ward Thomas had been sent the script because I had it mailed myself months before he agreed to put the money up. You can imagine how we all felt. It was one first night I shall never, ever forget.'

The episode was never made public. The Old Vic Company were not about to raise the cry of 'Stinking fish!' while there was still hope that the play might run. And Trident did not want Yorkshire's reputation as a promotor of new drama to be damaged at such a critical stage. But this was more than an echo of Bernstein's ejector-button touch.

Those on whom the tactic has been practised seldom forgive. Unlike Kenneth Griffith, who felt Lew Grade's iron hand at ATV, or the producer Michael Darlow, who fell out with Sidney Bernstein in a censorship quarrel, few employees of Ward Thomas who have lost a battle with him have sustained any admiration.

23

Although men like Ward Thomas have not been content to remain on the periphery of the giant network operation, it should not be assumed that the regional backwaters are inhabited only by minnows. Many of the biggest fish find the rewards of a regional station greatly to their taste. Lord Thomson of Fleet, perpetrator of the celebrated phrase which has dogged commercial television throughout much of its history, was only expressing his honest delight at owning Scottish Television when he described his franchise as a licence to print money.

Thomson had already had practical experience of the rewards commercial television could bring, back in his native Canada. Besides his chain of radio stations and newspapers, he had also acquired the franchises for two television stations in Kingston and Peterborough, Canada, just as the shape of ITV was being formulated in the United Kingdom. He had only recently come by the ownership of the ailing but influential *Scotsman* when the British franchises were put out to tender, and, being the sort of man he was – someone who had prematurely vowed to become a millionaire before he was thirty – he instantly grasped the potential of consolidating his foothold in Scotland. Ironically, few native Scottish financiers could be persuaded to join him in his bid.

So Thomson went it, bold but alone. If ever there was someone with a carpet-bagger's instincts it was he. When he bought up the *Scotsman* he had declared jubilantly: 'We're in the big league now!'

But it was not until the profits from his television company started to pour in that anyone realized how big he intended his league to be. It is no exaggeration to say that, from Scottish TV alone, Thomson made himself a separate fortune to put alongside those he had already amassed in his single-minded pursuit of wealth back home in Canada.

It was this financial power-base, more than any other factor, which enabled him to buy himself the most respected paper in Britain, and possibly in the world: *The Times* of London. Twice he had been rebuffed by Lord Kemsley in his attempts to get his hands on the Kemsley Scottish newspaper interests. These negotiations, though unsuccessful, had at least established a close contact between the two men, and when the latter decided to sell off his holdings in the largest newspaper group in the country, it was to Thomson that he turned.

The deal took six weeks to complete, during which time Thomson installed himself in London at the Savoy Hotel and breakfasted each morning in a transport café on the other side of the Strand in Covent Garden. It was a typical idiosyncracy of the man who had risen from the humble origins of a Toronto barber's son and sustained himself through several reversals of fortune solely with the unshakeable belief that one day, somehow, he would be rich. He was, in fact, approaching the age when most men are contemplating retirement before he attained the goal he had set himself. Though he had impressive holdings in his homeland, he was not on the same standing as his fellow countryman, Lord Beaverbrook, either in fortune or influence.

It was to put himself there, in pursuit of this early visionary gleam, that he crossed the Atlantic. The *Scotsman* was the toehold he needed; Scottish TV was the real means to his end. With the television fortune he made north of the border, he was better placed than anyone else to take over *The Times* and the Kemsley empire and to rank himself at last among the press barons Beaverbrook, Rothermere and Kemsley. But whereas these men were watching with some dismay their empires diminish in terms of sales, Thomson's star was in the ascendant, thanks to the revenue flooding in from his admittedly lacklustre enterprise at Scottish TV.

By the time the House of Lords came to debate the future of Fleet Street in 1967, Roy Thomson was not only ennobled and among their ranks, he was also the central figure in the proceedings. Lord Arran, himself a newspaper director and controversial columnist, condemned Thomson as 'the rogue elephant of British newspapers' and likened his take-over of *The Times* to the prospect of having the Royal Navy bought up by Aristotle Onassis. Arran's deluge of abuse was in full flood when Thomson took his seat for the debate, having been delayed by the 175th Anniversary luncheon of the *Scotsman*, an event he had just cause to celebrate.

'His avowed intention is making money,' Lord Arran told the Lords, who have not on the whole been known to condemn the practice to a man. 'He owns 108 newspapers,' he continued.

'I own 140 newspapers,' interrupted the object of his ire mildly.

For once Lord Arran was guilty of understatement, but undeterred, he continued demanding to know: 'Is Lord Thomson going to go on buying newspapers? Is he going to own, in the end, the whole British press? Is no government, Socialist, Liberal or Tory, ever going to stop him?' demanded the infuriated Arran, adding, for good measure, the accusations that his adversary was 'a compulsive buyer' and 'politically sexless'.

In both these assumptions, if in nothing else, Arran was probably right. Thomson bought where he saw the best opportunities and interfered remarkably little once he had made his killing. He enjoyed the means of power rather than its practice. As an employer, he could be the very model of sweet reasonability so long as things were run successfully. It was his fellow press baron, the late Lord Rothermere, who leapt to his defence in the Lords' debate. 'Lord Thomson will never take over or buy a newspaper which he is not absolutely certain he can save and make into a paying proposition,' Rothermere told the peers, adding to a roar of laughter, 'I know that, because I myself tried to sell him one.'

To the Lords, too, Thomson presented himself as a humane figure who hardly qualified for the odium heaped upon him by Lord Arran. He pointed out that he had staked his own personal fortune in Britain to make a success of his acquisition – adding, with his own brand of verbal Canadian dry ginger: 'Personally I don't think that will be necessary. And I'm going to make darn sure it isn't!'

In all of this he was right. He had used his own money to breathe fresh life into a dying industry; he did have the best interests of British journalism at heart, in so far as they coincided with his own ambitions. However, the far more thorny topic of the easy money to be made from a television franchise scarcely occupied their Lordships' minds at all. Yet, by that time, even commercial

197

television's old arch-enemy, the Beaverbrook organization, was forced to realize how much more lucrative a television station was – and how much freer from Fleet Street's cut-throat competition tactics – than a national newspaper. Lord Rothermere had rued the day he sold off his stake in the earliest consortium more or less on a whim. He had quickly rectified this momentary aberration by buying Associated Newspapers a sizeable share in Southern Television, the Southampton-based company over-lorded for much of its earlier life by the irascible and unloved Sir John Davis, head of the Rank Organization.

The Kemsleys, too, had lived to regret the day when they backed out so peremptorily from the Winnick–Collins consortium. The fact that Lord Thomson, with his television revenue to back him, was able to take over their once mighty newspaper empire spoke eloquently for itself, though Maurice Winnick, permanently embittered by their perfidy, could not be expected to draw much comfort from the fact.

In the year following the House of Lords' debate on the press, the ITA came belatedly to look into its own house and examine what holdings the press lords had managed to buy in the new medium. Their attitude on the subject was as quaintly ambivalent as it always has been. On the one hand, Lord Hill was urging more publishing interests on the new London Weekend consortium; on the other, he made it perfectly clear that the franchise for Scottish TV would only be renewed if Lord Thomson shed a considerable portion of his holdings. Many had prophesied that Thomson would lose his licence altogether as an arbitrary punishment for his embarrassing public gloating and his station's unimpressive track record. In the event, the ITA delivered no more than a smack on the wrist. Through S. G. Warburg, Thomson was forced to put 1,300,000 non-voting 'A' shares on the market, giving preference to Scottish buyers. The sale brought his stake down to 25 per cent, the maximum the ITA would tolerate.

The Annan Committee were also to emphasize that close control must be kept over newspapers extending their power and propping up their profitability by buying their way into commercial television. In fact, the committee members' disquiet at the whole system of diversification in this big money-making sphere was reflected in an unusually tough edict issued belatedly from the IBA itself as the new franchises came up for redistribution and the companies' profits soared to their record £320 million (embarrassing riches in view of the BBC's impoverished financial state and ratings victories):

> The Authority had adopted the rule that it would not want to see more than about one-third of a company's funds used outside television [declared the authority in their report]. But the consequences of the decision to diversify must be the responsibility of the company. The company has its own job to do in explaining the moves which are sometimes called taking money out of TV [it added rather ambiguously]. The company has also to convince the IBA – probably in competition with other applicants – when it makes an application for a new programme contract that it is financially and managerially in good shape to continue to hold a TV contract. Among the matters which will be of concern to the Authority is the general attitude of a company to the TV operation. Do they organize their affairs so as to give the clear impression both within and outside the system that their hearts and minds lie in broadcasting as a creative medium rather than a business enterprise?

The implication in the statement is obvious. The plain fact had at last dawned upon even the protective IBA that too many of their present licence-holders were putting in the least effort to reap the most rewards, especially in the smaller regions. Despite the inflated salaries they could offer to lure talent away from the BBC, their creative energy was often second rate and their training schemes lamentable by comparison.

Southern Television, to take a random example with which, as a viewer, I am more familiar, is often conspicuous by its under-achievements. Its current affairs programmes are often smugly parochial, its contribution to original creative output seldom more than negligible. This was the company chaired by the man one might have expected to contribute more than most to the television industry: John Davis, the aggressive, autocratic boss of the huge Rank Organization. Yet, by the time Davis was in charge of Rank's fortunes, its great film-making days were over and Lord Rank merely a memory. It had subsided into a giant financial conglomerate which marketed leisure activities as others manufacture fried chicken or factory furnishings.

Sir John's reign at Rank is remembered now largely through his inglorious boardroom battle with his chief executive, Graham Dowson, in which Davis scored a pyrrhic victory and Dowson received a £150,000 golden handshake. It was the beginning of the end for the man who had started a spectacular financial career as an accountant in a Welsh coal and steel combine and moved into the entertainment business by becoming chief accountant and company secretary to Oscar Deutsch, founder of the Odeon cinema chain. He became chairman of Rank in 1961, and steered its fortunes until its Rank Xerox copying machine interests were making no less than 90 per cent of the company's £62 million profits, while the leisure side, covering cinemas, bingo halls, bowling alleys, motorway service stations, hotels and Bush and Murphy television manufacturers, remained very much a poor relation. Sir John, in this respect, was the exact opposite of the IBA's ideal example of licence-holders, with 'their hearts and minds in broadcasting as a creative medium rather than a business enterprise'.

His row with his managing director back in 1975, however, effectively ended his days both at Southern and at Rank itself. The City was mortified by his conduct in the Dowson affair, especially as the row seemed to have more to do with the two men's domestic entanglements than any boardroom policy. Dowson had abandoned his mistress of many years and suddenly married a much younger woman. His jilted companion happened also to be the best friend of Felicity Rutland, the lady with whom Sir John at that time shared his Chelsea flat and his 600-acre Surrey estate and moated house, Crowhurst Place. Miss Rutland, a former débutante, later became Davis's sixth wife – though the reference books always cut the total by two and omit any mention of the children of these unions. By then, however, he had agreed to step down and his days of power were numbered.

At Rank, he gained the nickname of 'The Executioner', having reputedly been responsible for over seventy sackings of senior executives. Amid the mounting pressure for him to stand aside as chairman, personal affection for him was markedly absent.

'Perhaps the real trouble was that John was never a cinema man. He often said he wanted to sell the chain and flirted with getting rid of Pinewood,' a former colleague reported on the man who had inherited the mantle of Lord Rank, the British film pioneer, and had control of a rich TV area at his finger-tips.

His departure two years after the Dowson débâcle was marked by little but relief. The beautiful timber-framed house at Crowhurst, which had been his pride and joy, was sold for £225,000 to the pop-singer turned impresario, Adam Faith. Artistically he left no mark whatsoever on the television station which he had retired from in the previous year. Sir John was, first and foremost, a money mogul.

A no less charismatic character with a life-style as palatial as Sir John's (though with only half his tally of wives) also reinforced a vast personal fortune by moving into regional television. Peter Cadbury, heir to the chocolate family, built an empire of his own in the giant Keith Prowse ticket agency, of which he was chairman and managing director when he moved into the realm of commercial television. He, it will be remembered, was the television chief who was so incensed by the criticism made of ITV by the Pilkington Committee that he went to the extravagant lengths of burning an effigy of the offending report. The flamboyance of the gesture was typical of his quixotic style. Quaker educated in the family tradition, he vows that he does not believe in inherited wealth.

Cadbury, like Ward Thomas, distinguished himself in the air before finding his feet in commerce and television. He saw brief wartime service with the Fleet Air Arm before becoming a dashing test pilot. Nor, again like Ward Thomas, did he ever relinquish his passion for flying. After his business interests had made him executive chairman of Westward TV, he planned to operate his own commercial airline, Westward Air (but abandoned the notion), besides boasting his own private airfield on the country estate at the elegant Queen Anne house at Preston Candover near Basingstoke. There, in a hangar which could accommodate five aircraft at any one time, was always to be found an impressive array of planes plus his £100,000 helicopter. 'I find my private aircraft useful for ferrying the children, the dogs and friends around the place,' he once explained breezily, pointing out that he also needed an aircraft to commute daily to his Plymouth headquarters.

Anyone still misguided enough to assume that the small stations go only to the small fry only had to look at how Cadbury fought to hold on to his franchise as the 1980 deadline approached. At least two major consortia were built up to unseat him in strictest secrecy, lured on, no doubt, by Westward's announcement of a £9,120,000 advertising revenue the previous year. Cadbury's hopes of winning through were at first encouraged by an IBA survey of the regional stations which voted his company the 'most friendly', only to be daunted by the assessment that it was also the 'least professional' in

201

presentation. 'We are very much a local station,' said Cadbury, considerably ruffled by the latter accusation. 'I don't think our programmes would be at all suitable for the metropolitan area.' But he did concede that 'we do sacrifice a certain amount of professionalism for friendliness'.

By now Cadbury was ensconced in similar luxury to his Berkshire life-style on the 1,000-acre Lyneham estate at Yealhampton, just outside Plymouth and adjoining the property of one of the chief contenders for the South-West franchise, Simon Day. Day had, according to Cadbury, made the previous owner of Lyneham 'an offer he couldn't refuse' when he got wind that his arch-rival was bidding for the property. But Cadbury eventually won that particular tussle. 'I never go into anything without a hope of winning,' he once remarked, looking back over a chequered career which has included contesting Stroud for the Liberal Party and practising at the Bar from 1946 to 1954. 'I've never forgotten the thrill of getting a man off I knew to be guilty,' he reflected, showing a glimpse of the competitive streak which has marked out much of his life.

It began as far back as he can remember, but he dates it to the time when he was out walking with his father as a small boy and noticed a flock of wild ducks flying in perfect formation overhead. 'Who decides which duck flies in point?' he asked. His father replied: 'There are leaders among ducks as there are leaders among men,' and his son, Peter, knew instantly that, duck or man, he wanted to be that leader. 'You must be ambitious, to want to succeed and improve on what you're doing,' he explains. 'I never go into anything without a hope of winning. From school onward – wanting to be head of school, wanting to be captain of cricket, even at Stroud, surrounded by my Liberal supporters, I thought I'd certainly win.'

Interestingly enough, when he took on the ailing Keith Prowse Agency and put it back on its feet and into enviable profit virtually single-handed ('I did everything myself, down to interviewing the typists'), he reserved part of its sprawling office space for Westward Television. 'I *knew* I'd get the contract, though there were twenty-nine competitors,' he said later. Such men are not easily ousted.

Cadbury virtually sidled into the hurly-burly of commercial television, merely to guard his family's vested interests. His own laconic description of the events which turned him, eventually, into one of ITV's regional moguls has a disarming innocence about it which

202

entirely captures the flavour of those early pioneering days. However the ITA visualized their role as guardians of the medium's respectability, there is a Klondike image of hustling speculative enterprise in the manner the nuggets were mined.

'My Uncle Lance rang me up and said the *News Chronicle* was a member of the successful syndicate for the Tyne-Tees North-East ITV station,' says Cadbury cheerfully. 'Before that I really knew very little about television. He asked if I would look after their interests as the *News Chronicle* representative on the board of the new company.'

His qualifications, so far as the Cadbury family were concerned were sufficient unto the day. 'I'd taken over Keith Prowse in 1954, and before that I was at the Bar. Keith Prowse had been very successful and he asked me as the only person the family knew of who knew about the entertainment business, which he regarded as rather suspect anyhow. So I met up with George and Alfred Black.'

George and Alfred Black?

'They were other shareholders. They were agents, I imagine, weren't they?' recalls Cadbury with breezy self-assurance. 'I think they had their dance routine act; they were a variety act, I think, then they had an agency and then they had a stake in the syndicate. Sydney Box represented the films in that syndicate and the four of us set up Tyne-Tees. We started with nothing except a licence.'

It is hardly how the ITA, or the later IBA, like to imagine their precious franchises being distributed. Nor, presumably, do they welcome such enthusiastic assurances as Cadbury's assertion that 'I asked my uncle, as I was doing all the hard work, if there was any reason why I shouldn't have a small, perhaps even modest, stake in the enterprise, because I saw people being issued with £1 shares which were promptly valued at £80 each.'

From a personal point of view, his argument was irrefutable. During the mêlée of hiring staff, designing and equipping the entire operation in Newcastle in time to go on the air on schedule, Cadbury was receiving a director's fee of a straight £300 a year. A man of his spirit would have been a fool not to have cut himself in on a bigger slice of the action. And, having acquired a taste for what ITV offered a businessman of his ingenuity, he smartly began looking around for a station of his own. In the event he stayed with Tyne-Tees, representing his family's interests on the board, only as long as it took to get the station operational and to find pastures new but equally lucrative on his own account.

Having failed to deal himself in on the Anglia franchise – the next one on offer – he sallied forth to the West Country in the same spirit as Sidney Bernstein journeyed north to Manchester, but with a slightly different *modus operandi*.

'I went down to the West Country with just a copy of *Who's Who* and a road map. Nothing else', he chuckles. 'And I had an introduction to Sir John Carew Pole who was a great friend of my father's.'

Sir John also happened to be the Lord-Lieutenant of Devon. And it was with the aid of his *Who's Who* and family connections that he approached over two hundred men and women of influence in the area to become shareholders in his enterprise. His interpretation of 'people of influence' was broad and, given the regional nature of the venture, wise. Village midwives, postmasters and policemen were all involved in the operation to give it an authentic local flavour. As luck so often has it in success stories like this, in the middle of his tough negotiations Rediffusion announced that they had turned their depressing deficit into a multi-million pound bonanza. The tide had turned and recruitment was no longer any problem.

'People who had been reluctant to invest suddenly realized it was possibly a gold mine, and they started arguing between themselves as to having bigger shareholdings. So then we set up Westward and we got the licence,' he says. It was as simple as that.

For Cadbury, alas, it was not to be a happy-ever-after ending to his true-life fairy story. Yet, between the granting of the franchise and his own boardroom débâcle, the rewards have been rich from the £10,000 he paid for his original 5 per cent holding (the limit for everyone in the syndicate capitalized at £200,000). He himself admits that, at the time, he looked on the acquisition of a station merely as insurance for his Keith Prowse ticket agency. He also admits that, because the big fish were all biting at the bait Anglia was dangling, the small pool of the West Country was left wide open for his own consortium of the local butcher, baker and candlestick-maker.

Without Cadbury's connections with Prowse, of course, the station would never have got under way so cheaply or so soon. The agency provided the basic financial backing, staff and facilities needed to set up the operation. In Cadbury's own words: 'Keith Prowse was the sort of fairy godmother to Westward Television.' Soon, however, it became obvious that Cinderella needed no more magic to keep her at the ball; Westward's profits soared, its revenue rose steadily over the years until its chairman was talking of a £7 million turn-over prospect for the year that took them up to the new bidding. In the meantime, he had divested himself of his Keith Prowse holdings, selling them to Westward for £1 million, and then reselling them on behalf of his station shortly after for £1.5 million.

But, as the competition for the new franchises hotted up, so did the seat the mercurial chairman occupied. There had already been one palace revolution in which his fellow directors had voted him off the board, telling him, in effect, 'You have not been doing your job properly.' This he survived by brazening the whole matter out and threatening them with an extraordinary general meeting of shareholders which would call for *their* removal. The opposition cravenly collapsed.

Cadbury himself blames the entire business on the Iago-like intentions of his then managing director, Bill Cheevers. In the event it was Cheevers who went – in tears according to the victor – and Cadbury who stayed to collect the abject apologies of his rebellious board. 'I agreed to keep them on – rightly or wrongly. I think it was probably a generous offer to keep them on, but, in fact, I did because I felt that there'd been enough publicity about this to do the company no good. To have a new board of directors and to remove the existing board was not in the interests of the company and so I agreed, at their request, to allow them to stay on. Those who have not reached the age of seventy are still there.'

Time would prove that what he saw as a magnanimous gesture did not pay him dividends in loyalty. His opponents had been allowed to live and fight another day. Before the licences were back in the melting pot, Cadbury was again unseated. And this time *he* left the board meeting with tears in his eyes. A charge of wasting police time was hanging over the heads of himself and his wife at the time. He himself was complaining of being driven out of his magnificent estate because of police harassment. The ensuing embarrassment to a board defending its domain against some of the most fierce challenges in the franchise line-up proved too much for even Cadbury to withstand. In July 1980, refusing to say whether he jumped or was pushed, this high flyer vacated the pilot seat of Westward to Lord Harris. It was a bitter blow to someone who had entered ITV merely to keep an eye on the family shop. But he left his ex-colleague in no doubt that he would move heaven and earth to fight his way back and his past track-record proved this was no idle threat.

24

In solving the problem of who will take over the next batch of franchises, the IBA will also be considering who takes over the Fourth Channel. Against all Lord Annan's impartial and leisured recommendations aimed at breaking the duopoly of the BBC and ITV – which the committee found restricted rather than expanded the viewers' choice – the government have decided that the authority will have the responsibility for running it.

'A great opportunity will be missed if the Fourth Channel were seen solely in terms of extending the present range of programmes,' warned Annan, prompted by the writers, producers and directors who felt thwarted by the commercial requirements or personal idiosyncracies of their employers as well as the busybodying interference of the IBA.

The classic *cause célèbre* in station censorship was Kenneth Griffith's first documentary on Ireland for ATV. The Grade organization backed it financially, his idea being to produce a documentary on the life of the Irish patriot, Michael Collins, called *Hang Out Your Brightest Colours*. Griffith, a fiercely committed man to any subject that captures his imagination, felt passionately that viewers in England could not possibly understand the Irish question if they did not know the background to Irish history. With Antony Thomas as director, he set about tracing Collins's motivations and achievements.

'To the Irish, Collins is a hero every bit as great and glorious as

Wellington is to the English or Napoleon to the French,' says Griffith. On this basis, he made the film.

Significantly, Lord Grade did not even put the final product before the IBA for their comment. It was locked away and even Griffith himself now declares ruefully that he would find it extremely difficult to be granted a viewing if he were to ask today. There is no doubt that the IBA requested that the film should not be offered to them because of the inflammatory situation in Ireland. And Lord Grade, ever anxious to please, saw to it that neither he nor the board had their reputations singed by political controversy of this kind. The British Film Institute now hold a copy as part of their library of censored material.

If Lord Grade were acting from the highest motives, of course, the stench of personal censorship might be sweetened in this instance. It may remain odious to many that one man's taste is arbitrarily foisted upon so sensitive a medium, but then that has ever been so. That most public of bodies, the BBC, was itself for years dominated by the personality of one man, Lord Reith. Lord Grade had only to point out that, as he had paid for the film, it was his to do with as he pleased if it did not satisfy his expectations.

He did not put forward any such straightforward reasoning. In fact it became perfectly evident that his motives were lamentably self-interested. Griffith says that he was told by ATV: 'Our franchise is up for renewal.' This shabby excuse was all that was vouchsafed, and there is little reason to doubt that there was any higher motive in Lord Grade's actions.

'It would not be fair to say that Lord Grade acted in any other way than he saw fit,' Griffith told me. 'He has done a great deal of good for this country and I am sure that he felt the film was harmful. But it was an area largely outside his understanding. He is a patriotic man himself and I would be the last person to condemn him for being so.

'But I was extremely wounded by his subsequent behaviour towards me. When he was explaining to me the reasons for not showing my film – reasons which I understood even if I repudiated them – he offered me several very attractive posts within his organization. He never stopped being complimentary about my abilities, and if I had taken up any of the positions he offered me I would have been earning more than I had ever done in my life.

'What saddens me now is that I have been told directly by an ATV executive that I am now *persona non grata* there, that I would not be welcome in the building.

Yet what a strange contrast to all this ATV presented in 1980 as their franchise was about to come up for renewal yet again. Antony Thomas, the director Griffith has worked with on *Hang Out Your Brightest Colours*, found even greater notoriety with another 'factional' film, *Death of a Princess*. The political furore which erupted in the wake of ATV's screening of Thomas's reconstruction of the events surrounding the execution of a royal princess and her lover in Saudi Arabia are possibly without parallel in British television history.

The British Foreign Secretary, Lord Carrington, was forced to eat humble pie to the Saudi Arabians, important British exports were lost through a trade boycott, diplomatic relations were all but completely severed, and the repercussions reverberated in a ban being placed on education grants to Saudi Arabian women wishing to study abroad. Rightly or wrongly, the Saudi Arabians were mortified by what they interpreted as a grossly sensationalized attack on their way of life. The film had, indeed, represented women of the royal family using their limousines to cruise highways for sexual assignations. Not unnaturally, the ruling family took extremely personal offence at this particular section of Antony Thomas's portrait of life behind the Muslim veil. Would ATV have shown a similar insult to our own royal family, they asked, even if the moral behaviour of certain of its members left something to be desired? Why single out the Saudi Arabian princesses?

Antony Thomas, in reply, claimed that before transmission – indeed, during the course of its making – the script had been shown to 'a high-ranking minister' in Saudi Arabia and the producers had been assured that no diplomatic action would be taken. It was, said Thomas, on this advice that they proceeded. And, presumably, it was also on that advice that Lord Grade's company went ahead with the screening. If such an assurance had been given, it could not have been less reliable. Within hours of the film being shown, Lord Carrington was desperately trying to pour soothing waters on troubled oil. It was too late.

Of course, those who argued that Lord Grade's censorship of Kenneth Griffith's Irish film was a calculated smack in the face for free expression, could hardly blame ATV for showing Antony Thomas's Saudi Arabian enterprise. Screening it in the teeth of such heavyweight opposition might seem almost like an act of redemption.

208

But why? Why should the same organization on the one hand refuse to embarrass their watchdogs at the IBA by withholding one controversial documentary through self-confessed fear of losing their franchise and then adopt such a cavalier 'publish and be damned' attitude to an even more sensitive subject?

The conundrum opens up several worrying possibilities, one of which could be that Lord Grade's personal power within ATV has waned as he has concentrated his energies on film making. In which case, whose hand is now manipulating the massive powerbase he built up? Not that, for all his much-vaunted avuncular charm and winning ways, Lord Grade has proved himself to be a man who moves over or delegates real power readily. His organization has seen the rise of many ambitious young heirs-apparent, not least Robin Gill, once Lew's joint managing director. Brilliant and tough-minded, Gill was tipped by everyone as the man Lord Grade was grooming as his successor. Gill's fall from grace was even swifter and more unexpected than Val Parnell's. Having been treated almost like a son, he was dismissed by his mentor with a less than paternal 'pat' on the back. It reveals a side of Lew not often spoken of by his minions for reasons which must be obvious: in a precarious business like television, the fates are not readily tempted. But there is a saying at ATV which has a ring of gallows' humour: you can be walking down the corridors of power and not find that you've broken your leg until you reach the door. (*Sunday Times* profile by Nicholas Tomalin, 23 December 1968).

Lew's reported explanation of Gill's going was hardly fatherly. He let it be known that he considered that when his employees got too big for their boots it was time for them to walk on other people's carpets, not his. In other words, the lesson to Lew's heirs-presumptive is, never become too presumptive.

Yet, if the buck still rested on his own vast desk at ATV House when the Saudi crisis erupted, it represents a most confusing *volte-face* by a man known to go to almost any lengths not to offend anyone, especially anyone who matters. Almost anyone who mattered was offended in some way or another by *Death of a Princess*. Why did he allow such a calculated risk at such a stage in his company's fortunes? Indifference? Mischief? Lack of judgement? As a 'deeply patriotic' man who is delighted to remind people of his Queen's Awards for Industry, the loss of trade to Britain cannot have been a consequence he would willingly court in normal circumstances. Yet, though Parliament was in uproar at the news of large Saudi contracts being withdrawn from British firms, Lord Grade's feelings on the matter were never disclosed. Nor did the House of Lords hear a word of explanation from their noble member on this (or any other) vexed topic. The Baron Grade of Ealing has, at the time of writing, still to make his maiden speech.

Whatever one's views on the merits of the programme itself, the double standards operating at ATV must be disturbingly apparent. And, again, we are back to the troubled question of individual power being wielded within the commercial television set-up.

It would, of course, be unfair to depict Lord Grade as the sole culprit when it comes to inflicting erratic and quirky censorship on creative underlings. Lord Bernstein, that champion of free debate on television, was not above imposing similar restrictions on his programmes when he deemed it necessary, as many of his employees can testify. Michael Darlow is a former Granada producer who has been one of the main lobbyists for a truly independent Fourth Channel in the way that Norman Collins first intended when he spoke of a wholesome alternative. To men like Darlow, it seems invidious to have one's work sieved through the commercial or artistic considerations of others whose pre-television training has been confined to flying aeroplanes, running cinemas or booking variety acts. The butcher, the baker or the candlestick-maker could equally easily find themselves in control of a network as things are arranged within the IBA.

Michael Darlow, for instance, felt the Bernstein brand of discrimination when he made a documentary called *Johnny Cash in San Quentin*, a study of the effect of a concert by the ex-convict singer on the inmates of that prison. Darlow had allowed his cameras to linger on the special buttons and the prison insignia of Death Row. Granada objected to the shots being shown over a sound-track of Cash's harsh musical commentary sung from the executioner's point of view. Bernstein tacitly allowed the company's, i.e. his own, will to prevail. Darlow removed his name from the credits and himself from Granada.

In the meantime, he has dedicated a great deal of energy to freeing the medium from needless controls of vested interests. 'I cannot say that I have found myself victimized by my campaigns, though,' he once told me when the battle for the Fourth Channel was at its height. But he has not been helped by it, either.

The new Conservative government which came to power after the

1979 General Election threw out Annan's main proposals for the reorganization of the IBA; they decided not only to perpetuate the body but to make it largely responsible for operating the new Fourth Channel. However, Darlow and his campaigners continued to fight and to gain considerable concessions in the way of freedom for the artist and of choice for the viewer. To subject the Fourth Channel to the restrictions that have grown up around the IBA would be as futile as perpetuating the present duopoly. To reiterate Anthony Smith's statement to Lord Annan: 'If I am free to say anything except the thing I want to say, then I am not free.'

The affair of *Death of a Princess* may well be looked on in some quarters as a blow struck for just that freedom. But, besides the issues it raised about Lord Grade's enigmatic personal role within ATV, it also spotlights the complete muddle within the IBA itself on such matters. This is the body who, in a period of nine months, interfered on trivial minor matters no fewer than ten times in the various programmes produced by Thames's *This Week* team alone. In this they are in the stranglehold of their own good intentions. But what were their communications with Lord Grade's minions on the matter of Antony Thomas's film? Again, the wall of secrecy obscures the details of their dealings. But the outcome was clear: it was screened as filmed with the IBA shrugging their shoulders and murmuring piously about the proven integrity of ATV. When the touch-paper was lit and the rocket went up, the IBA had effectively retired from the scene.

Interestingly enough, the Danes, who on other occasions are wont to take broadminded freedoms to a level of excess, formed an entirely different view when their national television was offered the film by ATV (no doubt to help redress the balance of our exports in the wake of Saudi sanctions). Their powers-that-be decided that parts of the film were 'highly sensationalized' and promptly refused it a showing.

Now these are only contrasting opinions on one rather sore topic. The rights and wrongs of the case can, and no doubt will, be debated endlessly. But it has vividly exposed the power of the medium and the totally unpredictable whims of the men who run it. The men in ATV House, being in the business of commercial television, can surely have been only too alive to the commercial possibilities in Antony Thomas's film. By comparison, the martyrdom of an obscure Irish patriot could hardly rank with illicit royal love and summary death in the desert as a hot-selling property. If it had, the toothless watchdogs at the IBA would almost certainly have had their bark muzzled in the name of free expression and Lord Grade would have found some persuasive reasons against suppressing his company's own product.

For all Lord Annan's generous praise of men like Lords Grade and Bernstein, at the end of the day. They must be as much concerned with the profitability of their company as are the faceless men in pinstripe trousers. And this, as we have seen, is no less a prime consideration with the IBA. The lamentable lack of resolve among the members of the IBA over the London Weekend fiasco, their sudden policy of non-interference over the *Death of a Princess* affair set against their previous history of petty restrictions elsewhere are, in themselves, a catalogue which must raise the most serious doubts on their fundamental duties. Lord Annan recommended drastic restructuring of the IBA itself, and there can be few who give serious thought to the future of television who would not agree with him.

Back in 1967, when Lord Bernstein was champing at the bit against the then ITA restrictions on political debate, Bernard Levin was moved to comment in the *Daily Mail*:

> It is the ITA, under a succession of lamentable chairmen, that has forbidden the companies to do anything that might offend the Government or any potential government; that has made them knuckle under to the outrageous (and legally unenforceable) demands of the political parties at election-time; that has repeatedly stifled controversy at the behest of pressure groups; that has made even duly balanced comment tamer than it need be.
>
> Under the present ITA chairman [Lord Hill], this process has reached its nadir.

Of course, Mr Levin was not necessarily arguing for the kind of affront to 'potential governments and pressure groups' which Antony Thomas's film provoked. He was commenting on the authority's general ineptitude at keeping their own house in order while imposing quite unnecessary restrictions on free debate.

'The ITA is now engaged on the redistribution of the television contracts,' Levin concluded his *Daily Mail* article in 1967. 'But who shall redistribute the ITA?'

It is a question still to be answered. What the *Death of a Princess* affair did expose more glaringly than anything else was the dangerous anomaly built into the franchise system. On the one hand, the IBA is supposed to be responsible for its actions to the

212

government, yet, when a programme capable of adversely affecting the government's foreign policy and the export market is screened by one of its most powerful licence-holders, it stands by and answers to no one. This must, in one sense, smack at the roots of our democracy as hard as it strikes a blow for free speech. For it was the government, not Lord Grade or ATV, who was elected to conduct our diplomatic policies in these delicate and troubled times. If we feel that there has been a gross misconduct of those policies, we are at liberty to vote them out of office when the time comes. But who votes Lew Grade out of office if he makes a blunder of international magnitude? Certainly not the IBA, judging on past form.

Again the contracts are up for renewal, and again the industry is sunk in its own eternal dilemmas brought upon it by the series of laws, accidents and personalities from which it has evolved. Is this therefore really all we can hope for from the new Fourth Channel: more of the same for the majority and more licences to print money for the few; more barons, more men in pinstripe trousers?

It would surely be a wanton waste of opportunity if this were so. Mr Levin's question remains as pertinent as ever. Must it be repeated twenty years after he penned it, when the next contracts come up for renewal? Who, indeed, shall redistribute the IBA; and, more to the point, when?

Further Reading

The Mirror in the Corner by Peter Black, Hutchinson, 1971

With An Independent Air by Howard Thomas, Weidenfeld and Nicolson, 1977

Television, a Critical Review by Gerald Beadle, Allen and Unwin, 1963

Pressure Group, the Campaign for Commercial Television by H.H. Wilson, Secker and Warburg, 1961

David Frost by Willi Frischauer, Michael Joseph, 1972

You Can Get There From Here by Shirley MacLaine, The Bodley Head, 1975

The Future of Broadcasting: Report by Lord Annan's Committee of Enquiry, H.M. Stationery Office, 1975

The Pilkington Committee Report on Broadcasting, H.M. Stationery Office, 1962

The Beveridge Committee Report on Broadcasting, H.M. Stationery Office, 1949

Index